Within the Market Strife

STUDIES IN ETHICS AND ECONOMICS

Series Editor
Samuel Gregg, Acton Institute

Economics as a discipline cannot be detached from a historical background that was, it is increasingly recognized, religious in nature. Adam Ferguson and Adam Smith drew on the work of sixteenth- and seventeenth-century Spanish theologians, who strove to understand the process of exchange and trade in order to better address the moral dilemmas they saw arising from the spread of commerce in the New World. After a long period in which economics became detached from theology and ethics, many economists and theologians now see the benefit of studying economic realities in their full cultural, often religious, context. This new series, Studies in Ethics and Economics, provides an international forum for exploring the difficult theological and economic questions that arise in the pursuit of this objective.

Titles in the Series

Within the Market Strife

American Catholic Economic Thought from Rerun Novarum *to Vatican II*

Kevin E. Schmiesing

LEXINGTON BOOKS
Lanham • Boulder • New York • Toronto • Oxford

LEXINGTON BOOKS

Published in the United States of America
by Lexington Books
An imprint of The Rowman & Littlefield Publishing Group, Inc.
4501 Forbes Boulevard, Suite 200, Lanham, Maryland 20706

PO Box 317
Oxford
OX2 9RU, UK

British Library Cataloguing in Publication Information Available

Library of Congress Cataloging-in-Publication Data

Schmiesing, Kevin E.
    Within the market strife : American Catholic economic thought from Rerum
Novarum to Vatican II / Kevin E. Schmiesing.
        p. cm.—(Studies in ethics and economics)
    Includes bibliographical references and index.
    ISBN 0-7391-0880-8 (hardcover : alk. paper) —ISBN 0-7391-0963-4 (pbk. : alk.
paper)
        1. Economics—Religious aspects—Catholic Church—Congresses. 2. United
States—Economic conditions. 3. United States—Social conditions. 4. Christian
Sociology—Catholic Church. 5. Catholic Church—Doctrines—History. I. Title.
II. Series.
    BX1795.E27S36 2004
    261.8'5'08828273—dc22   2004017912

Printed in the United States of America
♾™ The paper used in this publication meets the minimum requirements of American
National Standard for Information Sciences—Permanence of Paper for Printed Library
Materials, ANSI/NISO Z39.48–1992.

To Anne

Lo, the Prince of common welfare dwells within the market strife;
Lo, the bread of heav'n is broken in the sacrament of life.

—Irish Hymn

CONTENTS

ABBREVIATIONS

Journals

ACQR	*American Catholic Quarterly Review*
AER	*American Ecclesiastical Review (Ecclesiastical Review)*
CHR	*Catholic Historical Review*
CW	*Catholic World*
OF	*Orate Fratres*
RSE	*Review of Social Economy*

Archival Sources

CCCV	Central Catholic Verein Manuscripts, Archives of the University of Notre Dame
CKEL	Edward A. Keller Manuscripts, Archives of the University of Notre Dame
CKLN	Frederick Kenkel Manuscripts, Archives of the University of Notre Dame
CLN	Patrick Henry Callahan Papers, Archives of the University of Notre Dame
JRP	John A. Ryan Papers, Archives of Catholic University of America
LMP	Louis J. Mercier Papers, Archives of Georgetown University
PKLN	Frederick Kenkel Printed Material, Archives of the University of Notre Dame

ACKNOWLEDGMENTS

I wish to express my appreciation to all those who assisted in the research for this book, in particular, Sharon Sumpter and Kevin Cawley of the Archives of the University of Notre Dame, and Brother David Richardson and Timothy Meagher of the Archives of Catholic University of America. I am grateful to the Cushwa Center for the Study of American Catholicism at the University of Notre Dame for providing a travel grant, and to Christopher Shannon, formerly assistant director of the Center.

The Acton Institute provided support throughout the research and writing processes and I thank its leaders, Father Robert Sirico and Kris Mauren. Those who furnished intellectual encouragement through conversation, criticism, and suggestion include Michael Coulter, Stephen Grabill, Samuel Gregg, John Quinn, Andrew Yuengert, and Gloria Zúñiga. John Zink graciously offered his personal remembrances of Father Edward Keller, C.S.C.

I appreciate the permission granted by editors Derek Davis of the *Journal of Church and State* and Ryan Barilleaux of the *Catholic Social Science Review* to use portions of previously published articles in chapters 3 and 4.

As in all my endeavors, my family provided motivation, edification, and distraction. Anne, John, Theresa, Maria, and Agnes testify that there are goods apart from those pursued within the market strife.

INTRODUCTION

This book examines the views of Catholics writing on economic questions in the period 1891–1962. Its thesis is that those views were dependent in large measure on factors other than the authors' adherence to the authoritative social teaching of their Church. Instead, Catholic thinkers' applications of that teaching to the American context were generally determined by the same complex set of factors that informed the views of non-Catholics. These include, but are not limited to, political loyalties, personal experience, and economic theories.

This study focuses on the last of these factors (while not ignoring the others) by placing Catholic social thinkers within the context of the American intellectual culture in which they operated. In this way, it hopes to show how these commentators interpreted that which was held in common—Catholic social teaching—as consistent with a wide variety of concrete political positions, depending on a given thinker's judgments, perspective, and allegiances.

The period chosen is illuminative because, among American Catholics, there were few disputes over core issues of Catholic theology or morality. Few Americans espoused the modernist positions condemned by Pope Pius X, and the rancorous debates over theological and moral issues that would characterize the post-Vatican II era lay in the future. At the same time, the pre-Vatican II period witnessed intense debate over the application of Catholic social teaching to the American economic and political situation. The juxtaposition of theological unity and economic policy disparity during the period demonstrates clearly, then, that positions on religious and economic issues were not inexorably connected.

The period under consideration has often been viewed by historians as one in which Catholics labored, intellectually and physically, within a Catholic ghetto, shut off from mainstream American thought and culture. The existence of a ghetto, in some places and in some ways, is hard to deny. Yet, a significant number of Catholic intellectuals were thinking seriously about the relationship between Catholicism and its American context. This book, then, dovetails with the work of contemporary Catholic historians who have similarly shown that Catholics were in conversation with, and that their debates mirrored those taking place in, the surrounding intellectual culture.[1]

At the same time, it is true that both native anti-Catholicism and its obverse, Catholic isolation, continued to be problems during this period. Non-Catholics who, on the theoretical level, might most naturally be considered Catholic allies (such as socially concerned evangelical Christians) retained a bias against their Catholic countrymen that prevented them from seeing the ways in which their concerns paralleled Catholic ones. Catholics, for their part, were sometimes overly smug in their belief that Catholic social teaching held the key to the solution of all social problems. They failed to see that their own theology did not require that kind of confidence, but was instead open to the insights of non-Catholics at the level of political and economic application of the moral norms that formed the bedrock of Catholic social teaching.[2]

One of the purposes of this book is to locate Catholic thought more definitely amid the contours of American intellectual history. The boundary lines of professional history have encouraged an emphasis on the distinctive nature of American Catholics' thinking vis-à-vis their Protestant and secular neighbors. That certain distinctive traits existed, in most cases, cannot be gainsaid. Yet, the segmentation of "secular" and "religious" histories has tended to obscure the ways in which the two are intrinsically tied. This book is intended, then, to contribute to historical understanding of not only American Catholic history, but also of American history more generally. Since American Catholics were participating in the same debates and using many of the same ideas as other Americans, their history should be seen not as a separate strain but as an integral part of the histories of, for instance, progressivism, the New Deal, and the fifties.

Two points need to be made concerning the scope of this book. The first is a clarification of its definition of *economic*. The book does not employ a strict theoretical definition of the term, but uses it loosely according to the popular understanding of what are economic issues. Its focus, therefore, is on two main areas: (1) *economic policy*, or the role of government in particular economic questions such as wages and labor; and (2) *economic systems*, or questions as to the nature of, and the technical and moral attractiveness of, the American economic order (called *capitalism* by most commentators).

By treating only economic commentary, this study sets itself off from most histories of American Catholicism, which tend to cover the more general area of *social thought*. There is nothing wrong with the broader approach, but a claim to cover social thought would entail treatment of many more issues including, for instance, Catholic commentary on race, on sexual morality, and on church and state. The choice of economics, the term's imprecision notwithstanding, helps to delimit the study and provide focus on an area relatively neglected by historians of Catholic thought. At the same time, the focus on economics does not mean a focus exclusively on professional economists. In addition to the fact that economics as a profession was still in the process of crystallizing during the early decades of the twentieth century, it is also true that much commentary on economic issues took place outside the confines of academic economics.

The second point concerning the book's scope has to do with its focus on economic *thought*. This study is an essay in intellectual history; as such it examines Catholic thinking on economic issues primarily through the writings of scholars and others acting within the sphere of Catholic intellectual life. Even within this sphere, the book does not aspire to be comprehensive. Figures such as John Ryan, Frederick Kenkel, and Edward Keller receive extensive attention because each of them represents a distinctive and significant approach to understanding the relationship between Catholicism and American economic life. It is hoped that the book has not neglected any major perspectives that were voiced during the discussions of the time, but it is possible that there are figures who deserve more attention than they are given here.

Notes

1. See, for instance, Patrick W. Carey, "Political Atheism: *Dred Scott*, Roger Brooke Taney, and Orestes A. Brownson," *Catholic Historical Review* 87 (April 2002): 207–29. Carey criticizes the "general attitude that American Catholics existed in such a religious ghetto prior to the Second Vatican Council that they were not much engaged in American public issues. They were preoccupied, so the argument goes, with their own internal religious or spiritual affairs. Such a view cannot be entirely sustained by close historical analysis of the public record. . . " (229). See also Carey's argument against the dominant historiography that views the papal encyclicals (*Testem Benevolentiae*, 1899; and *Pascendi Dominici Gregis*, 1907) as deadening influences on American Catholic intellectual life; Carey, "After *Testem Benevolentiae* and *Pascendi*," *Catholic Southwest* 7 (1996): 13–33. While he does not make the argument explicitly, the bulk of Jay P. Corrin's *Catholic Intellectuals and the Challenge of Democracy* (Notre Dame, Ind.: University of Notre Dame Press, 2002) demonstrates significant interaction between Catholic intellectuals and non-Catholic social theorists and political figures.

2. For a discussion of the distinction between Church social teaching and economic expertise (moral and economic spheres), see Jean-Yves Caldez, S.J., and Jacques Perrin, S.J., *The Church and Social Justice: The Social Teaching of the Popes from Leo XIII to Pius XII* (Chicago: Henry Regnery, 1961), chap. 3.

1

Early American Catholic Social Thought

Catholics in the New Republic

At the time of the Revolution of 1776, Catholics were a tiny minority among the population of the thirteen colonies. As many historians have observed, this minority status played a determinative role in the way Catholics thought about and related to a wider American society. Catholics were by most characteristics other than religion indistinguishable from non-Catholic Americans. Of British extraction, like most Americans at the time, Catholics participated for both sides in the Revolutionary War, and in numbers not appreciably different from that of the population at large. There were prominent Catholics among the signers of the Declaration and the Constitution eleven years later, including Charles Carroll of Maryland and William Fitzsimmons of Pennsylvania. In fact, Carroll was said to have been the wealthiest landholder among those who pledged their "lives, fortunes, and sacred honor" against their former sovereign.[1]

In the construction of the new nation, then, Catholics participated as enthusiastically as any other group. It was the era of what David O'Brien has called "Republican Catholicism."[2] Not only were Catholics much like other Americans in their ethnic and socioeconomic background, their status as a small minority in the midst of a dominant Protestant culture provided motivation to avoid highlighting any differences that might raise the ire of the majority. Thus, Catholics got along amicably, for the most part, in the new republic, and did not present themselves as critics of either the political or the social status quo.

At the same time, it would be too much to say that Catholics blended effortlessly into the mix of American cultural life. "No-popery" sentiment was still powerful in revolutionary America, and Catholics were, either de facto or de

1

jure, denied access to full citizenship in many of the nascent states. From the beginning of the nation's life, therefore, Catholics naturally assumed an element of otherness, a foreign character, if not based on ethnicity then based on devotion to a religion that for many Protestant and nonreligious Americans was identified with the forces of reaction and monarchy against which the colonists had rebelled.[3]

The story of Catholic life in the United States, then, is one of participating in and engaging American culture, politics, and social life, with varying degrees of comfort or criticism, depending on time, place, and other criteria. Indeed, for different Catholics of similar backgrounds, the same phenomenon might elicit very different responses, some critical and some less so. The story of Catholic views on economic and social issues fits into this larger pattern.

As the economic transformations of the early nineteenth century led to the first great wave of Protestant reform in the 1830s, therefore, Catholics "held to no specifically Catholic view of politics or economics." Robert Walsh, for instance, editor of the *American Review of History and Politics*, defended laissez-faire economics, while Mathew and Henry Carey attacked Adam Smith and championed protectionism. Neither cited Church documents in their arguments, and their social thinking thus did not appear to be self-consciously Catholic. From the early years of the Republic, there was a general understanding that Catholic doctrine did not demand adherence to one or another particular economic policy, system, or perspective.[4]

Such diversity is not a peculiarly American phenomenon, of course. From the beginning of the Catholic encounter with modern social problems—those arising from urbanization and industrialization—Catholics in Europe divided into a wide array of groups with conflicting opinions about the most appropriate response to those problems. Catholics concerned with the social question divided into liberal and conservative branches. Figures such as Charles de Coux and Edouard Ducpétiaux occupied the left, while Alban de Villeneuve-Bargemont and Armand de Melun aligned with the right. Concerning the major figures from the 1830s and forties, Villeneuve and Frederic Ozanam, historian Paul Misner explains, "social reform was not [their] chief preoccupation." Instead, social Catholics emphasized "the political defense of the freedom of the church or in the age-old works of mercy: direct succor for the poor and for those whose traditional livelihoods no longer supported them."[5]

The basic story of early European social Catholicism is that it was composed of both conservative and liberal elements, though it moved into a more reactionary stance as rejections of both liberalism and socialism came to define the social question in the latter part of the century (before *Rerum Novarum*). A less paternalistic brand of social thought arose late in the century as well, particularly in Germany, where corporatism was more open to government intervention and to self-direction of the working class. *Rerum* confirmed this move with its professed openness to government's role and provided a spur to Christian democracy.[6]

This characterization of the European Catholic approach to social problems mirrors Aaron Abell's description of American Catholic views through the 1880s. In 1845, Ozanam's brainchild, the St. Vincent de Paul Society, was established in the United States, in St. Louis, and began its extensive work of caring for the indigent. The society was an intrinsically local operation, organized at the parish level and emphasizing personal relationships between society members and the needy. Providing relief to the poor regardless of creed, members were nonetheless assumed to provide both spiritual and material aid, their most important contribution being their own example of Christian living.[7]

Catholics and Social Reform after 1830

What was unique to the United States, however, was the minority status of the Catholic population. This fact was important for determining Catholic response to the first major wave of social reform in the United States beginning in the 1830s. While that reform movement itself did not differ drastically from the Catholic emphasis on individual behavior over legislation, it was perceived to be a product largely of a vibrant Protestantism that combined social concern with proselytization. In religious terms, then, the main strands of American reform assumed a tone hostile to the growing number of immigrant (and indigent) Catholics who were increasingly the beneficiaries of charitable work. As an indication of the problems any cooperation between Protestants and Catholics would have to overcome, there was the fact that Lyman Beecher, an important reform-minded preacher, had caviled against Catholics the night before a mob burned the Charlestown convent to the ground.[8]

Because of this dynamic, Catholic efforts on social issues in the United States were driven to some degree by fear of Protestant proselytization. Protestant charitable efforts, from this perspective, provided an impetus for the creation of Catholic institutions that could serve the material needs of Catholics while buttressing their faith. From the early nineteenth century on, then, the arena of social problems was seen to be one not of cooperation among American Christians, Protestant and Catholic, but one of competition between them. This fact would color relations between the two groups in this field for more than a century.[9]

Large numbers of Irish and German Catholics altered the complexion of American Catholicism dramatically. Still a minority, Catholics were nonetheless a rapidly growing religious group. At the same time, Catholicism had come to be associated in most Americans' minds with ethnic identities other than the British. As Catholics became increasingly identified with foreign cultures and tongues and simultaneously became more numerous to the point of being a serious political force, fear of them grew among those "natives" who believed that the foreign Catholic masses represented a threat to traditional American life. The rise of nativist groups in the 1840s and fifties exacerbated the strain between Protestants and Catholics. Encouraged by the school controversies of the early 1840s, nativists organized to oppose what they regarded as a Catholic conspiracy to take control of the nation, and Protestant clergymen played a vital role in these organizational efforts.[10]

In the 1860s and seventies, the situation changed somewhat. Participation in defense of national unity during the Civil War brought respect to the previously suspect immigrant groups. "The clash that alienated sections reconciled their component nationalities," in John Higham's words. Anti-Catholicism remained, and flared again in various incidents during the 1870s; nonetheless, the period was one of general comity among native and immigrant, Protestant and Catholic.[11]

The phenomenon of increasing Catholic immigration and its implications for the relationship of Catholicism to America played out among Catholics themselves as well. The Americanist controversies[12] of the late nineteenth century can be seen in this light, as a contest between Catholics of old stock—exemplified by Cardinal James Gibbons, Archbishop John Ireland, and Bishop John Lancaster Spalding—and the newer arrivals, represented by Bishop Bernard McQuaid and the German Catholics of the Midwest.[13] The origins of the conflict revolved around disputes between Irish and Germans over issues of language in church and school, and the controversy prompted by the Cahensly affair, which involved financial ties between immigrants and the Old Country.[14]

The Americanist debates can also be seen, however, as a conflict between two fundamental approaches to understanding the relationship between Catholicism and American culture.[15] Americanists such as Archbishop Ireland believed that the United States represented an essentially friendly environment for the growth and prospering of the Catholic Church. Like many others around the world, he looked to the United States as the quintessentially modern society, but he saw modernism more as a promise than a threat. His attitude was summed up in his exclamation "Church and Age, Unite!"[16]

Other American Catholics saw pluralistic America as a dangerous place wherein the faith could be (and increasingly was) lost easily and where the prospects for the rise of a specifically Catholic culture were dim. The German Catholic Verein exemplified this position. Founded in 1855, it exerted a conservative influence on American Catholic life and served as a rallying point for those opposed to a too-facile rapprochement with the American social order.[17]

There is a longstanding debate concerning the question of whether any American Catholic actually held the positions condemned by Leo XIII in his 1899 apostolic letter, *Testem Benevolentiae*. The preeminent historian of Americanism, Thomas McAvoy, was noncommittal, although he implied that, while some Americans may have been tending toward the heretical form of Americanism, none really held forbidden views. French cleric Félix Klein's claim that Americanism was a "phantom heresy" remained the consensus for several decades. Some historians have interrogated that interpretation, however, and found it wanting.[18] It seems likely that, if some Americans did hold heretical views, their number was very small.[19] Certainly, most combatants on both sides saw themselves as firmly within the parameters of orthodoxy, although they sometimes accused each other of being otherwise.

It is important to note, also, that, as R. Laurence Moore has compellingly argued, the conservative-liberal split is not best described as a disagreement between pro-American and anti-American elements among Catholics, but as a debate over two different ways of being American.[20] Anti-Americanist Conde Pallen contended as much in 1898: "Americanism, that is to say what is politically and socially understood by that term in this country, has no more to do with [theology and doctrine] than the question of the rotundity of the earth. It is a confusion and misleading to speak of the dispute as a controversy between Americanism and something not American. . . ."[21]

Moore casts doubt, in addition, on the assumption that "Americanizers" were necessarily more palatable to non-Catholic Americans than non-Americanizers. Americanist Father Edward McGlynn, for instance, with his mentor Henry George, was not well-liked among most Protestant leaders.[22] Historians of American Catholicism, who have tended to occupy the liberal side of the political spectrum, have celebrated the Americanists because they share the same vision of the American project. Something similar is true of those conservative historians who have been friendlier toward the anti-Americanists. The issue, then, is not one of liking or disliking America; the issue is determining what "America" means.

One aspect of the American social order under contention was liberal capitalism. The conservative group notwithstanding, it has been widely noted that American Catholics were much more open to phenomena such as democracy and liberal capitalism than were their European counterparts. As Eugene McCarraher has suggested, the Americanist debate itself can be seen as a referendum on capitalism. "Conservatives," in McCarraher's schema, who guarded doctrinal orthodoxy and ethnic traditions, "could be seen not only as defenders of 'tradition' but also as critics, however narrow-minded, of the emerging corporate order." Liberals, on the other hand, "affirmed the progress of science and corporate industry."[23]

One, less plausible, explanation as to why American Catholics resisted the rise of capitalism and democracy less strenuously is that they were less informed of or devoted to their faith than their European counterparts. Confronted with minority status in a Protestant nation, American Catholics were amenable to compromising some of the tenets of their faith so as to assimilate more fully into their American context. An alternative possibility is that the so-called "modernist" phenomena of democracy and capitalism appeared under forms in the United States that were different from the way they appeared in Europe. Accordingly, they were imbued with different ideological commitments and were, therefore, less threatening to Catholic belief and practice. This latter hypothesis is more compatible with Thomas McAvoy's contention that the bitter discord on political and cultural matters characteristic of the Americanist controversy both masked and was made possible by remarkable doctrinal and spiritual unity.[24]

Any assessment of capitalism by a Catholic social thinker depended, of course, on what exactly that thinker meant by "capitalism" or the "American economic system." Confusion, inconsistency, and imprecision regarding the use of these terms regularly plagued Catholic commentary on the subject. As will be seen, this fact accounts for some of the differences among Catholic thinkers as they talked past each other in their attempts to substantiate their positions with the teachings of their Church. At the same time, there were genuine differences in interpretation of that teaching and in empirical judgments of economic realities, which led to varying opinions as to the necessity and nature of social and political reform.[25]

The Rise of the Social Gospel

As has been noted, Catholics had little to do with the reform movements that swept Protestant circles in the 1830s and forties. Besides the fact that there were few Catholics relative to the American population as a whole, the movement itself was closely identified with the Protestant churches and therefore did not lend itself to Catholic cooperation. In the 1880s, another powerful reform movement arose within Protestantism, that combination of disparate strands, which has been called the social gospel movement.

It is important to examine the social gospel movement in some depth because it dominated American religious engagement of social problems from the late nineteenth century through the rise of progressivism in the early twentieth century. (Its own links to progressivism will be discussed in chapter 2.) In this way, the attitude of American Catholics toward the social gospel and the ideas it represented defined to a large extent the way social Catholics viewed their relationship to mainstream America. If, in the 1880s, there were a significant number of Catholics in the United States at the same time as there was a significant movement of social concern among Protestants, then there was for the first time an important area of potential cooperation between Protestants and Catholics. If Catholics did not view the social gospel in this way, as a moment for alliance with fellow Americans to effect a religiously motivated improvement of society, then it is important to understand why this was the case.

One reason Catholics and Protestants found no common ground in the social gospel is that theological modernism had made significant inroads into American Protestant theology, while not yet doing the same with respect to Catholic thought. Beginning with the Unitarian controversies of the first decades of the nineteenth century, a large segment of Protestantism over the course of the century came to accept a variety of modifications to traditional Christian doctrines. The degree to which one accepted these modifications was a marker of the degree to which one was identified (often both by self and by others) as a "modern" or "liberal" Christian.[26]

Catholics, meanwhile, had little sympathy for modernist modifications of the faith. While scholars such as Richard Cross and R. Scott Appleby have located and highlighted the extent to which there were modernist or liberal tendencies among Catholics in the nineteenth and early twentieth centuries, their studies indicate clearly that modernism made little headway among American Catholics prior to the middle part of the twentieth century.[27]

It is not enough to cite the theological liberalism of the social gospel movement as the reason that Catholics had nothing to do with it, however. The popular tendency to link the social gospel with liberal theology is only partially justified. While it is true that theological liberals came to dominate the movement, in its beginnings the social gospel was a form of unity among a diverse set of groups, including theological conservatives. George Marsden has argued on this basis that the relationship "between evangelical orthodox Protestantism which emphasizes rescuing men from sin and preparing them for heaven, and a lack of a social Christianity responsive to the needs of the day, is not a necessary relationship, but rather largely an accidental one—or, more precisely, a coincidental one." Such a relationship, in Marsden's estimation, is due in part to "the historical coincidence of the post-Darwinian intellectual crisis with the Gilded Age."[28] The later identification of liberals with social concern and evangelicals with conservatism, then, was founded on historical developments in the late nineteenth and early twentieth century, culminating in the multifarious debates of the 1920s. Far from discouraging active concern for social and economic problems, evangelical theology lent itself to the project, a fact recognized in the reform movements earlier in the nineteenth century, and not entirely lost even in the latter half.

In addition, there was a strong backlash against modernism within Protestantism itself, especially by the time of the closing decades of the century. While Catholics may not have had much in common with strict fundamentalists, not all such opposition came from those quarters. As will be seen, other powerful movements within Protestantism would rise up against modernizing tendencies, including neoorthodoxy early in the next century.[29]

In the 1880s, then, as a concern for social issues was again gaining steam in the Protestant world and Catholics were beginning to amass the numbers and resources necessary to make an impact on the American scene, there was nevertheless little if any cooperation between the two groups. To a large extent, the explanation for Catholics' failure to engage the social gospel movement lies in the history of the nineteenth century. In the 1860s and seventies, there were powerful forces united in opposition to the presence and flourishing of Catholics on American soil. While there was nothing particularly Christian about the Know-Nothings, religious groups were not exempted from an anti-Catholic bias.

Various figures associated with the rise of the social gospel, for instance, wrote about immigrants in ways that could be perceived as anti-Catholic. Josiah Strong was an early social gospeler genuinely concerned with urban problems, but his popular book, *Our Country*, has been described as the "first sweeping

indictment of immigrant influence since the 1850s," for its linking of immigration to urban crime, political corruption, Catholicism, and socialism. Strong's
fellow muckraker, Jacob Riis, in his major work, *How the Other Half Lives*,
brought sympathetic attention to the problems of the cities, but did so at times
with an evident "class and race snobbery." Edward Bemis, University of Chicago
economist (and student of social gospel advocate Richard Ely), wrote against
immigration.[30]

Among evangelicals, moreover, adherence to the Republican Party and anti-
Catholicism were important aspects of their identity through the 1870s.[31]
Evangelical Christians, who might be closer theologically to Catholics, were
therefore precluded from an alliance with them because of obstacles in their own
cultural outlook. Catholics, as has already been noted, reciprocated by viewing
evangelicalism in the social sphere as a threat rather than as a potential ally.

Threats to Capitalism in the 1880s

The last two decades of the nineteenth century were characterized by intellectual
challenges to traditional Christian orthodoxy. In theology, adherents of Christianity attempted to reconcile the claims of revelation with the claims of
Darwinian science. In philosophy, the pragmatism of Charles Peirce, William
James, and John Dewey was in the ascendancy.[32] Catholics, like other Christians,
engaged Darwinism and its challenge to traditional religious thinking. Like
Protestants, too, Catholic response ran the gamut from broad acceptance of the
evolutionary account to outright denial.[33]

The view that "socialism could not happen in America" is a brand of
American exceptionalism belied by the appearance of socialism as a real possibility in the 1880s. Historian of American social science Dorothy Ross has made
the case well. "The failure of socialism to secure a permanent and substantial
presence in America," she observes, "has made it easy to forget that its fate was
still an open question in this period." Ross details the ways in which scholars in
the fields of economics and sociology, during the 1880s and 1890s, considered,
debated, and dispatched the alternative of socialism as a viable economic system.[34]

In this context, the Catholic Church's overriding concern with socialism in
this period becomes intelligible.[35] As the threat of socialism gave way to increasing American disapproval of it over the course of the 1880s and nineties, it might
be expected that the Church's unflinching opposition to socialism would improve
its reputation.[36] Instead, antiradicalism cut in the opposite direction. Catholicism
was still too closely tied to immigration, which was in turn too closely tied to
radicalism, to permit such distinctions to be made among broad swaths of
American opinion.

The 1880s, therefore, saw the rise of significant anti-immigrant sentiment.
Urban reformers accomplished the enactment of the first federal immigration

controls, but the restrictions were minor. Organized labor tended to see foreigners as tools of the capitalists, used to break strikes and drive down wages. Business leaders, meanwhile, also saw immigrant laborers as a threat, but for a contrary reason: Immigrants represented a radical element. Neither labor nor management was driven by xenophobia as much as self-interest. The 1886 unrest epitomized by the Haymarket incident in May, however, prompted the rise of new nativist organizations and reinvigorated old ones. In the same decade that the social gospel movement picked up momentum, antiradicalism and anti-Catholicism became strongly linked in the minds of many Americans. A crisis in Protestant-Catholic relations in this period, prompted by the issues of school funding and urban politics, fomented this development.[37]

Catholics became entangled, meanwhile, in a broader controversy that pressed against and highlighted the limits of official toleration for diverse applications of social teaching to the American economy. Henry George's *Progress and Poverty* (1879) and the movement it inaugurated represented for some Americans (and some Catholics) a promising reform impulse. For others, it seemed to be a threat to the foundation of capitalism and tantamount to socialism in its abrogation of the right of private property.

The Church was forced to deal with George's ideas, including his central reform of the single tax, by the popularity and public visibility of a George enthusiast, Father Edward McGlynn. McGlynn's superior, New York Archbishop Michael Corrigan, who viewed George's ideas as contrary to Church teaching, ordered McGlynn to cease his public promotion of them. When McGlynn refused, the matter was referred to the Vatican, where the Holy Office declared McGlynn excommunicated. Two years later, in 1889, the Vatican condemned George's writing as contrary to the faith.[38]

Here was a case, it seems at first glance, in which an individual judgment regarding economic issues had crossed the lines of acceptable debate. This synopsis, however, obscures a number of complications that reveal that, even in the McGlynn case, the parameters of orthodoxy with respect to economic issues were not clear and bright.

The first complication concerns the decision against McGlynn. In the course of the Vatican's deliberation on the matter, McGlynn received support from important members of the hierarchy, including Cardinal Gibbons. Within the Vatican curia itself, discussions noted carefully a distinction between the issues of McGlynn's defiance of ecclesiastical authority and his commission of doctrinal error.[39]

The second complication is the fact that McGlynn's excommunication was lifted in 1892. The reversal reflected the realization that McGlynn's position did not involve a question of doctrine; in the reported words of one curial official: "There is no right or wrong implied in the question. If you people in the U.S. want [a] single tax, why take it; it is nobody's business but your own."[40]

The final qualification concerns the method of condemnation of George's writing. The decision of the Holy Office was conveyed by the Congregation for the Propagation of the Faith to the American bishops via their primate, Cardinal Gibbons. In an unusual move, however, the bishops were placed under obligation of secrecy regarding the condemnation, and simply urged to pastoral vigilance. This fact does not undermine the Vatican's verdict on George—it clearly considered his writings to contain "false theories" concerning private property—but it does indicate Rome's caution against fostering a public (and false) impression that Catholics were excessively constrained in their consideration of matters of non-doctrinal character.[41]

As the last decade of the nineteenth century approached, Catholic immigration continued unabated. Meanwhile, a Catholic cohort of older immigrant stock (Irish and German) had begun its rise in status and wealth. While the Church's opposition to socialism and revolution made it appear to be a force of conservatism in the view of some Americans, its active social apostolate, manifested in groups such as the St. Vincent de Paul Society and the Catholic Central Verein, simultaneously presented the Church as the friend of the poor. Some Catholics emphasized one or the other side of their faith's social face, but most attempted to preserve both in a balance. The details involved in maintaining that balance, however, could be disputed. The Americanist controversy proved that Catholics were capable of disagreeing strenuously over the application of Church teaching to the American situation. With the advent of modern Catholic social teaching and the rise of powerful social reform movements in the 1890s, there would be new impetus for such debate, especially with respect to economic questions.

Notes

1. Jay P. Dolan, *The American Catholic Experience: A History from Colonial Times to the Present*, (Garden City, N.Y.: Doubleday, 1985), 96–97; Thomas T. McAvoy, C.S.C., *A History of the Catholic Church in the United States* (Notre Dame, Ind.: University of Notre Dame, 1969), 37–45. For the most comprehensive treatment of American Catholic social thought during the period preceding 1900, see James Edward Roohan, *American Catholics and the Social Question, 1865–1900* (New York: Arno, 1976 [reprint of Ph.D. diss., Yale University, 1952]).

2. David O'Brien, *Public Catholicism*, 2d ed. (Maryknoll, N.Y.: Orbis, 1996 [1988]).

3. For a summary of the anti-Catholic strain in American history, see John Higham, *Strangers in the Land: Patterns of American Nativism, 1860–1925* (New Brunswick, N.J.: Rutgers University Press, 1955), 5–7. See also Francis D. Cogliano, *No King, No Popery: Anti-Catholicism in Revolutionary New England* (Westport, Conn.: Greenwood, 1995); and Ira M. Leonard and Robert D. Parmet, *American Nativism, 1830–1860* (New York: Van Nostrand Reinhold Co., 1971).

4. O'Brien, *Public Catholicism*, 29. There has been considerable debate about the timing and the precise nature of the change, but there is agreement that sometime between the Revolution and the middle of the nineteenth century, the American economy underwent a fundamental shift; see Charles Sellers, *The Market Revolution: Jacksonian*

America, 1815–1846 (New York: Oxford University Press, 1991); Sean Wilentz, *Chants Democratic: New York City and the Rise of the American Working Class, 1788–1850* (New York: Oxford University Press, 1984); and Joyce Appleby, *Capitalism and the New Social Order: The Republican Vision of the 1790s* (New York: New York University Press, 1984). For criticism of Sellers's treatment of religion's relationship to the market revolution, see Daniel Walker Howe, "Charles Sellers, the Market Revolution, and the Shaping of Identity in Whig-Jacksonian America," 54–74; and Richard Carwardine, "Charles Sellers's 'Antinomians' and 'Arminians': Methodists and the Market Revolution," 75–98, in *God and Mammon: Protestants, Money, and the Market, 1790–1860*, ed. Mark A. Noll (New York: Oxford University Press, 2002).

 5. Paul Misner, *Social Catholicism in Europe: From the Onset of Industrialization to the First World War* (London: Darton, Longman and Todd, 1991), 4, 35.

 6. Misner, *Social Catholicism.* Misner's helpful summary of the period appears in pages 319–25. See also Franz H. Mueller, *The Church and the Social Question* (Washington, D.C.: American Enterprise Institute, 1984 [1963]), 72–78.

 7. Aaron I. Abell, *American Catholicism and Social Action: A Search for Social Justice, 1865–1950* (Garden City, N.Y.: Hanover, 1960), chap. 2. On the foundation of the Vincent de Paul Society in the United States, see 22. On the early St. Vincent de Paul Society, including differences between it and other American social assistance groups, see Deirdre M. Moloney, *American Catholic Lay Groups and Transatlantic Reform in the Progressive Era* (Chapel Hill: University of North Carolina Press, 2002), 124–41. For a summary of the work of the society and its animating spirit, see Sister Vera Gallagher, R. G. S., *Hearing the Cry of the Poor: The Story of the St. Vincent de Paul Society* (Liguori, Missouri: Liguori Publications, 1983), esp. chap. 2.

 8. See Abell *American Catholicism*, 19–20; and O'Brien, *Public Catholicism*, 64. For the convent burning, see James T. Fisher, *Communion of Immigrants: A History of Catholics in America* (New York: Oxford University Press, 2002 [2000]), 46. For a collection of essays on diverse topics related to Protestantism and economic questions in antebellum America, see *God and Mammon: Protestants, Money, and the Market, 1790–1860*, ed. Mark A. Noll (New York: Oxford University Press, 2002). A case study of Protestant social reform is Paul E. Johnson, *A Shopkeeper's Millennium: Society and Revivals in Rochester, New York, 1815–1937* (New York: Hill and Wang, 1997 [1978]).

 9. Abell, *American Catholicism*, 19–20. On the fear of Protestant proselytization as a spur to Catholic social action, even through the progressive era, see Moloney, *Catholic Lay Groups*, 117–22.

 10. Leonard and Parmet, *American Nativism*, chaps. 6–8.

 11. Higham, *Strangers*, 13, chap. 2.

 12. Temperance, schooling, labor unions, and secret societies were among the issues that contributed to the various Americanist debates of the late nineteenth century. For a comprehensive treatment of the controversies, see Thomas T. McAvoy, C.S.C., *The Great Crisis in American Catholic History, 1895–1900* (Chicago: Henry Regnery, 1957). John Quinn has explicated the ways in which attitudes toward liquor became markers of the desire and willingness to be assimilated: "Temperance was by and large a concern for progressives, promoted in the same breath with American democracy and church-state separation." John F. Quinn, "Father Mathew's Disciples: American Catholic Support for Temperance, 1840–1920," *Church History* (December 1996): 631.

13. This view has its limitations. Gibbons's archenemy during the Americanist controversy, Archbishop Michael Corrigan of New York, was of old-immigrant stock. I have followed the lead of many historians of the period by lumping together a series of different debates under the heading of the Americanist controversy. Thomas McAvoy, in distinguishing the Americanist debate immediately preceding and following the apostolic letter *Testem Benevolentiae* (1899), has argued that the battle was cultural not racial (ethnic). But the lines of debate were not always clearly delineated at the time, as McAvoy admits: "That these distinctions were clearly seen at the time by many of the controversialists is apparently not so, because the earlier controversies over the rights of foreign languages in churches, over the parochial schools, and over Catholic membership in certain secret societies were dragged into the battle when occasion offered." McAvoy, *Great Crisis*, x.

14. McAvoy, *Great Crisis*, 64ff.

15. This interpretation is similar to that of Thomas McAvoy: "The major problem of the Catholic hierarchy in the decades following the Third Plenary Council [1884] was: whether to concentrate on the theological and eternal principles of the Universal Church, hoping in this way to preserve the faithful from modern errors; or, as some 'progressive' prelates urged, to enter more wholly into the modern American political, social and economic problems, hoping that by supplying the Church leadership there to bring the masses back to the eternal teaching and practices of the Church." McAvoy, *Great Crisis*, 42–43.

16. See R. Scott Appleby, *"Church and Age Unite!": The Modernist Impulse in American Catholicism* (Notre Dame, Ind.: University of Notre Dame Press, 1992). As Appleby notes, Ireland was not really a theological modernist in the sense usually associated with European modernism (8).

17. For the story of the Verein, see Philip Gleason, *The Conservative Reformers: German American Catholics and the Social Order* (Notre Dame, Ind.: Notre Dame, 1968).

18. McAvoy, *Great Crisis*, 353–54. Klein, *Americanism, A Phantom Heresy* (Cranford, N.H.: Aquin Book Shop, 1951). At one point McAvoy calls the controversy "theological and cultural" (x). He apparently means theological not in the sense of concerning doctrinal issues, but of concerning the nexus of Catholic theology and American culture, because elsewhere he writes that it was not theological (42–43), and that seems to be the argument of the book. See also his distinction between "heretical" and "non-heretical" forms of Americanism and his characterization of the reaction to Leo XIII's condemnation of Americanism: "none of the Americanists defended in any way the doctrines condemned by the Pope. Heretical Americanism was dead. . . . The blow to the non-heretical Americanism became the subject of a debate which is not yet complete" (280). Among those who have detected Americans holding Leo's condemned views are Jay Dolan and Thomas Wangler. Dolan, *American Catholic Experience*, 316; Wangler, "Americanist Beliefs and Papal Orthodoxy, 1884–1899," *U.S. Catholic Historian* 11 (Summer 1993): 37–51.

19. See McAvoy, *Great Crisis*, 298–99, for the general reaction to the encyclical among Catholic periodicals. The result of the encyclical, in McAvoy's estimation, was that it "merely stopped the public discussion and allowed the forces in the controversy to work out quietly a series of practical solutions, some of which were unsatisfactory to the leaders of the controversy" (xi).

20. R. Laurence Moore, *Religious Outsiders and the Making of Americans* (New York: Oxford University Press, 1986), chap. 2. Moore observes a bias in American Catholic historiography for Americanists, against conservatives. Even among the critics of liberals (e.g., David O'Brien), Moore continues, there is no admiration for conserva-

tives. Moore, on the contrary, wants to defend the program of conservatives. Moore, then, represents the argument he is making; that is, as a non-Catholic American, he finds much merit in the views of those characterized by their opponents as too Catholic and insufficiently American. Another example of the same phenomenon is D. G. Hart, "The Church with the Soul of a Nation" [Review of Jay P. Dolan, *In Search of an American Catholicism*], *Books and Culture* (May/June 2003): 39.

21. Quoted in McAvoy, *Great Crisis*, 259.

22. Moore, *Religious Outsiders*, 63.

23. Eugene McCarraher, *Christian Critics: Religion and the Impasse in Modern American Social Thought* (Ithaca, N.Y.: Cornell University Press, 2000), 22–23.

24. McAvoy, *Great Crisis*, 37 and passim. Jacques Maritain made the same point, distinguishing capitalism in the United States from its counterpart in Europe. See chap. 6 below.

25. There were, of course, some Europeans who shared "American" ideas about the promise of the free society, versus the explicitly "Christian society" or "Christian economic order," for promoting Christian ideals. Peter Reichensberger, a Catholic layman trained in economics, is one interesting case. See Misner, *Social Catholicism*, 74–76.

26. William R. Hutchison, *The Modernist Impulse in American Protestantism* (Cambridge, Mass.: Harvard University Press, 1976), chaps. 1–5. This explanation does not pretend to avoid any of the difficulties associated with the use of the terms "modernism" or "liberalism" with respect to theology. Hutchison's description of modernism, for instance, cites the following three criteria: (1) conscious adaptation of religion to modern world; (2) God immanent in and revealed through human culture; (3) human society moving toward (though maybe never attain) Kingdom of God (progress) (p. 2). With the possible exception of the belief in progress, few religious foes of modernism would have problems with these criteria as articulated. The real differences between modernists and non- or antimodernists would be revealed in the course of a detailed discussion about what exactly is meant by terms such as "adaptation" and "immanent."

27. Robert D. Cross, *The Emergence of Liberal Catholicism in America* (Cambridge, Mass.: Harvard University Press, 1967); Appleby, *Church and Age Unite*.

28. George Marsden, "The Gospel of Wealth, the Social Gospel, and the Salvation of Souls in Nineteenth-Century America," in *Protestantism and Social Christianity*, ed. Martin E. Marty (Munich: K. G. Saur, 1992), 11; first published in *Fides et Historia* 5 (Fall 1972 and Spring 1973): 10–21.

29. Hutchison, *Modernist Impulse*, 105ff. On nonfundamentalist opposition, see 199–206, on the Princeton conservatives.

30. Higham, *Strangers*, 39–41. For a sympathetic interpretation of Strong, see Keith J. Hardman, *Issues in American Christianity: Primary Sources with Introductions* (Grand Rapids, Mich.: Baker Books, 1993), 252–53; James B. Lane, *Jacob A. Riis and the American City* (Port Washington, N.Y.: Kennikat Press, 1974), 67. Ironically, Ely would also be a mentor to a prominent Catholic priest and writer on social questions, John A. Ryan (see chap. 2).

31. Sandra Sizer, "Politics and Apolitical Religion: The Great Urban Revivals of the Late Nineteenth Century," in *Protestantism and Social Christianity*, 15–32; first published as "Politics and Apolitical Religion: The Great Revivals of the Late Nineteenth Century," *Church History* 48 (March 1979): 81–98.

32. George Cotkin, *Reluctant Modernism: American Thought and Culture, 1880–1900* (New York: Twayne, 1992), chaps. 1–2. See also Bruce Kuklick, *Churchmen*

and Philosophers: From Jonathan Edwards to John Dewey (New Haven: Yale University Press, 1985), chaps. 14–16.

33. Appleby, *Church and Age*, chap. 1.

34. Dorothy Ross, *The Origins of American Social Science* (New York: Cambridge University Press, 1991), 98, chap. 4. For an overview of American economic views in the 1880s, see Joseph Dorfman, *The Economic Mind in American Civilization*, vol. 3, 1865–1918 (New York: Viking Press, 1959 [1949]), chap. 5.

35. Some observers have unfairly criticized the Church for its focus on socialism. A case in point is Francis Downing's survey of Catholic participation in the labor movement; Francis Downing, "Catholic Contributions to the American Labor Movement," in *Church and Society: Catholic Social and Political Thought and Movements 1789–1950*, ed. Joseph N. Moody (New York: Arts, 1953), 845–904. Downing's article is a particularly egregious example because, having earlier criticized the Church's concern with socialism in a nation unlikely to embrace it, he later in the same piece admits that workers were turning to socialism in significant numbers (866). See also Neil Betten, *Catholic Activism and the Industrial Worker* (Gainesville: University Presses of Florida, 1976), 20–22, on the activity of communists within the CIO.

36. Pope Leo XIII's second encyclical, *Quod Apostolici Muneris*, prefigured the later *Rerum Novarum* by condemning socialism while insisting on the social responsibilities of the wealthy and the value of labor unions. See Lillian Parker Wallace, *Leo XIII and the Rise of Socialism* (Durham, N.C.: Duke University Press, 1966), 111–14.

37. Higham, *Strangers*, 43–62. The American Protective Association was founded in 1887.

38. For an overview of the McGlynn affair, see Abell, *American Catholics*, 61–80. For a discussion of the relationship between George's ideas and those of Leo's in *Rerum Novarum*, see J. Brian Benestad, "Henry George and the Catholic View of Morality and the Common Good I," *American Journal of Economics and Sociology* 44 (July 1985): 365–78. See also Robert Emmett Curran, S.J., "The McGlynn Affair and the Shaping of the New Conservatism in American Catholicism, 1886–1894," *Catholic Historical Review* 66 (April 1980): 184–204.

39. C. Joseph Nuesse, "Henry George and *Rerum Novarum*," *American Journal of Economics and Sociology* 44 (April 1985): 243, 247. Nuesse's excellent article is marred by the repetition of John Coleman's erroneous claim that Leo held an "un-Thomist," overly metaphysical view of the right of private property (250). Benestad's article cited above (n. 38) notes the limits that Leo placed on property rights.

40. Nuesse, "Henry George," 250.

41. Nuesse, "Henry George," 242–43, 251 n. 4.

2

Catholics in the Age of Reform

Richard Hofstadter's classic work *The Age of Reform* describes three waves of American reform—populism, progressivism, and the New Deal—dating the age of reform from 1890 to 1940.[1] Coincidentally, the modern era of Catholic social teaching was ushered in by Pope Leo XIII's 1891 encyclical, *Rerum Novarum*. How, then, did American Catholics relate to the broader phenomenon of reform?

Marginal within the predominantly rural populist movement, Catholics engaged more fully the city-based progressive movement. In general, Catholics, growing in numbers and influence through the period, gradually assumed a more vocal role in public discussions of economic questions. Catholics' relationships to American reform depended on their approaches to the problem of applying Catholic social teaching to the American situation. Catholic thinkers disagreed vigorously among themselves as to whether and in which ways American political and economic structures could be enlisted to promote, in Leo's words, "public well-being and private prosperity." While the 1891 encyclical provided impetus for some Catholics to take up stances in line with American reform movements, others were critical of various aspects of those movements.

Fin-de-siécle America and *Rerum Novarum*

The three decades following the Civil War witnessed dramatic changes in American life. Urbanization and industrialization on an unprecedented scale created both enormous benefits and enormous problems. These developments challenged observers to reconsider the nature of economic life and the role of the state in it.

The rapid growth in the size of firms after the war resulted not immediately in a centralization of power, but in its dispersion. Company owners at first operated as though the old ways were still good enough, as though a paternalism that worked reasonably well in the context of a small enterprise could be equally effective in the context of a large one. In politics, too, although urban political machines were formed as one method of dealing with increasing size and complexity, this development did not lend itself automatically to centralization at the national level. Instead, national political leaders had little control over the running of local machines. Citizens were attached to a party as a show of local and personal loyalty, but usually saw national affairs as irrelevant to their daily lives.[2]

The organization of capital in the closing decades of the century gave rise to the organization of labor. Relations between labor and capital became by many estimates the foremost issue of the day. Labor violence and economic depression in the 1890s tinged the labor question with nativist overtones. Anti-immigration sentiment increased as immigrant labor came to be perceived less as an asset to employers than as competition for native-born laborers. The rise in nativism coincided with a general rise in nationalistic fervor, which would culminate in war with Spain in 1898. As with earlier manifestations of nativism, anti-Catholicism was closely related. Anti-Catholicism in the 1890s, however, had a limited impact because it generally remained unfashionable among the elite and remained excessively focused on Irish immigrants at a time when new immigrant groups from southern and eastern Europe were beginning to predominate. Although these new groups would come to be associated with radicalism, legislative attempts at immigration restriction in the decade achieved only modest success.[3]

With the labor unrest and economic downturn of the early 1890s behind, anti-immigrant activity waned after 1896. The chief historian of nativism, John Higham, notes that this change included a dramatic shift in business sentiment, which became strongly pro-immigrant. The rise of progressivism in the new century, moreover, was predominantly a favorable development for immigrants. Some aspects of progressivism, such as the settlement house movement, forthrightly embraced the interests of immigrants. While nativism did not disappear, the tendency of reformers was to blame big business rather than immigrants themselves for the plight of the urban poor. This tendency reflected a general shift in social reformers' attitudes with respect to the relative importance of environmental versus personal behavioral factors as causes of poverty and unemployment. The shift in turn was tied to the professionalization of welfare provision and an increasing reliance on government assistance.[4]

Into the midst of these developments came the publication of Leo XIII's 1891 encyclical, *Rerum Novarum*. The encyclical combined a defense of private property and condemnation of socialism with an insistence on the rights of workers to organize and to receive just wages. Among Catholics, reception of the encyclical was positive, though interpretations of its application to the American situation varied widely. Catholics continued to argue, for instance, about whether or not papal teaching condemned the single tax scheme promoted most notably by Henry George. Another main point of difference was the degree to which the encyclical allowed and even demanded government action in the economy.[5]

Jesuit René J. Holaind, writing for fellow priests in the *American Ecclesiastical Review*, saw in the encyclical's tone a mandate for pastors not to favor either workers or businessmen in their congregations, but to treat members of each group with equal solicitude. Holaind emphasized Leo's upholding of the inviolability of private property and noted that the encyclical's principles were in "perfect harmony with the teaching of standard economists." Holaind shared the assessment of most American Catholic commentators that *Rerum* struck a wholesome balance between the competing concerns of workers and capitalists, recognizing the value of both groups to a properly functioning economy and thereby urging reform without indulging in fantastic schemes detached from economic reality.[6]

Monsignor John J. Keane articulated the dominant view that the encyclical located Church teaching on the economy in a position between laissez-faire liberalism, "which has been everywhere prevalent since the days of Adam Smith," and state socialism, with its denial of the right of individual property ownership and its substitution of public authority for individual initiative and "domestic society." In economics, the encyclical represented a condemnation of "the Manchester school and whole tribe of '*laissez-faire*' political economists," with their "fundamental notion" of "economic man."[7]

Leo taught that the state was not to be merely a "gendarme," Keane wrote. Government action was warranted especially in two areas: Sunday work and wages. With his teaching on wages, Keane averred, Leo "cuts with trenchant force the knot of difficulty which has occasioned controversies innumerable, not only among political economists but even among Christian moralists," namely, the question of "how far the relation of wages to the cost of living is a matter of justice." The encyclical's declaration that "justice demands that wages shall be sufficient to support the laborer in frugal comfort, is startlingly decisive."[8]

The implication that Leo had settled the thorny question of wages in either political economy or Catholic moral teaching was tempered by Keane's caveats. First, in Keane's estimation the encyclical left open the question of whether the paying of a "family wage" was a matter of justice. Second, Keane noted that the pope dealt only in principles, not in application, and that the "practical determination of figures"—that is, the determination of the exact level of a sufficient wage—would have to occur within particular circumstances. Keane ended on an optimistic note, observing that the trend in the United States was toward rather than away from the wider ownership of property that was among the goals exhorted by the encyclical.[9]

Others were even more certain that the encyclical should not be viewed as fundamentally critical of the American economy. Bishop John Lancaster Spalding of Peoria used the encyclical as a springboard to articulate a defense of the American system and a warning against assertions of government power. Rejecting the labor theory of value espoused by Karl Marx and David Ricardo, Spalding endorsed the right of the capitalist to a return on his investment. Conceding that Catholics shared with socialists a concern for the poor, Spalding insisted that the American system already contained the mechanisms necessary to alleviate poverty. "We began," he wrote, "as the most completely individualist people of which history makes record, and our experience has not tended to weaken our faith in the power of freedom, intelligence, and industry to solve the great social problems." "The tendency of good government," he continued, "is to make government less necessary...."[10] Spalding, usually considered one of the three main "Americanist" bishops in the context of that controversy, exemplified the Americanists' positive evaluation of the capitalist system.

Many non-Catholics also received *Rerum* graciously. John Graham Brooks wrote an appraisal of the letter for the American Economic Association, and economist Carroll Wright favorably commented on it. Protestant organs similarly found the encyclical to their liking. Progressive clergyman Lyman Abbott extolled the letter, while the more conservative *Andover Review* praised its balancing of a defense of private property with the concession that the state must undertake some economic functions.[11] Catholics noted the tremendous positive reception of the encyclical and thought that it enhanced significantly the Church's reputation as a serious moral voice on modern problems.[12]

While *Rerum Novarum* clearly articulated certain positions (e.g., the validity of labor organizing, the moral repugnance of socialism), plenty of room remained for Catholics to consider and dispute the best means for bringing about social justice in the United States. Leo's missive had served to remind Catholics that the Church's moral teaching was relevant not only to private behavior but also to public economic life. The precise way in which that teaching could be applied to the economic sphere remained an issue of contention. The unsettled character of Catholic opinion on such issues after *Rerum* was demonstrated by debates at the Columbian Congress of 1893.[13]

Catholics and Populism

In the estimation of historian Elizabeth Sanders, "Agrarian movements constituted the most important political force driving the development of the American national state in the half century before World War I."[14] The best-known such movement was populism. Like all such major interpretive devices in American history, the meaning of *populism* has varied somewhat according to historians' sympathies and perspectives. For some, agrarian populists were champions of American democracy; for others, they were avatars of American anti-intellectualism and demagoguery.[15] Some have seen the heart of populism in the call for silver coinage, while others view that effort as a "shadow movement" that obscured the driving force of populism—the urge for political and economic empowerment felt by downtrodden rural folk.[16]

The origins of the movement lie in what populists called the "Crime of '73," the demonetization of silver. While the specific source of discontent to some extent varied geographically, the monetary issue was symbolic of the injustice that the rural populace perceived to be endemic in the machinations of powerful economic and political interests. This perception fueled the rise of populism's institutional manifestation, the Farmers' Alliance. Founded in 1877, the alliance counted 100,000 members by 1886. The People's Party grew out of the National Farmers' Alliance, a union of hundreds of local chapters.[17]

Catholics were not intimately involved in the populist movement. This fact represented an intractable problem for populists desirous of national political clout; in the words of one historian of the movement: "What could a Protestant, Anglo-Saxon Alliance organizer say to the largely Catholic, largely immigrant urban working classes of the North?"[18] As the question implies, there are good reasons that most Catholics did not attach themselves to populism.

Tom Watson was one of the best-known populist leaders. There was always an undercurrent of nativism in Watson's thought, but, as C. Vann Woodward notes, this current came to the fore in the years 1910 to 1917. "During those seven years," Woodward writes, "Tom Watson became almost as closely identified in the public mind with the anti-Catholic crusade as he had once been with the populist movement."[19] Watson complained that "the scum of creation has been dumped on us. Some of our principal cities are more foreign than American." He described immigrants as "dangerous and corrupting hordes," and "Goths and Vandals," bringing in their wake "vice and crime." Having established the danger, Watson turned his attention to the question of culpability: "The manufacturers are mainly to blame. They wanted cheap labor: and they didn't care a curse how much harm to our future might be the consequence of their heartless policy.[20]

By such harangues, Watson skillfully exploited common fears and prejudices to support his political agenda. Urban crime and immorality were the problems against which the rural Protestant populace could readily unite, but Watson shifted the focus from immigrants themselves to the native group he deemed responsible for the problem—big business. In this way the populist platform—for example, of decreasing tariffs and of railroad price legislation to aid farmers—could be pushed by utilizing the sentiment of many who did not necessarily stand to benefit personally from such policies.

Shorn of its anti-immigrant and anti-Catholic tones, however, agrarian populism could be an attractive idea to the many Catholics skeptical of the triumph of industrialism. Populism, together with the artisanal movements of the late nineteenth century, represented "the producer's last stand," the doomed effort by defenders of the "producer ethic" to stave off the domination of the economy by industry and wage labor.[21] Although populism has variously been seen as both proto-capitalist and radically anticapitalist, it is probably true that populists exhibited a variety of attitudes toward market capitalism, ranging from outright rejection to measured acceptance.[22]

In fact, some Catholics did grab onto some strands of populism. The brand peddled by Minnesotan Ignatius Donnelly, for instance, appealed to Baltimore's Cardinal James Gibbons. A young John Ryan (future priest and social theorist; see below), whose father was a National Farmers' Alliance member, listened approvingly to Donnelly's speeches. Donnelly himself wanted nothing to do with the American Protective Association, the main nativist organization.[23]

There is further evidence that nativism and anti-Catholicism were not at the heart of the movement. Walter Nugent, historian of Kansas populism, makes a compelling case that populism and anti-Catholicism were not substantially linked, at least in that state. Nugent further shows that non-native-born farmers, far from being ostracized, were solicited to support and to join the movement. In at least one case, Catholic and Populist leadership were able to overcome initial hesitation and establish friendly relations. Catholic Bishop Louis Fink of Leavenworth, skeptical of the alliance because of what he perceived to be its secret society characteristics, worked out an agreement with the Kansas state committee, which addressed the bishop's concerns on that score. Fink came to be an enthusiastic supporter of populism.[24]

The lack of extensive Catholic involvement in populism, in light of these points of contact, seems to be due more to demographic realities than to any intrinsic ideological conflict. Populism's main impulse was rooted in agricultural economic conditions, particularly in the South and the West. Because Catholics in these years were predominantly located in the cities of the East and Midwest, they naturally had little opportunity or motivation to ally with the People's Party.[25] Insofar as Catholics were located in places such as rural Kansas and Minnesota, they could find common ground with populism and become part of the movement.

Catholics, Progressivism, and the Social Gospel

It has been said that progressivism so dominated the country that "creative figures who did not fit the pattern found that they had to cooperate with the progressive ethos in order to find places for themselves within American life; the alternatives were to leave the country or be ignored."[26] In light of this assessment, it will be important to consider the relationship of Catholic social thinkers to progressivism. Even more than populism, though, *progressivism* admits of a wide variety of interpretations and many disparate phenomena have found a home under the appellation. This variety notwithstanding, it still seems possible, as with populism, to use the term to describe "a real, vital, and significant phenomenon, one which contemporaries recognized and talked and fought about."[27]

Whereas populism had been a provincial and rural phenomenon, progressivism differed markedly by being national in scope and strongest among the urban middle class. The "first full-scale attempt to come to terms with the rapidly emerging multicultural, urban, industrial society," progressivism owed its genesis in some respect to the changes brought about by the rapid industrialization and urbanization of the previous decades. Yet, the particular problems progressives sought to address had not been previously unknown. "A change in the quality of perceptions not in the quantity of unique evils," Robert Wiebe observes, "produced a broad reappraisal of the cities around 1900." Poverty and vice had ever been present in American cities; after 1900, a considerable number of Americans determined not only that their presence was intolerable, but also that they had certain causes and therefore had to be addressed in certain ways.[28]

Progressives initially were impelled not by a statist political philosophy, but by a concern that the self-reliant individual, the idol of American political philosophy since Jefferson, would be trampled on by conglomerations of business. This motive prompted ever-increasing reliance on government as an antidote to big business, a strategy that, ironically, led to greater centralization and increasing danger that the individual would be lost amid the bureaucracies created to save him. Insofar as progressives achieved political success, moreover, they themselves became participants in the wielding and distributing of power, thereby benefiting by and creating their own ties to other powerful interests, including business.[29]

The situation reflected an intellectual problem at the heart of all social reform movements. Progressive intellectuals claimed to promote democracy, defined as the self-determination of the American people. But how could the people be convinced to pursue the ends that the intellectual leadership identified as good? Given the institutions of modern society, moreover—the state, in particular—how could progressives participate in its power structure without ineluctably becoming part of the system that was to be reformed? The desire by experts to direct democratic choice in certain ways, and the institutional implications of that desire, were in tension with progressive paeans to democracy.[30]

Theodore Roosevelt, for instance, a champion of progressivism, was no zealous trust-buster; he remained friendly with business. The relationship between progressives and big business was an ambivalent one, for businessmen, looking to gain advantages from the state and strengthen their own positions, also had an interest in allying with the dominant political trend of the day. The progressive strategy also overlooked (or masked) the fact that government had generally played the part of contributing to, rather than curtailing, the rise of monopolistic business.[31] Woodrow Wilson, for example, like Theodore Roosevelt identified as a progressive politician, presided over the creation of a business-government alliance stronger than any previously seen in the United States.[32]

The seeming comity between business and government during the progressive era has led some scholars to argue that progressivism was essentially conservative, coopting radical movements and thereby saving capitalism.[33] Other historians argue that, whatever its end result, reform during the populist and progressive eras was prompted by sincere motives.[34] In light of these conflicting views, it seems safe to say that a variety of interests, including Protestant moralists, acquisitive businessmen, and agitated farmers, sought to use government to their ends during the progressive era. To say as much is not necessarily to denigrate either the motives or the results of these groups' efforts. Sorting out the admixture of motives ranging from crass self-interest to disinterested concern for the common good is beyond the scope of this study. It is certain that progressive-era reforms changed the character of the American economy and enhanced the state's role in it, while preserving its essential nature as a market economy.

It can be argued that the social gospel movement, introduced in chapter 1, was part of the progressive movement and that it is, therefore, misleading to separate a discussion of social gospelism from a discussion of progressivism more generally. White and Hopkins, for instance, observe that social gospel advocates and progressives "knew each other well, operated from many of the same premises, and employed similar strategies."[35] At the same time, White and Hopkins and other historians have usually maintained that social gospelers were distinguishable from their more secular counterparts on the basis of their explicitly theological vision.[36] Some historians argue that religious concerns were an influential component of the progressive movement; others consider progressivism to be a postreligious phenomenon.[37]

Gary Scott Smith's important recent synthesis on social Christianity has helped to clarify the movement at various points. One clarification is Smith's argument that, prior to 1920, the American Protestant world was more unified than it would be following the fundamentalist/modernist controversy of the 1920s. Historians must be careful, Smith reminds us, not to apply the typologies common since the controversy to the period before it.[38]

Put simply, it is not correct to identify social concern with liberal theology, or social apathy with conservative orthodoxy in the period under question. A strong link between revivalism, evangelism, and social concern, evident in earlier eras, persisted through the turn of the twentieth century.[39] Evangelical social concern might be politically expressed, moreover. William Jennings Bryan, the man who would come to be associated with the defense of fundamentalist Christianity against the progress of science during the Scopes Trial, ran presidential campaigns that Garry Wills has called "the most leftist mounted by a major party's candidate in our entire history."[40]

For Smith, then, the social movement of American Christians in the late nineteenth and early twentieth centuries should be delimited not according to theological positions but according to commitment to social reform. The decision is justified, he observes, because "before 1915 many Protestants did not perceive social Christianity as being connected with a specific theological position."[41] Smith's definition excludes Catholics, but others have implied that some Catholics were part of the social gospel movement.[42]

Smith's characterization notwithstanding, many historians have seen in the social gospel a trend toward theological liberalization.[43] Susan Curtis, for instance, claims that social gospel programs and literature "reflected an important transformation of Protestant theology." In her view,

> social gospelers redefined salvation, the nature of God, and religious commitment and in so doing, made an important departure from the Protestantism of the Second Great Awakening in the early 1800s. . . . Instead of the angry Jehovah of the eighteenth century or even the judgmental God of the "burned-over district," the God of the social gospel was "immanent," "indwelling," and indulgent.[44]

All of these changes, Curtis argues, represent social gospelers' effort to straddle Christianity and modern life, to try to make Christianity relevant to the modern world. This effort, however laudable, led to an uncritical embrace of modernity. "The all-consuming passion for social justice of early Christian reformers . . . had become by the 1920s an assertion that the various dimensions of modern life—the corporation, the state, technological sophistication, and an ethos of consumption—could bring about the kingdom of God on earth." Social gospel proponents began from premises different from their secular progressive counterparts, Curtis observes, but ended in the same place. "When social gospelers themselves tried to occupy the bully pulpit of American politics, they sacrificed the independent authority of their religion to the social dynamic of the state. In this way the social gospel became a gospel of social salvation, and the authority of Christian religion was absorbed into the authority of secular culture." The movement of much of the social gospel movement into closer alliance with secular progressivism at the expense of orthodox Christianity can be seen as one of the factors leading to the "fracturing of the united front" of social Christianity in the 1920s.[45]

One of the genuine differences among social Christians was in their varying degrees of willingness to enlist government as an instrument for bringing about the Kingdom of God. Even here, the lines of difference did not parallel necessarily the lines of theological disagreement. Conservative Protestants, for instance, could be vigorous supporters of using government to bring about social reform, but their definitions of social reform might differ widely from those of liberal social gospel advocates.[46]

There were also Christians at the time who, to varying extents, called into question the whole social gospel project. These critics denounced what they perceived to be an exaggerated emphasis on the role of social environment in creating social problems (and in solving them). A good social order, they pointed out, does not inevitably produce good men.[47]

Finally, Smith notes that many social gospelers were too cavalier in their use of Scriptures. Failing to distinguish sufficiently biblical principles from the application of those principles to the American economy, social gospel proponents tied the Bible too tightly to specific economic policy recommendations. Such carelessness offended more cautious Christians who saw the danger of squandering the genuine moral authority of the Scriptures by yoking them to political or economic positions that were necessarily provisional and open to being discredited.[48] All of these differences among Protestants—inside and outside the social gospel movement—provided one source of instability that would contribute to the fissures about to be opened in American Protestantism.

That religion is an important factor in any explanation of progressivism seems obvious. As a group, progressives tended to be sons and daughters of devout believers, who abandoned the Christian orthodoxy—but not the religious zeal—of their parents. They channeled this zeal into secular professions geared to social reform (economics, social work, law, journalism, education), rather than into the calling of the ministry. In this way, progressives tended to conflate politics and culture, emphasizing the cultural sphere as a venue for political reform. Education, for instance, became a focal point for progressives' "hopes for a democratic future." The involvement of clergy themselves in progressivism led Richard Hofstadter to claim that no other major movement in American history "had ever received so much clerical sanction."[49]

Progressives' typical abandonment of orthodoxy is significant. Christopher Lasch has traced the religious element in the work of the prominent urban reformer Jane Addams. Addams, he observes, is an example of the way in which progressivism was an outgrowth of New England moralism, but her moralism was one stripped of its theological content. "It was the waning of theology rather than the persistence of piety," Lasch explains, "that created the cultural climate out of which the social settlement in particular and progressivism in general emerged." Addams herself claimed that the settlement house was not a continuation of, but a "revolt" against Puritan ideas—a substitution of works for dogma.[50]

James Kloppenberg's treatment of the intellectual foundations of progressivism supports the view that the movement was largely a postreligious phenomenon. Progressivism's intellectual icons, such as Herbert Croly, Walter Lippman, and John Dewey, departed from traditional metaphysical ideas connected to Christian orthodoxy and adopted a stance of philosophical uncertainty. The argument is similar in its basic outlines to Morton White's earlier contention that progressive-era social thought was a "revolt against formalism," construed in such a way as to be fundamentally at odds with any Catholic understanding of philosophy.[51]

It is too simplistic, however, to read such portrayals as definitive statements of Catholics' relationship to progressivism. First, Kloppenberg's and White's depictions of progressive thought depend on a certain cast of characters. But identifying the main actors in the progressive movement is itself a matter of contention.

Second, even accepting the proposed cast, it is too much to say that these thinkers' views were diametrically opposed to the theologically driven approach taken by Catholic thinkers. Kloppenberg's description of the progressives shows that they viewed a religious approach to social questions as the obverse of that of the ideologues of socialism, fascism, and communism. Like dogmatic Marxists, in this view, Catholics were seen as operating from a position of "certainty," seeking to impose order on society for the sake of the common good. For Marxists, the order was dictated by Marxist theory; for Catholics, it was divinely mandated and proclaimed by the authority of the Church. Both the Marxist and the Catholic approaches, then, were fundamentally at odds with a radically empirical approach that left the shape of society up to the working out of scientific method applied socially, that is, to the will of individuals expressed through social democracy.[52]

Leaving aside the intellectual problems that social democracy failed to solve, the approach of men such as Croly, Lippman, and Dewey was not as far from Catholic thinkers' as it has been portrayed (by both sides, at times). Admittedly, the proclamations of Catholic publicists as to the solution to the social question being found in Catholic teaching could easily be taken in the way in which social democratic intellectuals took them. An example of this brand of triumphalism appeared in a 1918 book review. Having mentioned the problems of profiteering, exploitation, sabotage, strikes, and revolutions, the reviewer avowed, "the Catholic Church believes she has the answer, and that she could bring about unity and harmony among all men if they would only submit to her direction."[53] On this score, then, American Catholic purveyors of the Church's social teaching deserve some blame.

Yet, as has been seen and will be substantiated more thoroughly over the course of remaining chapters, most Catholics were clear about the fact that the economic reform they advocated did not involve coercive measures along the lines of communism or fascism.[54] Catholics did insist that a just social order depended on the moral goodness of citizens (and the Church served as the guarantor of sound moral teaching), but, as the common disagreements among Catholic social thinkers demonstrated, Catholic teaching left open the question of the precise nature of the economic order. Catholics, too, were open to what experience and economic science taught.

As a group, Catholics were not a major part of the progressive movement. Progressivism was largely a phenomenon of the urban middle class, a segment not yet well-populated by Catholics. Additionally, ethnicity and Catholicism represented threats to the many progressives who identified progress with Americanization. The Catholic Church, for its part, continued to be wary of non-Catholic charitable groups. Some saw Catholic attachments to unions and political machines as conflicting with the aims of progressivism. Finally, most Catholics were skeptical of the legislative, statist approach to social reform, judging it to be a slippery slope to socialism.[55]

Assessing the relationship of Catholics to progressivism involves grappling with the peculiar position of Catholics in the United States during the era of reform. David O'Brien has captured well the character of that position:

As an organization and as a people, Catholicism became a subculture within, not outside of, American culture. From the viewpoint of other Americans that subculture seemed divisive, separatist, too Catholic, not American enough. From the viewpoint of Rome and that of converts or unusually committed Catholics, it seemed narrow, more social than religious, preoccupied with material rather than spiritual measurements of success, too American, not Catholic enough. Voluntary, self-consciously constructed, it was a uniquely American phenomenon.[56]

Deirdre Moloney's description of American Catholic social reformers fits O'Brien's characterization of a janus-faced subculture, at once American and non-American. Social reform, in Moloney's depiction, was a way for Catholics to fit into American society by displaying their middle-class credentials, but the particular character that reform assumed among Catholics allowed them to retain connections to the European contexts out of which their forbears had emigrated.[57]

The difficulty of defining alignments among Catholics and progressives is indicated by the example of Herbert Croly. Considered by many to be the prototypical intellectual spokesman for the progressive movement, Croly's *The Promise of American Life* has often been viewed as a representative progressive text.[58] Robert Crunden, on the other hand, reads Croly out of the progressive movement because he lacked the moralistic tone and clear religious background of other progressives.[59]

Others argue that Croly was not a progressive, not because he was not religious, but because his economic and political views were radical.[60] In this characterization, Croly advocates a corporatist economic system that looks similar to that embraced by Catholics such as Frederick Kenkel and the German Catholic Central Verein (see below). Further complicating the picture is the position that shares the view of Croly as radical but sees him nonetheless as squarely within the progressive movement. In this view, Croly's corporatist vision was one strand among the intellectual influences of progressivism.[61]

Explanations posited for the participation of the Protestant clergy in progressivism, it must be admitted, seem impotent when applied to Catholic priests. It is unlikely, for instance, that priests attached themselves to progressivism as a result of the status revolution of the late nineteenth century, since the status of Catholic priests could hardly be paralleled to that of Protestant ministers in their heyday.[62] Even the intellectual influence of the social gospel, definitely a key source of inspiration for progressive Protestant clergy, could only be indirectly related to the formation of a priest such as John Ryan. With rare exceptions, the Catholic priests who advocated progressive political programs over the next few decades remained untouched by theological liberalism of the sort that deeply influenced Protestant social gospelism. Although John Ryan has been called "the outstanding social gospeler of American Catholicism," he specifically criticized the Protestant social gospel advocate Walter Rauschenbusch for failing to emphasize sufficiently the Church's primary concern as being the salvation of souls.[63]

Any attempt to sort out Catholics' relationship to progressivism, then, is necessarily provisional and contingent. It depends on an assessment not only of Catholics' relationship to progressive ideas but also on decisions concerning what those ideas are. The following survey of Catholic economic thought during the progressive era will help to illuminate some of the various ways in which Catholic thinkers interacted with the dominant reform movement.

William Kerby

Born in Lawler, Iowa, William Kerby (1870–1936) was ordained a priest in 1892. After studying at Catholic University, he traveled to Berlin, Bonn, and Louvain for training in sociology. He returned to his alma mater in Washington, where he constituted the sociology department for more than a decade and left his mark on a distinguished list of students.[64]

In a series of articles penned around the turn of the century, Kerby displayed affinity for progressive reform, but at the same time strove to maintain a critical distance. "As a rule," he wrote, "we may trust a social movement in its general character, but we must beware of the danger there is in its disregard for accuracy, its impatience of restraint and its failure to count consequences before acting." To minimize these dangers, Kerby sought to demonstrate the kind of even-handedness that he believed should characterize any approach to reform. He recognized that both capitalist and laborer had been unfairly maligned and equally unfairly lionized by various groups, and so he tried to present them both sympathetically. He wrote of the "essential rightness in Reform," but decried the partisanship that made polemics prevail over genuine progress: "Right and wrong, understanding and misunderstanding, merited and unmerited criticism abound on both sides. . . . One must be Reformer or Conservative and adopt the language, spirit, and methods of his party, or be ruled out."[65]

Kerby wrote insightfully about the character of reform movements. "All men are to an extent reformers," he pointed out. "The most determined conservative will not resent all efforts at reform. He merely has his peculiar views about what is needed, of what is possible and advisable." He also expressed skepticism of the effort to portray a particular era as entirely unique in its emphasis on social reform. "Need of reform," he observed, "effort for it and opposition to it are practically constant in history." He noted the tendency of reformers to ignore the "limitations of life" in their focus on ideals, specifically highlighting the Populist Party's 1892 platform as a case in point.[66]

In several subtle ways, however, Kerby revealed his own perspective, which helps to place him within the boundaries of progressivism. In describing the differences between employer and laborer, Kerby portrayed the employer as taking a "business view" of life, which means that he does not see the relevance of moral law for the workings of business. In distinction, laborers "insist on the validity of moral law and ethical views in all the relations of life." Kerby also

located much of the fault for inadequate business standards in the fact of competition. In so doing, he implicitly sanctioned efforts to curtail or modify business
competition. Finally, he exhibited a Hegelian faith in the trajectory of history.
"Nature thus brings face to face, conservative and reformer as types of social
processes," he explained, "both necessary and each an obstacle, both narrow,
intolerant, impatient. Out of the conflict of the two tendencies comes much of
the elevation of the race, which we call progress."[67]

Kerby joined other American Catholics in producing a spate of articles critical of socialism during the progressive period. His treatment, however, was
more irenic than some, including as it did an admission of the veracity of many
of the socialists' criticisms of capitalism and a recommendation that Catholics
should not dismiss such complaints lightly. He strongly disagreed with the materialist philosophy that underpinned the Weltanschauung of many socialists, yet
he did not view socialism as an unmitigated evil. In fact, socialism, along with
unionism, deserved credit for bringing the "social question" to the fore; in
so doing, it had done Americans a service. For the United States lacked self-
consciousness on many social issues: "The social conscience is still largely dor-
mant in the United States. It is appalling that in the presence of the gigantic evils
of modern society there should remain so much of indifference in public opinion." To the socialists, he conceded, "we must give credit for forcing society to
know its wrongs."[68]

Kerby's work contained an inherent tension. He went to extensive lengths to
explain the creation of "the capitalist," "the laborer," "the reformer," and "the
conservative," stressing the circumstances that conspired to give each of these
his particular perspective on economic affairs. Simultaneously, he criticized
reformers and socialists for locating social ills in institutions and for neglecting
the role of the individual. "Reform's great error," he declared, "is in assuming
that social wrongs are created by institutions and that they are cured by them.
They are caused by *men*, and men alone can cure them." It was the reform of
men, moreover, in which the Church had a conspicuous part to play: "There can
be and will be no social reform without individual reform; there will be no individual reform that is not moral and religious."[69]

Kerby's views seem to have developed over the next fifteen years, as his
ambivalence toward reform disintegrated. War was one catalyst. As is well
documented, World War I entailed the rapid organization and centralization of
many facets of American life. The organizational spirit of the times had an effect
on Catholics as well. The war years saw the collaboration of the nation's bishops
in the National Catholic War Council, to be continued later as the National
Catholic Welfare Conference.[70]

Kerby viewed this nationalization as a hopeful sign, endorsing the idea that
duty to one's country constituted a religious obligation. On the vast efforts of the
nation during the war, he declared, "Being duty, it is religion. Being religion, it
is of God. Being of God it is destiny. All of this must be seen in the glow of
supernatural sanction." In addition, Americans, given the exigencies of a total

war, came to accept a broadened view of the role of the state. Again, Kerby approved, encouraging only that "our re-education must lead us to the understanding of this wider concept of state functions."[71] The experience of the wartime extension of state power convinced Kerby that the application of that power to the social question would produce beneficial results.

John Ryan

Probably the best-known Catholic progressive was William Kerby's student, and later colleague, John A. Ryan. In his politics and in his economic thought, Ryan (1865–1945) shared much with the American progressive movement and may even be considered part of it.[72] Ryan championed the rights of workers and emphasized the beneficial role that could be played by government in bringing about social justice through industrial regulation and wage law.[73]

Ryan was born in Vermillion, Minnesota, in 1865 and attended seminary near Minneapolis, training to be a priest for the archdiocese led by the outspoken Americanist, Archbishop John Ireland. He was sent to the newly formed Catholic University of America in 1898 for training in moral theology where he studied under Kerby, among others. At Catholic University, Ryan developed an abiding interest in economic questions and wrote his dissertation in moral philosophy on the subject of justice in wages. In 1915, Ryan returned to Catholic University as a professor of political science; he soon switched to moral theology, a position he held until his retirement in 1939.[74]

Joseph McShane has argued that Ryan accomplished the task of renewing natural law thinking, showing its compatibility with American thought and showing how it led to progressive reform ideas. Ryan understood himself, McShane observes, as integrating scholastic moral theology and social and economic reform. It seems clear that Ryan's progressive views predisposed him to interpret Catholic social teaching in certain ways. For Ryan, Leo's 1891 encyclical did not prompt a move to social reform; it simply provided a new lode from which to mine nuggets of support for political and economic views already held. Ryan was progressive before he ever read Leo.[75]

Ryan's own understanding of the relationship between Catholic social teaching and the progressive political agenda is perhaps most succinctly stated in a letter he wrote to Frederick Kenkel. Commenting on an address by an English Catholic social thinker, B. W. Devas, Ryan recounted Devas's views:

> He maintained that all the specific doctrines of Pope Leo's social encyclicals are already accepted by the majority of persons, and that specific legislative measures looking to the realization of these principles already have been, or soon will be among the living programs of political parties. Hence, he said, all that we can do is try to assist these legislative movements, and try to infuse a Christian spirit into social reform generally.[76]

Devas exaggerated, Ryan thought, but "he is to a great extent right." It was certainly the case, Ryan observed, that the principles of Catholic social teaching "are not *in opposition* to progressive labor and social legislation," and, he added, "if we want to do anything besides talking generalities, we ought to cooperate with these definite and practical proposals."[77]

Straddling the two identities of Catholic and American never posed for him the problem it did for some of his coreligionists.[78] An unproblematic understanding of the relationship between his Americanism and his Catholicism did not mean that Ryan swallowed whole the raft of ideas that tended to float together down the stream of American progressivism. He shared none of the nativist fear of immigrants that tinged many progressives, and he was, perhaps as a result, friendlier toward organized labor. He was also a caustic critic of prohibition.[79]

In other words, his alliance with non-Catholic progressives was for Ryan a means, not an end, and it was conditioned always on the truths that he believed were embodied in the Catholic faith. On the issue of birth control, for instance— the promotion of which was an important cause for many progressives—Ryan was never other than a staunch defender of his Church's traditional position.[80] In fact, Ryan's economic positions were often tied logically to his moral positions. His concern that working men be paid a living wage, for instance, derived at least partially from his belief that a large family headed by a male breadwinner should be normal.[81]

On some counts, Ryan's religiously motivated positions located him within the American mainstream. Opposition to socialism, for instance, was typical of progressives. Socialism remained an attractive option for many Americans, especially workers, in the early twentieth century. Socialists held a third of the top positions in American Federation of Labor unions, despite Samuel Gompers's concerted effort to keep them out.[82] Socialist Eugene Debs garnered almost a million votes in his campaign for president in 1912—a figure that represented 6 percent of the electorate and more than twice the share ever previously received by a socialist candidate. In this environment, Catholics were not alone in viewing socialism as a serious threat to the American political order. Ryan's seeking of a middle way between corporation-friendly laissez-faire liberalism and state socialism was in line with the efforts of other progressives.[83]

Ryan and Richard Ely

One important influence on Ryan's economic thought was Richard Ely, a major figure in the social gospel and progressive movement.[84] Ely (1854–1943) was also instrumental in the rise of the New Economics in the United States, an offshoot of the German Historical School.[85] Ely was introduced to the German school through Johannes Conrad and Karl Knies, while studying at Halle and Heidelberg. Ely promoted the movement in the United States, first at Johns Hopkins and later at Wisconsin. He had contact with most of the major players in the movement, including Thorstein Veblen, John R. Commons, Albion Small, and Edward A. Ross.[86]

As will be seen, many of Ely's ideas on economics would be reflected in Ryan's writings. Ely stressed the "positive" character of liberty (e.g., the freedom to be employed) and saw the state as the guarantor of that liberty. Ely assaulted the assumptions of "classicism" (classical economics), including that of the existence of natural laws of economics from which policy could be deduced. Instead, he insisted, empirical research would provide the basis for economic reform. Ely also accepted the arguments of English economist John A. Hobson, whose theory of underconsumption demanded that a greater share of corporate income be directed to workers' wages.[87]

Ely's expansive concept of the role of the state in modern life was rooted in a peculiar historical view of church-state relations. The earlier Christian (Catholic) Church had considered the state base and the church exalted, he claimed, thereby justifying domination of the state by the church. "The Protestant Reformation," he continued, "meant the exaltation of the State." He viewed positively the extension of the state into education, universities, extension of civil courts, and curtailment of ecclesiastical courts all good things: "The only limit to the functions of the State is that laid down by Aristotle. . . . 'It is the duty of the State to do whatever is in its power to promote the good life.'" Paying tribute to the theology of Richard Rothe, who thought that the fulfillment of the church would be in the state, Ely implied that progress involved a kind of withering of the church to be replaced by the state.[88]

Ely argued that "the main purpose of the State is the religious purpose" and "the nation must be fully recognized as a Christian nation." What he meant by "Christian nation" was not that the state would recognize any particular theological position, but that the nation's laws would promote social and economic well-being: "Factory acts, educational laws, laws for the establishment of parks and of playgrounds for children, laws securing honest administration of justice, laws rendering the courts accessible to the poor as well as the rich."[89]

Tending theologically to a liberal form of Christianity, Ely nonetheless had respect for certain aspects of Catholicism. He appreciated the Catholic Church's insistence on the reality of suffering as part of the Christian life: "The cross is still a reality," he noted, and "the Roman Catholic Church provides opportunities for self-renunciation the most complete. To Protestants this often appears worse than useless; but it is, nevertheless, one source of its strength. . . . Let us, at any rate, see to it that for us religion is something more than a 'graceful and pleasing appendix to life.'"[90]

Ely encouraged American Catholics to become more active as social reformers. He saw a happy trend aborning in the early work of John Ryan and wrote the preface for Ryan's first major work, the published form of his dissertation on wages. Ryan argued there that a wage sufficient for workers to support families was morally required. The book was, in Ely's words, "the first attempt in the English language to elaborate what may be called a Roman Catholic system of political economy."[91] Viewing Ryan's work as consistent with his own efforts to reform American economics, Ely welcomed this new Catholic contribution to economic thought.

Catholics and Professional Economics

Understanding the broad trends in the academic world of the late nineteenth and early twentieth centuries is instrumental for considering the views of American Catholic thinkers on economic issues. One of these trends was the professionalization of economics as a discipline, itself part of a broader trend of academic professionalization and specialization. Such disciplinary specialization evolved out of the efforts of American universities to emulate the model of scientific inquiry that they admired in their German counterparts.[92] As departmental divisions arose and solidified during this period, economics became one of the "social sciences," a term first used in the United States in the early twentieth century.[93] Whether by coincidence or some necessary connection, the establishment of the social sciences was almost coterminous with the secularization of universities.[94] The tandem development of professional economics and secularization presented a special problem for Catholics concerned with engaging the discipline of economics as it existed in the American academy.

At the same time, at its roots, professional economics was linked to religious concerns.[95] Richard Ely was one key link between the budding academic field of economics and the social gospel and progressive movements. Ely was the stimulus behind the organization of what would become the major professional economics organization, the American Economic Association (AEA). Founded in 1885, the association had as its specific purpose to offer a critique of classical economics from the perspective of New Economics.[96] Ely was not the only link between the social gospel/progressive movements and the AEA. At its inception, the AEA was closely tied to the social gospel: Twenty-three of fifty founding members were ministers or former ministers.[97]

The New Economics (or the "American historical school") did not last as a coherent movement, although it might be more accurate to view its dissipation not so much as demise; instead, it was integrated into and appropriated by the older discipline of political economy.[98] For the older tradition of economics was itself in a process of revision at the end of the nineteenth century, with more emphasis being placed on empirical methods.[99]

In the United States, even historical economists joined other progressive-era social scientists in carefully distinguishing their positions from socialism. The increasing professionalization of the discipline, too, militated against radicalism.[100] Historian Dorothy Ross has portrayed economics in the progressive era as a battle among three competing ideas: marginalism, the liberal economic interpretation of history, and the socialist historic-evolutionary economics of Veblen. While marginalism won a clear victory over Veblen, the debate over historicism continued.[101]

The American reception of the marginalist revolution, in Ross's account, was especially propitious for several reasons. One reason was the favorable climate of positivist and liberal assumptions that already characterized economics in the United States. In addition, the labor theory of value was discredited in America because of its association with Marxism. Marginal theory benefited, then, by providing intellectual ammunition in the political fight against the enemies of liberalism.[102]

Professional economics in the progressive era, as in other periods, was not characterized by absolute consensus, but by various individuals and schools battling over wide ranges of disputed territory. Defenders of orthodox economics confronted challenges from dissenters who questioned traditional assumptions. Although a kind of *Methodenstreit* between marginalists and historicists continued in the United States in the twentieth century, there was no real institutionalist school until World War I, nor was the debate as heated as in Germany and Austria. Some economists would draw on Veblen in offering an institutionalist challenge to orthodox economics. Although Veblen himself, with his sometimes behaviorist assumptions, presented a problematic approach from the perspective of Catholic anthropology, many Catholics shared the institutionalist critique's skepticism toward orthodox assumptions.[103]

Catholics did not ignore these developments within economics. Besides William Kerby and John Ryan, a number of other Catholic scholars produced meaningful work in the discipline.[104] Catholic thinking on economic issues, moreover, was not monolithic. Most Catholics tended more toward the ambivalence of Kerby than the enthusiasm of Ryan with respect to progressive-era reform, but many shades of difference could be descried. On particular matters of economics, too, such as wages, Catholics engaged in debates that reflected differing views of economics more than differing moral theologies. The divisions common to economics during the progressive era also characterized Catholic discussions of economic topics.

Francis Howard argued for a position consonant with that of the historical economists in *American Catholic Quarterly Review*. Howard articulated the relationship between political economy and the natural sciences, observing that, even in the case of physical laws, such laws are not absolute but dependent on a given set of conditions. The relativity of political economy, he claimed, is more pronounced than that of the natural sciences. The errors in economics, he argued, "and all the popular prejudice against it, have resulted because it was not understood that its laws are true only of certain conditions, and that these conditions are in a state of constant change; and because, moreover, economists have endeavored to extend their generalizations beyond legitimate premises."[105]

Howard, like Ely and other historical economists, denied the absolute character of economic laws. Even supply and demand, he pointed out, is not a distinctive economic law, but "the economic statement of the general problem of equilibrium that is found in all the sciences." If premises such as self-interest and perfect competition needed extensive qualification, as Howard thought that they did, then any theory founded on them as premises was of limited value as a description of reality. Howard explicitly praised the "new school" of historical economics, Wilhelm Roscher in particular, for demonstrating the relativity of economic laws to historical circumstances.[106]

Howard argued that economics "must be studied with reference to human happiness and well-being, for, otherwise, it will degenerate into a mere academic discipline for the edification of the erudite." In this way, Howard explained, ethics was intrinsically valuable to economics, giving it its purpose and value. Howard found evidence for this claim even in the *Principia* of Alfred Marshall, where Marshall observed that poverty is the problem "which gives to economic studies their chief and highest interest," and poverty, Howard concluded, was a problem only because of "the growth and prevalence of ethical feeling."[107]

Economics was a matter of importance for the *American Ecclesiastical Review*, which sought to keep its clerical readers informed of the latest economic scholarship through frequent book reviews on the subject. In this venue, the nature of the editors' economic views surfaced. They accepted, for instance, the subjective value theory that lay at the root of the marginalist revolution and rejected the labor theory of value that enjoyed a distinguished pedigree from Adam Smith to Karl Marx. They described Henry George's single tax as "a doctrine which not a few Catholics ignorant probably or heedless of its theoretical principles and practical bearings, still strongly advocate." The editors criticized a reading of the gospels that understood Christ to be condemning wealth (as opposed to its abuse): "Christ preached no socialistic creed. He was no popular demagogue denouncing capitalism as a crime."[108]

The editors had strong words of praise for the first volume of German priest-economist Heinrich Pesch's *Lehrbuch der Nationalökonomie*. Critical of economics that was either overly empirical or excessively abstract, the *AER* perceived Pesch's book as being "harmoniously inductive and deductive, analytic and synthetic." In another review, the editors bemoaned the severing of the historical connection between moral philosophy and economics, but expressed pleasure that "during the past century," the sundering had been somewhat repaired. The *AER*, through such reviews, deliberately aimed at the extension of economic knowledge among Catholic clergy, for "on none more than the clergy and seminarians preparing for efficient work in the Master's vineyard is it incumbent to be and keep acquainted with the economic problems and conditions affecting society in these times."[109]

Most of *AER*'s contributors shared Kerby's early views of progressive reform, taking up a stance that might be regarded as cautiously positive. Such was the tone set by the editors themselves in 1905. Priests ought to approach reform somewhat differently from economists, they noted, with a particular emphasis on its spiritual dimension. At the same time, there was a need for "a well-informed priesthood, a clergy which, whilst not permitting itself to be consumed by externals, does not at the same time refuse to take cognizance of progressive methods in reform legislation and the operations that improve the conditions of the people." Economic and political knowledge, they predicted, would allow the priest to discern prudently, "to make effective whatever is good in the efforts of the economic reformers, and to preserve his people from admitting those false maxims and motives of success which are being taught by the irreligious socialist."[110]

For many priests, this process of discernment led to a series of positions that were, in the American context, a peculiar mix. William Stang, who produced a raft of articles and books on socialism in the first decade of the century, at times sounded like an ardent defender of capitalism. Stang, who became bishop of Fall River, Massachusetts, staunchly opposed measures that diminished private property rights. The answer to the social question, he insisted, following Leo, was not in the abridgment of private property holding but in its extension. The state's role in the solution of social problems, then, was quite limited. Stang opposed the "evident tendency among men to increase the power of the State, to favor a more paternal government. . . . The State should not absorb the rights of individuals, but should keep them inviolate, unless they clash with the common good and interests of others."[111]

Stang allowed for the intervention of government for the remediation of certain evils, including "danger to morals" in workshops or factories, the laying of "unjust burdens" on employees, or the endangerment of the health of workers by working conditions. "But the State should not intervene in or meddle with private concerns," he concluded, "any further than is required for the remedy of the evil or the removal of the danger."[112]

He observed that the "position of the workingman . . . is constantly improving," and he opposed the movement toward government ownership of productive enterprises, doubting that it would aid this process. The "present industrial system has its defects," he admitted, "but it has its great advantages. . . . Individual capitalists are more economical and more enterprising managers than public boards or state officials." "Our biggest capitalists in this country," he continued, "became rich by hard work; and not by 'mere luck' as some imagine. . . . And while they grew rich themselves, they enriched thousands of their poor fellow-citizens and made hundreds of thousands comfortable in life."[113]

Such commentary notwithstanding, Stang favored economic reform and cannot be viewed as an apologist for business. Following Leo, he denied that an employer could justly pay as low a wage as the market would bear, if it was not up to *Rerum*'s standard. Trade unions were a force for good and he advised employers that they "will not get rid of them by ignoring them or treating them with ridicule and contempt. Unionism has to be recognized and respected." He upheld the worker's right to strike, writing that it could be an effective tool and was sometimes necessary in the face of an intractable employer. "A priest who would indiscriminately condemn strikes," he wrote, "should not be praised for pastoral prudence." Finally, he argued that existing legislation in the United States was inadequate with respect to worker protections such as accident insurance. The reason was the untoward union of employers and state: "Our magnates have owned or at least controlled municipal and State legislators." In line with progressive urban reform aimed at machine politics, Stang urged priests to do their part in eradicating this problem by promoting clean government: "An occasional instruction on the solemn and sacred trust of voting and on the hideous crime of selling or purchasing votes is within the priestly line of duty."[114]

Stang's concern with reforming urban politics did not make him a natural ally of Protestant reformers, however. Stang shared what was among Catholics a common understanding of history, which viewed the Reformation as the source of all the evils that subsequently befell human society. The severity of the modern social problem, Stang asserted, was a result of the forces unleashed in the sixteenth century. "After an exaggerated individualism and an insane liberalism, both children of the Protestant heresy, had done their deadly work, and had plunged the poor laborer into deeper misery and desperation," the Catholic Church appeared on the scene to attempt to rebuild a Christian social order. Focusing on nineteenth-century Germany, Stang praised the accomplishments of Catholic reformers such as Bishop Ketteler, while mocking the efforts of Protestant antisocialists. Stang did not restrict his criticism to Protestants; the French Catholic hierarchy, he opined, had also failed to lead on economic reform and thereby abdicated the field to socialism.[115]

Stang's perspective demonstrated well the ambivalence with which many Catholics regarded progressive-era reform. It was characterized by an insistence that Catholics be deeply involved in social and economic reform, but that they carefully assess whether or not their aims could be best served by existing models and movements for reform. Catholic voices calling for reform continued through the second decade of the century. "There is abroad a cry for social reform, and the Church cannot but be interested in the methods adopted to bring it about," wrote one commentator in 1910. He argued further that knowledge of social issues was central, not peripheral, to the mission of the priesthood. Arguing that the study of social problems should be part of seminary education, he also urged priests not to refrain from social reform on the grounds that such activity required the "extraordinary knowledge" of the specialist.[116]

The suggestion was merited as far as it went; however, in the exhortation for priests to enter the sphere of social reform, one could also glimpse a twofold danger. First, there was the danger that already troubled parts of the social gospel movement: the neglect of the Church's salvific and spiritual mission in favor of an overemphasis on economic reform. Second, if care was not taken in bringing moral training to bear on the economic sphere, clerics and others would lay themselves open to the charges that would in fact be made by Catholic businessmen in the following decades: that moralists too flippantly pronounced on economic matters without having a full understanding of the workings of business.

The Problem of the Just Wage

The *AER*'s review of John Ryan's *A Living Wage* highlighted one disputed area among Catholic economists and moral philosophers, the problem of the just wage. The review was largely favorable and agreed with Ryan that there existed an ethical obligation on the part of the employer to pay a living wage. The reviewer was less certain than Ryan, however, that the obligation was one of justice.[117]

The question of the just wage had been discussed in Catholic circles since the beginnings of the spread of wage labor in the sixteenth century. Catholic moralists generally took their cue from Thomas Aquinas, who had described the nature and obligations of justice based on Aristotle's foundational work on the subject. The central question, which stimulated the most vigorous debate, was: How is the level of a just wage determined? Since the beginning of the debate, moralists had tried to balance two realities: the right of a worker to a dignified living and the economic feasibility of wage rates. Inevitably, economic and moral questions were entwined. If wage rates were determined strictly by economic law (the price of labor as a function of supply and demand), then no room existed for human moral agency for the adjustment of wages. If, however, wages could fluctuate at employers' discretion, then wage rates became a matter for ethical consideration.

One piece of the debate focused on the question of whether the payment of a living wage was an obligation of justice or an obligation of charity. As noted above, John Ryan argued that the living wage was a matter of justice. Many Catholic commentators disagreed. Some of the disagreement stemmed from different interpretations of *Rerum Novarum*.

René Holaind treated the question in a commentary two years after the publication of *Rerum*. Holaind surveyed the various economic theories dealing with wages, including the minimum theory of Ricardo, the wage-fund theory, and a more recent theory proposed by George Gunton, based on the worker's standard of living. Holaind found each of these deficient in some way and examined the relevance of Leo's principle that wages "must be enough to support the wage-earner in reasonable and frugal comfort." Given this assertion by the pope, the question arose as to whether this requirement represented an obligation in justice. The difficulty, as Holaind noted, was that it was difficult to square with the traditional notion of commutative justice concerning the exchange of things of equal value. That is, if one worker performed a job that was of greater economic value than that performed by another worker, how could justice demand an equal standard for payment of the two?[118]

To answer the question, Holaind reported on a letter written by Cardinal Zigliara in response to a query from the archbishop of Mechlin. Zigliara argued in his response that a minimum wage according to the standard Leo stated was an obligation of commutative justice. Wage levels above this minimum, however, including the "family wage" (to support not only the worker but also his

family) would not fall under commutative justice; there may be such an obligation in some cases, but it would fall under charity, not justice. Zigliara also added
an important qualification to the minimum wage requirement, which mirrored
Leo's teaching in *Rerum*. In cases in which it was impossible for the employer to
pay the minimum, he would be justified in paying what could be afforded.[119]

In sum, Holaind presented Zigliara's answer as encapsulating Church teaching on wages. There was an obligation in justice to pay a living wage and sometimes an obligation in charity to pay a family wage. The Church recognized economic reality, however, and did not insist that an employer cease operations
rather than pay a below-standard wage to willing workers. It also recognized
the normative role of wages as prices to determine the level of compensation
demanded by commutative justice. Ryan, for his part, was convinced of his own
position and believed that Zigliara's explanation "leaves something to be desired,
both in clearness and conclusiveness."[120] The family wage, he continued to argue,
was a requirement of justice, not charity.

Ryan tussled similarly with another interlocutor over the issue of "stockwatering" (the effort by a corporation to increase nominal capital by the issuance of
new shares). To simplify what was an extended and complex debate, T. Slater, a
Jesuit at St. Bruno's College in Wales, thought that what was sometimes called
stockwatering was justifiable in some cases, provided that it occurred in a competitive (not monopolistic) context, so that commodity prices were not affected.
Ryan believed that stockwatering tended to pressure profits (and therefore prices)
higher and was, therefore, unjust to consumers. Part of Ryan's argument involved
the claim that stockholders were in justice entitled to no more than the competitive rate of interest. Slater countered that shareholders "are the owners of a company's property, and whatever that property produces belongs to the owners of
it." Again, the perspectives at play among Catholics mirrored those in the broader
American milieu.[121]

The lack of agreement among moralists such as Slater and Ryan ensured
that uncertainty existed with respect to the moral dimensions of many economic
issues. J. A. Dewe of Duquesne University expressed as much in the *AER* in
1914. Dewe was the author of a history of economics, in which he demonstrated
his debt to current trends in the historical profession by noting that history had
been raised to the level of a "science," studying "the workings of unseen laws
and influences." In the *AER* article, he complained that contemporary Catholic
treatises on morality and the law had not adequately taken into consideration
modern economic developments.[122]

As with the Slater-Ryan dispute, Dewe focused attention on the stock market. Dewe's article was less a full-scale treatment than a call for as much, but he
did hint at how a moral analysis of certain stock trading practices would look.
Dewe examined briefly short-selling, buying and selling on margin, and the use
of "puts" and "calls." On the topic of margins, for instance, he noticed that one
of the criteria conventionally required for validity of contract, namely, "that the
thing sold should be both physically and morally within the disposal of the

seller," was missing. On the other hand, he concluded, "to abolish the whole system of margins would mean the practical suspension of the operations of the exchange, and the loss of so much necessary good accomplished by them." Faced with such dilemmas, Dewe demanded that some Catholic, "an expert economist as well as a theologian," undertake to make "perfectly plain the links between the grand old principles and present conditions."[123]

Catholics against Progressivism

Often no more friendly toward capitalism than Ryan or Kerby, another group of Catholics were nonetheless more critical of the mainstream of American reform. Antiprogressives such as Frederick Kenkel approached the social question from another perspective.[124]

Kenkel (1863–1952) was one of the "conservative reformers," the ethnic Germans associated with the Catholic Central Verein (CCV).[125] Founded in 1855 and headquartered in St. Louis, the CCV was one of the oldest Catholic social institutions in the country and maintained a long tradition of charity and publication on social questions. Until the first decade of the twentieth century, the CCV was primarily a mutual aid society, little concerned with systemic reform. In the latter part of the century, it played an important role in the Americanist controversy, opposing what it viewed as the dangerously assimilationist policies of Archbishop Ireland and his allies. Its countercultural stance toward Americanism continued in some ways as it entered the field of social reform. In its first significant statement on social reform in 1905, the Central Verein advocated a full-fledged corporatist system. This plan "aroused little enthusiasm," however, and was "never again presented . . . in so extreme or rigid a formulation."[126]

In 1909, Kenkel assumed control of the Verein's Central Bureau and directed it for more than four decades until his death in 1952. In the year of Kenkel's accession, the CCV began publication of the *Central-Blatt and Social Justice*. The publication mirrored the development of the organization, beginning as a predominantly German-language periodical but gradually shifting to English-only by 1946, having changed its title to *Social Justice Review* six years earlier.[127]

Under Kenkel's leadership, the CCV remained devoted to the teachings of the Church as expressed in papal encyclicals and also continued to draw on the legacy of German social thought emanating from Bishop Ketteler and the corporatists of the late nineteenth century, particularly Heinrich Pesch. At the level of policy, in the 1910s, the CCV supported organized labor, state legislation concerning minimum wages and the labor of women and children, workmen's compensation laws, and government regulation of industrial safety.[128]

While the CCV never embraced capitalism and was generally critical of the U.S. economic system, it also stressed the dangers of centralization of economic functions in government, especially at the national level. It was the latter concern that led to disillusionment with the New Deal. Kenkel foresaw the problem in the tilt toward government action indicated by progressive-era reform. "I see the day coming," he predicted in 1916, "when we, who for twenty years have said there is a social question, who have been called socialists, may be forced to ... protest against the radical tendencies of the day. I believe I will see the day when I will ... [be] forced to say: 'This is the hour of state-socialism.'"[129] As will be seen in subsequent chapters, Kenkel could detect the glimmerings of state socialism not only among irreligious socialists but also among some Catholic commentators who paid too little attention to the dangers of state centralization.

Catholic antiprogressives were not the only group that set themselves against what they perceived as the dominant trends of the day. Jackson Lears has described well the diverse array of individuals, groups, and movements in the early twentieth century that in one way or another can be seen as impelled by an "antimodernist" impulse.[130]

Lears's account demonstrates the difficulty, however, of Catholics finding real allies among American antimoderns. In many cases antimodern intellectuals and aesthetes could be seen as coopting Catholic ideas to secular purposes—the phenomenon designated "antimodern modernism" by Lears. The Arts and Crafts movement, for instance, ostensibly an effort to restore communal values to modern economy, "became less a path to satisfying communal work than a therapy for tired business men."[131]

Catholic mysticism, art, and ritual, similarly, "became instruments for promoting intense experience, rather than paths to salvation."[132] Among many non-Catholic intellectuals, there was a marked attraction to "Catholic forms" in art and architecture around the turn of the twentieth century. Most did not actually become Catholic (though some did embrace Anglo-Catholicism, a more respectable alternative). Charles Eliot Norton (1827–1908), G. Stanley Hall (1844–1924), and Van Wyck Brooks (1886–1963) were among those whose aesthetic sensibilities led them to Catholic art and ritual. But this attraction ultimately was, as Brooks himself put it, "dilettantish Catholicism."[133] Even Henry Adams, whose attraction to Catholicism was more than just aesthetic, encountered the Catholic religion selectively. Drawn to the emotional and "irrational" aspects of medieval Catholicism, such as devotion to the Virgin Mary, Adams had no use for the scholastic philosophy that had also been an integral part of the medieval faith.[134]

Architect Ralph Adams Cram provides an example of the slippage between professed positions and actions characteristic of American antimoderns. Cram wrote disdainfully of modern commercial capitalism and expressed his disdain through art, but he was totally reliant on capitalists to sponsor his architectural projects.[135] On the social question, Cram displayed both socialist and monarchist tendencies, neither of which held much attraction for most American Catholic thinkers.[136] He wrote movingly of his religious experiences in Assisi and Rome, but his idiosyncratic views on evolution and his aristocratic sensibility combined to engender a claim that not all human beings were of equal dignity or worth.[137]

From the perspective of most Catholics, Cram's form of antimodernism would furnish at best an imperfect prospect for intellectual alliance.

Catholic forms in art could be exploited and detached from their sacred purpose by modern Americans to serve a utilitarian function, but the phenomenon of antimodern modernism should not be viewed with too much disdain. Even if they did not wish to acknowledge the theological background of medieval forms of societal organization or Catholic art, the intellectuals and others Lears describes at least recognized the attraction of community and the aesthetic appeal of sacred art. Lears observes, for instance, that the affinity of non-Catholics for Catholic forms in art represented genuine religious longing (not merely conspicuous consumption or dilettantism). He recognizes that the revolt of the antimodernists did have value: Their "accommodation was never complete. When antimodernists preserved higher loyalties outside the self, they sustained a note of protest against a complacent faith in progress and a narrow positivist conception of reality."[138] Finally, given that modernity, though it could be excoriated, could not really be escaped, most American Catholics themselves fit the description of antimodern moderns. Not completely at home in modern, industrial America, they attempted both to live within it and to reform it by drawing on the social and intellectual resources of their faith.

Bishops' Program and Pastoral of 1919

As the progressive era drew to a close, the intersection of various forces in American society threatened to stifle Catholic voices in the public forum. Social Darwinism combined with the burgeoning field of hereditary science to provide authoritative backing to nativist racism. The racist note reflected in the eugenics movement and Madison Grant's *The Passing of the Great Race* spilled into anti-immigration efforts (and, therefore, anti-Catholicism), providing them with an especially virulent character in the 1910s. The new anti-Catholicism found its supporters primarily among the rural populace and characterized the Church as a force of reaction. Although presidential candidates had courted the immigrant vote in 1912, anti-Germanism prompted by the outbreak of war in 1914 reinforced the nativist mood. Following the war, the Red Scare shifted nativist concerns away from German-Americans and back to radicalism.[139]

These developments notwithstanding, it was clear that by the end of the second decade of the century, Catholics were asserting a more vocal role in debates over economic ideas and policies. As has been seen, many of these Catholic voices were raised in favor of increasing government intervention. John O'Grady discussed the issue of compulsory health insurance and, while recognizing the threat it posed to existing groups providing such insurance (such as fraternal organizations and labor unions), ultimately leaned in favor of legislation on the issue. A reviewer in the *Catholic World* identified himself as "progressive-minded" and was clearly sympathetic to a larger role for government activity in the economy.[140]

J. W. R. Maguire, professor of social sciences at St. Viator College in Illinois, wrote optimistically about the possibility of combining the disparate reform movements so as to achieve smashing success. Explicitly abandoning the strident antisocialism of earlier Catholic treatments, Maguire distinguished the "economic reform" of socialists from their "materialistic interpretation of history" and "unethical doctrines concerning the family," without the least hint that there could be some connection between these positions. Maguire waxed enthusiastic about the possibility of uniting labor unions, progressives, charity workers, and Catholic social reformers on "a platform providing for merely practical, fundamental, economic social reform." He rightly pointed out that the moderating of some socialists such as Gustavus Meyers provided an opportunity for dialogue, but he seemed too facilely to chalk up differences among reformers to "misunderstanding."[141]

O'Grady and Maguire would both be involved in one of the strongest Catholic voices on economic issues, that which emanated from the Social Action Department of the National Catholic Welfare Conference (NCWC). The NCWC was founded during the war, in 1918, to serve as an instrument of cooperation for the nation's many bishops and dioceses. The Committee on Special War Activities (CSWA), out of which would be formed the Social Action Department, charged John Ryan with writing a program for reform that could be released under the aegis of the American bishops. The Bishops' Program of 1919 brought the bishops into the fray of the debates of the day.[142]

The program began by summarizing several other programs for reconstruction that had recently been proffered, most notably that of the British Labor Party. It pointed out, from a Catholic perspective, the highlights and drawbacks of each of the plans. It observed, for instance, that the British plan was one of "radical reforms, leading ultimately to complete socialism," and, therefore, "cannot be approved by Catholics."[143]

On the issue of wage rates, the program declared that the raising of wages that the war entailed should not be reversed. It observed that a "living wage is not necessarily the full measure of justice." Instead, the living wage is only the "minimum of justice," and the tremendous wealth of the American nation created a situation that demanded that most workers' compensation exceed the minimum. To ensure at least a living wage, the program stipulated, states should enact laws establishing wages at rates "sufficient for the decent maintenance of a family, in the case of all male adults, and adequate to the decent individual support of female workers."

The program recommended a comprehensive scheme of social insurance, "against illness, invalidity, unemployment, and old age," funded by taxes on industry. It saw this program as a "lesser evil," a needed stopgap until all workers had the means through sufficient wages to provide for present and future contingencies. It also proposed several other reforms, including more extensive use of the shop committee, the expansion of vocational training opportunities, and the abolition of child labor. On the last point, the document came short of proposing a child labor amendment to the Constitution, a proposal that would incite controversy among Catholics when it was raised in the 1920s and again as part of the New Deal.

On the question of whether or not the current American economic system required fundamental overhaul, the bishops' statement answered in the negative. "It seems clear," it said, "that the present industrial system is destined to last for a long time in its main outlines." The program doubted that private ownership of capital would be replaced by collectivism in the foreseeable future, and it offered this prediction approvingly, observing that the evils of socialism far outweighed those of capitalism.

At the same time, the program identified three major areas in which it thought that the capitalist system was deficient: inefficiency and waste in production and distribution of commodities, insufficient incomes for most wage earners, and exorbitant incomes for a small minority.

The first problem, it believed, would be resolved in large part by implementation of reforms cited earlier in the text. It could only be fully addressed, however, by a wider distribution of ownership and management of productive capital, brought about by worker-owned firms and "copartnership" arrangements in which workers owned a substantial portion of the company stock and held some decision-making power. If moves were made in these directions, the program observed, the wage system would disintegrate, but private ownership would remain.

The second problem, insufficient income, would also be addressed significantly by the aforementioned reforms, including living wage legislation. To confront the third problem, the program endorsed anti-monopoly initiatives, government regulation of public service monopolies, and "heavy taxation" of incomes, excess profits, and inheritances.

The program concluded by calling for a "reform in the spirit" of both labor and capital, without which any economic or political reform would be inconsequential. The worker, the statement exhorted, must give his employer an "honest day's work" and stem the desire to exact a "maximum of return for a minimum of service." The employer, it continued, must see wealth as stewardship, not view profit as "the basic justification of business enterprise," and, above all, recognize the worker's "right to a decent livelihood."

Response to the program among both Catholics and the American public more generally was varied. Most Catholics, rooted as they were in working-class urban backgrounds, reacted favorably, seeing the program as taking the side of labor against capital. Most of the Catholic press and Catholic academia lauded the program's publication. Catholic businessmen, however, were generally critical, and there were other, scattered voices of dissent as well.[144]

For example, Conde Pallen, a prominent Catholic journalist, joined his non-Catholic colleagues at the National Civic Federation in deploring what they perceived to be the document's radical implications.[145] Frederick Kenkel was also troubled by a growing tendency toward state centralization. In an article

published a month after the promulgation of the program, Kenkel warned against
the state's aggrandizement of economic functions and, in what appears to be a
veiled reference to the program, wrote, "If the last state of things is not to be
worse than the first, no Catholic program of social reform or reconstruction
should be drawn up which does not make reference to his peril . . . and to the
safeguards to be set up against state socialism."[146]

Most non-Catholics, whether critical or appreciative, saw the statement as
aligning the Church with American progressivism. Historian Joseph McShane
shares that assessment: "In recommending Ryan's program to the bishops for
their approval, the members of the CSWA were endorsing and asking the church
in America to espouse Progressive idealism and rhetoric in a significant way."[147]
In McShane's view, the very notoriety the program achieved was due in some
part to its consonance with progressivism.[148]

It should be noted in this connection that the CSWA did not represent a
diverse cross-section of Catholic opinion on economic matters. The major figures over the course of its first few decades—Fathers William Kerby, John
O'Grady, John Ryan—were all affiliated with Catholic University and shared a
similar perspective on the social question. O'Grady, its first head, indicated that
he wanted the CSWA to represent a diversity of views, but that this excluded
"ultraconservative businessmen."[149]

One problem with the program's reception was confusion over its authority
as a teaching document. Sophisticated lay observers, such as Pallen and Kenkel,
understood well that such a document stood outside the normal hierarchical structure of the Church, in which individual bishops exercised authority within their
own dioceses. Statements by groups of bishops on behalf of a national episcopal
body, in contrast, carried no more weight than what their authors could personally command. This fact was highlighted by the objections voiced by a number
of bishops who took exception to various pieces of the program.[150]

Pallen, offended by the general impression that the statements of the council
represented binding teaching, attacked John Ryan and the NCWC on precisely
this point. "Pardon me if I fail to see in you and Dr. [Father Raymond] McGowan
in Washington the sole depositories of the wisdom of the Holy Ghost in matters
economic," he wrote to Ryan. "I am content to accept Leo XIII's principles and
teachings on these matters as set forth in his Encyclical '*Rerum Novarum.*'
Indeed I am quite confident that Rome has a much stronger and juster claim to be
the seat of infallibility than Washington." Pallen thought that his differences
with Ryan and his collaborators were not on matters of doctrine but on matters of
economics, and he therefore chided Ryan: "You seem to think that the only economic orthodoxy is your 'doxy, and that anyone who presumes to criticize any
phase of your 'doxy is a knave, a prevaricator and a conspirator against the peace
of injured innocence."[151]

The administrative committee conceded in their foreword that the "practical
applications" the document broached were "of course, subject to discussion."
This caveat notwithstanding, the level of specificity with respect to economic

and political policy recommendations displayed by the program opened it to charges of improperly aligning the Church with one or another side in a number of contemporary debates in which doctrinal issues were not at stake.

While historians have tended to emphasize the Bishops' Program as the position of the Catholic hierarchy on social issues, it is probably the case that the Pastoral Letter of 1919, released later in the year, reflected more accurately the consensus view of the bishops. The most thorough historian of the documents, Joseph McShane, has argued that the two letters are essentially similar, though the pastoral lacked the specificity of the earlier program.[152] This difference is actually quite important. Instead of taking firm positions on various policy debates of the day (including minimum wage, child labor laws, etc.) as the program did, the pastoral confined itself mostly to the stating of principles. By leaving the working out of such principles to the prudential judgment of those in decision-making positions, the pastoral maintained politically neutral ground.

The program contained the language cited above on the subject of wages, recommending specific legislative initiatives to establish wage rates. The pastoral clearly shared the goal of the program, based on what it called the "right of labor to a living wage." It left open, however, the method by which such a wage could "be made universal in practice," stipulating only that it be "through whatever means will be at once legitimate and effective." In addition, the pastoral noted the rights of employers, including "a fair day's work for a fair day's pay" and "the right to returns which will be sufficient to stimulate thrift, saving, initiative, enterprise, and all those directive and productive energies which promote social welfare."[153]

On the question of labor organization, there was a similar divergence between the two documents. The program specifically endorsed the National War Labor Board and called for its continuation and endowment "with all the power for effective action that it can possess under the federal constitution." The pastoral again shared much with the program. It recognized the right of workers to organize and to deal with employers through their chosen representatives. It did not, however, endorse any particular governmental activity with respect to labor. Its only recommendation was a general one: to establish cooperative associations that embrace both employers and workers. Also, unlike the program, the pastoral warned against the danger of union radicalism in the mode of some European labor groups.

The pastoral, then, with input from more bishops and with less direction from John Ryan, gave less specific guidance regarding the implementation of the principles it articulated. The document may have indicated that there was less agreement among bishops on such specific proposals than the program had led some to believe. It also may have indicated that the bishops were concerned about avoiding the confusion that arose from the perception that, in the program, they had overstepped their roles as teachers of faith and morality.

All Catholics writing on the social question during the age of reform paid tribute to Leo XIII's landmark encyclical, but the ways in which they applied its mandates to the American situation varied widely. This is the only sense in which Catholic commentary on economics during the period can be said to have followed a uniform pattern. The Catholic Central Verein, with its spokesman, Frederick Kenkel, envisioned a corporatist economic order that was radical, by American standards. As Kenkel detected a shift toward government activism and moved to counter it, however, his views seemed increasingly to parallel those of other American conservatives. John Ryan and the Social Action Department of the NCWC, on the other hand, began to establish a reputation for the Church as progressive on economic matters, in contrast to its previous image as a force of reaction. Kenkel's and Ryan's different economic views and political judgments would shape the ways in which they would react to developments in the United States over the next quarter century.

Notes

1. Richard Hofstadter, *The Age of Reform: From Bryan to F. D. R.* (New York: Alfred A. Knopf, 1989 [1955]).

2. Robert H. Wiebe, *The Search for Order, 1877–1920* (New York: Hill and Wang, 1967), 17–37.

3. Alan Dawley, *Struggles for Justice: Social Responsibility and the Liberal State* (Cambridge, Mass.: Belknap, 1991), 38. See also John Higham, *Strangers in the Land: Patterns of American Nativism, 1860–1925* (New Brunswick, N.J.: Rutgers University Press, 1955), 70–105. Catholics were not the sole targets of antiradical nativism, of course; in New York, Jewish immigrants were similarly perceived.

4. Higham, *Strangers*, 114–22. On the professionalization of welfare, see Michael B. Katz, *In the Shadow of the Poorhouse: A Social History of Welfare in America* (New York: Basic Books, 1986). For a treatment of the same development from a more critical perspective, see Marvin Olasky, *The Tragedy of American Compassion* (Washington, D.C.: Regnery Gateway, 1992).

5. Aaron I. Abell, *American Catholicism and Social Action: A Search for Social Justice, 1865–1950* (Garden City, N.Y.: Hanover, 1960), 85–89; Abell, "The Reception of Leo XIII's Labor Encyclical in America, 1891–1919," *Review of Politics* 7 (October 1945): 464–95. On the European context for the issuance of *Rerum*, see Lillian Parker Wallace, *Leo XIII and the Rise of Socialism* (Durham, N.C.: Duke University Press, 1966), chap. 11. The encyclical can be viewed at <http://www.vatican.va/holy_father/leo_xiii/encyclicals/documents/hf_l-xiii_enc_15051891_rerum-novarum_en.html>.

6. R. J. Holaind, S.J., "The Encyclical '*Rerum Novarum*,'" 5 *AER* (August 1891): 81–93. The journal was called the *American Ecclesiastical Review* until 1905, when it was shortened to the *Ecclesiastical Review*. It reacquired its previous title in 1944. To avoid confusion, it is referred to throughout this book as the *American Ecclesiastical Review (AER)*.

7. Rt. Rev. John J. Keane, "The Encyclical 'Rerum Novarum,'" *ACQR* 16 (July 1891): 595–96. Keane later became rector of Catholic University and an Americanist ally of John Ireland.

8. Ibid., 600–601, 605–6.

9. Ibid., 606–9.

10. J. L. Spalding, "Socialism and Labor," *CW* 53 (September 1891): 801–2, 806.

11. Abell, "Reception," 476.

12. See, for instance, Holaind, "Encyclical," 81; Keane, "Encyclical," 595; and E. B. Brady, "The Pope and the Proletariat," *CW* 53 (August 1891): 633–44.

13. Abell, *American Catholicism*, 114–15. The conventioneers debated, for instance, the respective roles of the state and voluntary organizations in the provision of social insurance. On the congress, see also Deirdre M. Moloney, *American Catholic Lay Groups and Transatlantic Reform in the Progressive Era* (Chapel Hill, University of North Carolina Press, 2002), chap. 1.

14. Elizabeth Sanders, *Roots of Reform: Farmers, Workers, and the American State, 1877–1917* (Chicago: University of Chicago Press, 1999), 1.

15. Walter Nugent summarizes the historiography through the 1950s in chapters 1 and 2 of Walter T. K. Nugent, *The Tolerant Populists: Kansas Populism and Nativism* (Chicago: University of Chicago Press, 1963). Nugent's main concern is countering what he sees as the overly negative (and politically motivated) portrayal of the populists by Richard Hofstadter in *Age of Reform*. Another critical summary of the literature on populism appears in Lawrence Goodwyn, *The Populist Moment: A Short History of the Agrarian Revolt in America* (New York: Oxford University Press, 1978), 334ff.

16. Goodwyn argues that the mistaken focus on the free silver movement derives from the early history of populism. John D. Hicks, *The Populist Revolt: A History of the Farmers' Alliance and the People's Party* (Minneapolis: University of Minnesota Press, 1931); Goodwyn, *Populist Moment*, 334ff.

17. Goodwyn, *Populist Moment*, 8–19, chaps. 2, 4, 5.

18. Ibid., 177.

19. C. Vann Woodward, *Tom Watson: Agrarian Rebel* (New York: Oxford University Press, 1963), 419.

20. Tom Watson, *Andrew Jackson*, 326, quoted in Hofstadter, *Age of Reform*, 83.

21. Christopher Lasch, *The True and Only Heaven: Progress and Its Critics* (New York: W. W. Norton, 1991), 205, 217.

22. Norman Pollack, *The Humane Economy: Populism, Capitalism, and Democracy* (New Brunswick, N.J.: Rutgers University Press, 1990), chap. 1. See also Bruce Palmer, *"Man Over Money": The Southern Populist Critique of American Capitalism* (Chapel Hill: University of North Carolina Press, 1980). Palmer seems to concur with Lasch, describing populism as "the last major political attack on capitalism and its business culture in America" (xviii.). Later, however, Palmer concludes that populists' attitudes toward modern industrial society were ambivalent. They recognized its benefits and did not want curtailment of private property or profit; instead, they wanted reform that would ensure more equitable distribution (199–221).

23. Hofstadter, *Age of Reform*, 67ff.; Francis L. Broderick, *Right Reverend New Dealer: John A. Ryan* (New York: Macmillan, 1963), 8–9; Nugent, *Tolerant Populists*, 62.

24. Nugent, *Tolerant Populists*, 154–55, chap. 10, 67–68.

25. The geographical focus of populism is emphasized in Palmer, *Man Over Money*, xiv. It may be that the populism of the West was more amenable to Catholics than that of the South. Tom Watson, for instance, was from Georgia, and Palmer's description of the

religious character of southern populism depicts it as radical and anti-institutional in a way that would not appeal to Catholics (24–27).

On the paucity of Catholic settlement in rural areas in the nineteenth century, the efforts by Catholic groups to encourage such settlement, and the reasons for the general failure of such efforts, see Moloney, *Lay Groups*, 73–90.

26. Robert M. Crunden, *Ministers of Reform: The Progressives' Achievement in American Civilization, 1889–1920* (New York: Basic Books, 1982), 277.

27. Arthur S. Link and Richard L. McCormick, *Progressivism* (Arlington Heights, Ill.: Harlan Davidson, 1983), 3. Link and McCormick offer a summary of the major contributions to the historiography of progressivism prior to the 1980s (3–10).

28. Hofstadter, *Age of Reform*, 131; John Whiteclay Chambers II, *The Tyranny of Change: America in the Progressive Era, 1900–1917* (New York: St. Martin's Press, 1980), v; Wiebe, *Search for Order*, 167.

29. Hofstadter, *Age of Reform*, 225ff; Wiebe *Search for Order*, 145ff. On American progressive intellectuals (e.g., Croly, Lippman, and Dewey) as part of an international transition from liberalism to welfare statism, see James T. Kloppenberg, *Uncertain Victory: Social Democracy and Progressivism in European and American Thought, 1870–1920* (New York: Oxford University Press, 1986), chap. 8.

30. Leon Fink, *Progressive Intellectuals and the Dilemmas of Democratic Commitment* (Cambridge, Mass.: Harvard, 1997), chap. 1; Kloppenberg, *Uncertain Victory*, 381–84.

31. On this phenomenon, and for an important distinction between *market entrepreneurs* and *political entrepreneurs* among the "robber barons" of the Gilded Age, see Burton W. Folsom Jr., *Urban Capitalists: Entrepreneurs and City Growth in Pennsylvania's Lackawanna and Lehigh Regions, 1800–1920* (Baltimore: Johns Hopkins University Press, 1981); and Folsom, *The Myth of the Robber Barons: A New Look at the Rise of Big Business in America*, 3d ed. (Herndon, Va.: Young America's Foundation, 1996).

32. Hofstadter, *Age of Reform*, 242–54; Wiebe, *Search for Order*, 167; Dawley, *End of Reform*, 158–65.

33. In this view, it is wrong to assume that government intervention in the economy contributed to the general welfare. Instead, the nature of government is such that business itself controls political interference with business, in the interest of business's goals of economic stability, predictability, and security. Progressivism, limited as it was by its belief in the fundamental justice of the system of private property ownership, could not undo big business's grip on the American economy. See Gabriel Kolko, *The Triumph of Conservatism: A Reinterpretation of American History, 1900–1916* (New York: Free Press, 1963), 2–4, 279–87, and passim. See also Martin Sklar, *The Corporate Reconstruction of American Capitalism, 1890–1916* (Cambridge, Mass.: Harvard University Press). Link and McCormick discuss responses to Kolko's thesis in their bibliographical essay; *Progressivism*, 132–33.

34. Elizabeth Sanders argues that agrarian interests played a decisive role in state expansion as a "drive to establish public control over a rampaging capitalism." Sanders, *Roots of Reform*, 3–4. James Kloppenberg similarly avers that the realities of political implementation distorted what were the genuinely democratic intentions of progressive-era intellectuals. Kloppenberg, *Uncertain Victory*, 411.

35. Ronald C. White and C. Howard Hopkins, *The Social Gospel: Religion and Reform in Changing America* (Philadelphia: Temple University Press), xviii.

36. William McGuire King, for instance, argues that the social gospel was genuinely theological and thereby differed from secular progressivism. Social gospelers claimed as much, King points out, and were disturbed at the secularization of social movements; William McGuire King, "An Enthusiasm for Humanity: The Social Emphasis in Religion and Its Accommodation in Protestant Theology," in *Religion and Twentieth-Century American Intellectual Life*, ed. Michael J. Lacey (New York: Cambridge University Press, 1989), 63–74.

37. Robert Crunden sees progressivism as tied intrinsically to nineteenth-century American Christiainty; *Ministers of Reform*, chaps. 1–3. Gary Scott Smith also argues that religious ideas were more influential in the progressive movement than is generally recognized; see *The Search for Social Salvation: Social Christianity and America, 1880–1925* (Lanham, Md.: Lexington Books, 2000), chap. 9. Smith thinks that the connection between social Christianity and progressivism was tight, and that progressivism did not represent a secularization of Christianity but was impelled mostly by genuinely religious people (346–47). Christopher Lasch and James Kloppenberg see progressivism as a post-religious phenomenon (see above).

38. Smith, *Social Salvation*, 4. Smith's argument was adumbrated in an earlier article: Gary Scott Smith, "The Men and Religion Forward Movement of 1911–1912: New Perspectives on Evangelical Social Concern and the Relationship between Christianity and Progressivism," in *Protestantism and Social Christianity*, ed. Martin E Marty (Munich: K. G. Saur, 1992), 166–193.

39. Donald K. Gorrell, *The Age of Social Responsibility: The Social Gospel in the Progressive Era, 1900–1920* (Macon, Ga.: Mercer University Press, 1988), ix. Timothy L. Smith has documented evangelicalism's role as the main force in the rise of social Christianity in the 1850s; *Revivalism and Social Reform: American Protestantism on the Eve of the Civil War* (Baltimore: Johns Hopkins University Press, 1980 [1957]), esp. chap. 10.

40. Garry Wills, *Under God: Religion and American Politics* (New York: Simon and Schuster, 1990), 99.

41. Smith, *Social Salvation*, 5. Smith's unique view of the social gospel is due in part to his desire to define it more broadly than is usual. To demonstrate his different view, he names the movement under consideration "social Christianity" and defines it as "the campaign of Protestants, who belonged to numerous denominations and held varied theological perspectives, to combat a host of social ills that plagued the United States in the years from 1880 to 1925" (46). Charles Hopkins concurs, showing how the movement served as a unifying force, allowing Christians of diverse theological viewpoints to cooperate in social action; Charles H. Hopkins, *The Rise of the Social Gospel in American Protestantism, 1865–1915* (New Haven, Conn.: Yale University Press, 1940), 161.

Other historians disagree. William Hutchison, for instance, by his emphasis on social versus personal salvation, seems to rule out conservative Christians from the social gospel movement; Hutchison, *Modernist*, 165. Other treatments are not necessarily in conflict with Smith's, recognizing the broader movement of *social Christianity*, but still distinguish a more specific *social gospel* movement, which is identified with liberal theology. See, for instance, Henry F. May, *Protestant Churches and Industrial America* (New York: Harper Torchbooks, 1967 [1949]); and Robert T. Handy, *Undermined Establishment: Church-State Relations in America, 1880–1920* (Princeton, N.J.: Princeton University Press, 1991).

42. White and Hopkins suggest connections between Catholics and the social gospel in chapter 19 (which includes the quotation concerning John Ryan cited below), and characterize Abell's *American Catholicism and Social Action* as "the full story of Catholic involvement in the social gospel." White and Hopkins, *Social Gospel*, 214.

43. In William McGuire King's summary of social gospel theology, which focuses not on popularizers such as Rauschenbusch but on academic theologians such as Francis McConnell and Douglas Macintosh, he claims, "it is doubtful that the social gospel theologians were encouraging modern man to turn away from historic Christianity" (165). But the substance of King's presentation demonstrates otherwise. The theologians he treats advocated a method of drawing theology from the process of social engagement rather than vice versa. This method led them to contradict outright the doctrine of the immutability of God and to reformulate the doctrine of the Trinity. King, "'History as Revelation' in the Theology of the Social Gospel," in *Protestantism and Social Christianity*, 145–65.

44. Susan Curtis, *A Consuming Faith: The Social Gospel and Modern American Culture* (Baltimore: Johns Hopkins University Press, 1991), 5.

45. Curtis, *Consuming Faith*, 6–8, 11, 127; Smith, *Social Salvation*, 382–85. See also page 350 for Smith's thesis that the efforts by liberal social gospelers to align social Christianity with liberal theology in the 1910s and twenties "drove a deeper wedge" between them and evangelicals at the level of social cooperation.

Curtis's critique of social gospel Protestants mirrors Kolko's appraisal of progressivism. "The social gospel contributed to the reorientation of American culture that validated abundance, consumption, and self-realization," she explains. "Social gospelers, reformers though they were, created, not a critique of modern capitalism, but rather a consuming faith in the material abundance it promised" (278).

46. Smith, *Social Salvation*, 407. On conservative reformers, see, for instance, Gaines M. Foster, "Conservative Social Christianity, the Law, and Personal Morality: Wilbur F. Crafts in Washington," *Church History* 71 (December 2002): 799–819. Foster details the public career of Crafts, who saw himself furthering the Kingdom of God by lobbying for legislation designed to curb personal immorality (such as prohibitions on liquor, prostitution, and immoral films).

47. Smith, *Social Salvation*, chap. 10. Smith argues that most social Christians recognized the problems observed by contemporary conservative Christians and by historians such as Curtis. Most recognized a close link between individual and social salvation, for instance. They also believed that the church should not sacrifice its authority by aligning with a particular political party or program. Smith admits, however, that some social Christians themselves voiced worries that other social gospelers were drawing too close a connection between religious obligation and specific political positions (402–4). The existence of such criticism shows that probably some social Christians did not maintain sufficiently the distinctions that most of the movement's theoreticians stressed.

48. Smith, *Social Salvation*, 374–80.

49. Crunden, *Ministers of Reform*, 3–15; Christopher Lasch, *The New Radicalism in America, 1889–1963: The Intellectual as Social Type* (New York: W. W. Norton, 1965), xiv. See also Kloppenberg, *Uncertain Victory*, chap. 9. On education, see Fink, *Progressive Intellectuals*, 25, and Kloppenberg, *Uncertain Victory*, 373–80; Hofstadter, *Age of Reform*, 152.

50. Lasch, *New Radicalism*, 11. For a recent biography of Addams, see Jean Bethke Elshtain, *Jane Addams and the Dream of American Democracy* (New York: Basic Books,

2002). Elshtain's sympathetic account of Addams's work does not contradict Lasch's observation that such work, in Addams's view, had little or no connection to a specifically Christian belief system.

51. Kloppenberg, *Uncertain Victory*. Kloppenberg views Herbert Croly's reconsideration of the importance of Christian belief and skepticism toward the "special gods of natural science, politics, economics, and the world" as a "retreat" from democratic reform of capitalism (391); Morton White, *Social Thought in America: The Revolt Against Formalism* (Boston: Beacon Press, 1957 [1949]). White's major figures are Oliver Wendell Holmes Jr., John Dewey, and Thorstein Veblen.

52. Kloppenberg, *Uncertain Victory*, 413.

53. Unsigned review of Joseph Husslein, *The World Problem: Capital, Labor, and the Church* (New York: P. J. Kennedy and Sons, 1918), *ACQR* 48 (October 1918): 697–98.

54. That American Catholics eschewed communism has been generally recognized. There is less consensus concerning their antipathy toward fascism during this period. In this connection, it is important to note two facts. First, while some American Catholics did advocate a corporatist system that has at times been identified with fascism, such advocates were usually careful to distinguish their proposal from that of the totalitarian version implemented in Italy by Mussolini. American corporatists such as Frederick Kenkel had no sympathy for Mussolini's program. Second, it must be conceded that there was sympathy for totalitarian fascism among some Catholics, although their number in the United States was small. Some observers have conflated American Catholic support for General Franco and the Nationalists during the Spanish Civil War with support for fascism. That is an oversimplification that ignores the way in which American Catholics perceived the conflict as primarily religious in nature. An outstanding treatment of these issues that respects both the complexity and the diversity of Catholic opinion is Jay P. Corrin, *Catholic Intellectuals and the Challenge of Democracy* (Notre Dame, Ind.: University of Notre Dame Press, 2002); see also Wilson D. Miscamble, C.S.C., "The Limits of American Catholic Antifascism: The Case of John A. Ryan," *Church History* 59 (December 1990): 523–38.

55. Joseph M. McShane, S.J., *"Sufficiently Radical": Catholicism, Progressivism, and the Bishops' Program of 1919* (Washington, D.C.: Catholic University, 1986), 13ff.

56. O'Brien, *Public Catholicism*, 128.

57. Moloney, *Catholic Lay Groups*, 42. Thomas E. Woods Jr., argues similarly that Catholics engaged progressivism without compromising their distinctiveness. Woods, "Assimilation and Resistance: Catholic Intellectuals and the Progressive Era," *Catholic Social Science Review* 5 (2000): 297–312.

58. For Dorothy Ross, it is also the key text in "the transformation of American exceptionalism," the shift in reading American history from a republican, millennial perspective to a modern, liberal perspective. See Dorothy Ross, *The Origins of American Social Science* (New York: Cambridge University Press, 1991), 151.

59. Crunden, *Ministers of Reform*, 209.

60. Lasch, *True and Only Heaven*, 341–42.

61. Kloppenberg, *Uncertain Victory*, chaps. 8 and 9. Like Lasch, Kloppenberg points to *Progressive Democracy* rather than *Promise of American Life* as the key piece of the Croly corpus.

62. Hofstadter, *Age of Reform*, 149–52. Smith lists the various explanations that have been posited for the rise of the social gospel, including the rise of industrialism and urban

problems, the desire of Protestants to maintain social control, the response of clergy to the threat to their status coming from the rise of a new professional class. *Social Salvation*, 30–32.

63. White and Hopkins, *Social Gospel*, 220; Broderick, *Right Reverend*, 74. Joseph Husslein, S.J., another Catholic social theorist, also criticized Rauschenbusch as an example of failing to retain the supernatural dimension of Christian social reform. Rauschenbusch's concept of Christianity, Husslein claimed, might include atheists and agnostics, since it required only social activism not doctrinal adherence. Husslein, *The Church and Social Problems* (New York: America Press, 1912), 95. Catholic opinion regarding Rauschenbusch was not uniformly critical, however. Charles P. Bruehl, in a later book, highlighted Rauschenbusch as an example of a social activist who took care not to reduce Christianity to social reform; Bruehl, *The Pope's Plan for Social Reconstruction: A Commentary on the Social Encyclicals of Pius XI* (New York: Devin-Adair, 1939), 2–3.

64. This biographical information derives from Rev. Paul Hanly Furfey, "Sociology at the Catholic University," *Catholic University Bulletin* 23 (January 1956): 1–2.

65. Rev. W. J. Kerby, "The Capitalist and His Point of View," *ACQR* 24 (July 1899): 18–36; "The Laborer and His Point of View," *ACQR* 26 (January 1901): 108–24; "Reform and Reformers," *ACQR* 28 (April 1903): 227–47. Quotes are from "Capitalist," 18, and "Reform and Reformers," 227. Kerby recognized the ambiguity of the term *capitalist* and specified his subject as "the employer" ("Capitalist," 24).

66. Kerby, "Reform and Reformers," 229, 237. See also Kerby, "Social Reform," *ACQR* 28 (July 1903): 521–34.

67. Kerby, "Capitalist," 30, 34; Kerby, "Reform and Reformers," 233.

68. Kerby, "The Socialism of the Socialists," *ACQR* 26 (July 1901): 468–84. See also Kerby, "Catholicity and Socialism," *ACQR* 30 (April 1905): 225–43.

69. Kerby, "Reform and Reformers," 239, 247.

70. For Catholics' response to World War I, including other instances of organizational activity, see James Hennesey, S.J., *American Catholics: A History of the Roman Catholic Community in the United States* (New York: Oxford University, 1981), 223–28.

71. Kerby, "Re-education by War," *CW* 106 (January 1918): 451–61.

72. Not everyone agrees. Robert Crunden, correct in his estimation that Catholics were not central to formation of progressive ethos, argues further that the progressive movement, even for those Catholics trying to participate in it, "remained to them an intrinsically alien world." He contends that Ryan and his Catholic allies were precursors of social democracy (with its more collectivist ethos) rather than progressives. *Ministers of Reform*, 278.

73. Two examples of Ryan's earliest thought on economic questions are *A Living Wage: Its Ethical and Economic Aspects* (New York: Macmillan, 1906); and "The Morality of the Aims and Methods of the Labor Union," *American Catholic Quarterly Review* 29 (April 1904): 326–55. For a comprehensive account of Ryan's economics, see Patrick W. Gearty, *The Economic Thought of Monsignor John A. Ryan* (Washington, D.C.: Catholic University Press, 1953), esp. chaps. 2, 5.

74. Ryan's life is recounted in Broderick, *Right Reverend*.

75. McShane, *Sufficiently Radical*, 25–26, 32 fn. 49, 32–33.

76. Ryan to Kenkel, October 1, 1911, CKNA 3/24.

77. Ibid. That Ryan's thought can fruitfully be seen in conjunction with the history of progressivism is demonstrated as well by the historiographical assessments of his legacy.

McShane, for instance, from a perspective basically sympathetic to American progressivism, sees Ryan as a successful Americanist. By synthesizing the Catholic tradition and progressive thought, he brought Catholics out of their ghettos and into dialogue with modernity. Eugene McCarraher's more critical appraisal, meanwhile, like Curtis's critique of the social gospel, echoes the interpretation of progressivism offered by anti-capitalists such as Gabriel Kolko. For McCarraher, Ryan was an Americanist, too, but his legacy is, therefore, ambivalent at best. "At the very moment that Ryan's progressivism heralded a more decentralized, democratic political economy," McCarraher explains, "it also augured the incorporation of workers into the competitive, accumulative mores of corporate capitalism—suggesting that its third way was a repaving of the first way." Eugene McCarraher, *Christian Critics: Religion and the Impasse in Modern American Social Thought* (Ithaca, N.Y.: Cornell University Press, 2000), 47.

78. In the words of his biographer, Ryan "could never understand people, inside or outside the Church, who set Americanism and Catholicism in opposition to each other." Broderick, *Right Reverend*, 16.

79. For progressive views on immigration and labor unions, respectively, see Hofstadter, *Age of Reform*, 172–84; 239–42. On the relationship between prohibition and progressivism, see Hofstadter, *Age of Reform*, 287–91.

80. On birth control debates during the progressive era, including Catholic participation, see Kathleen A. Tobin, *The American Religious Debate Over Birth Control, 1907–1937* (Jefferson, N.C.: McFarland and Company, 2001). Ryan was, in fact, invited to join the Birth Control League, and his sharp letter declining was published in *Harper's Weekly*. Tobin, *American Religious Debate*, 68. For a comprehensive history of birth control in the United States, see Linda Gordon, *Woman's Body, Woman's Right: A Social History of Birth Control in America* (New York: Grossman Publishers, 1976).

81. See, for instance, Ryan, *A Living Wage*, 118–19.

82. Dawley, *Struggles for Justice*, 99.

83. Ibid., 101. For Ryan's views on socialism, see his debate with Morris Hillquit. Hillquit and Ryan, *Socialism: Promise or Menace?* (New York: Macmillan, 1914).

84. Social gospel historian Robert Handy calls Ely the "most influential lay exponent of the movement." Robert T. Handy, "Introduction," in *The Social Gospel in America, 1870–1920: Gladden, Ely, Rauschenbusch*, ed. Handy (New York: Oxford University Press, 1966), 15. See Kloppenberg, *Uncertain Victory*, chap. 7, on Ely and Rauschenbusch as part of the international social democratic movement.

85. The German historical school was not unknown in the United States prior to the work of Ely and his colleagues. See Joseph Dorfman, *The Economic Mind in American Civilization*, vol. 3, 1865–1918 (New York: Viking Press, 1959 [1949]), 87–110.

86. Benjamin G. Rader, *The Academic Mind and Reform: The Influence of Richard T. Ely in American Life* (Lexington: University of Kentucky Press, 1966), 11–15, 20–27. On the new school, see Dorfman, *Economic Mind*, vol. 3, chaps. 7 and 8. On the related Wisconsin school of labor history, which arose around Ely and Commons, see Fink, *Progressive Intellectuals*, chap. 2.

87. Rader, *Academic Mind*, chap. 2, 230.

88. Ely, "The State," in *The Social Law of Service* (New York, 1896), in *Social Gospel*, 246–47. James Kloppenberg has detailed the way in which Ely was part of an international movement of social democracy. Ely, like other social democrats, attempted to apply socialist principles within the context of American realities. Social democracy, as a result, involved a critique not only of classical economics, but also of the philosophical

assumptions that undergirded both classical and Marxist economics. His reliance on the ostensible certainties provided by deductive reasoning rendered Marx's predictions about capitalism wrong, social democrats thought. Capitalism might develop peacefully into socialism by a trajectory different from (and more peaceful than) that posited by Marx. Kloppenberg, *Uncertain Victory*, chap. 7, 289.

89. Ely, "The State," 248–49.

90. Ely, "The Social Law of Service," in *The Social Law of Service*, in *Social Gospel*, 234.

91. Richard Ely, Introduction to John Ryan, *A Living Wage: Its Ethical and Economic Aspects* (New York: Macmillan, 1906), xii.

92. Laurence R. Veysey, *The Emergence of the American University* (Chicago: University of Chicago Press, 1965), chap. 3.

93. Ross, *Origins*, xx.

94. Ross, *Origins*, 63–67. See also Veysey, *Emergence*, 203–5. On the secularization of American universities, see George M. Marsden, *The Soul of the American University: From Protestant Establishment to Established Nonbelief* (New York: Oxford University Press, 1994), esp. chapter 9, concerning "methodological secularization."

95. Delving further into the history of economics solidifies its connection to religious thinkers. Scholastic thinkers (especially the Late Scholastics) provided economic analysis of "all the phenomena of nascent capitalism," from the fourteenth to the seventeenth centuries. Their work was the "basis of the analytic work of their successors, not excluding A. Smith." Joseph A. Schumpeter, *History of Economic Analysis* (New York: Oxford University Press, 1954), 94.

96. Rader, *Academic Mind*, chap. 2. See also David Seckler, *Thorstein Veblen and the Institutionalists: A Study in the Social Philosophy of Economics* (Boulder, Colo.: Colorado Associated University Press, 1975), 14–15. See Dorfman, *Economic Mind*, vol. 3, chap. 9, on the founding of the AEA and its early development.

97. Fink, *Progressive Intellectuals*, 59, n. 21.

98. Seckler, *Veblen*, 18–19. See also Rader, *Academic Mind*, 117–23, on the passing of control of the AEA from Ely and its opening to conservatives.

99. Ross, *Origins*, 77ff. See also Paul F. Boller, *American Thought in Transition: The Impact of Evolutionary Naturalism, 1865–1900* (Washington, D.C.: University Press of America, 1981 [1969]), chap. 4. Boller's summary of the relationship between the Old and New Economics is helpful, although he treats too carelessly the concept of *natural law* in his characterization of the period as a critique of the natural law across the disciplines of biology, philosophy, and economics.

100. Ross, *Origins*, 115, 117, 145–46. Ross's argument is that this fact is due to economists themselves being part of the capitalist power structure. See Rader, *Academic Mind*, chap. 6, for the way in which Richard Ely's professional position led him to avoid radicalism.

101. Ross, *Origins*, chap. 6.

102. Ibid., 176–77.

103. Dorfman, *Economic Mind*, vol. 3, chaps. 11–13, 15–19. Ross, *Origins*, 217, 371ff. On Veblen as at once embracing contradictory behaviorist and humanist assumptions, see Seckler, *Veblen*, 6–8. Throughout this book, the terms *mainstream*, *orthodox*, and *heterodox* are used to refer to different approaches to economics. The terms are meant to be broadly descriptive rather than precise, since an extensive debate might be had about exactly which views fall under which term. *Orthodox* refers to the approach that has pre-

dominated among American economists. It includes the classical and neoclassical schools, although the latter in some ways transformed the former, and, in the contemporary context, the classical might be considered in some ways heterodox (see Ross, *Origins*, 174–75). *Mainstream* is used as a synonym for orthodox. *Heterodox* encompasses a variety of approaches united by the fact that each criticizes orthodox economics in some important way. It includes, for example, institutional economics and historical economics. Austrian economics probably falls into the orthodox category, although a case could be made that its rejection of mathematic modeling aligns it with the heterodox approaches.

104. One of the difficulties attending any study of "Catholic" thought involves distinguishing Catholics from others writing on the same subject. This study follows the convention of focusing on those figures who wrote for important Catholic journals, or who otherwise had roles in specifically Catholic enterprises. There were Catholic economists, not treated in this study, who worked within mainstream academia and whose writing was not distinctively Catholic. One example is David A. McCabe, professor of political economy at Princeton and author of *The Standard Wage Rate in American Trade Unions* (Baltimore: Johns Hopkins University Press, 1912).

105. Francis W. Howard, "The Relativity of Political Economy," *ACQR* 21 (January 1896): 17–19.

106. Ibid., 21–24.

107. Ibid., 25.

108. Unsigned review of Albert C. Whitaker, *History and Criticism of the Labor Theory of Value in English Political Economy* (New York: Columbia University Press, 1904), *AER* 32 (May 1905): 546; Unsigned review of *The Fundamental Fallacy of Socialism*, ed. Arthur Preuss (St. Louis: B. Herder, 1908), *AER* 38 (April 1908): 480; Unsigned review of Orello Cone, *Rich and Poor in the New Testament* (London: Adam and Charles Black, 1903), *AER* 28 (February 1903): 229. A later review exhibited more openness to the legitimacy of the single tax. Whether this represented a change of view or a change of editorial personnel is unclear; unsigned review of C. B. Fillebrown, *The Principle of Natural Taxation* (Chicago: A. C. McClurg, 1917), *AER* 57 (August 1917): 218–19.

109. Unsigned review of Pesch, *Lehrbuch* (St. Louis: B. Herder), *AER* 33 (October 1905): 204; Unsigned review of W. Cunningham, *Christianity and Economic Science* (New York: Longmans, Green, 1914), *AER* 52 (January 1915): 121; Unsigned review of Haney, *History of Economic Thought*; Nearing, *Wages in the United States*; and Clark and Wyatt, *Making Both Ends Meet, AER* 45 (December 1911): 737–38.

110. Unsigned review of Father Cuthbert, O.S.F.C., *Catholic Ideals in Social Life* (New York: Benziger Bros., 1904), *AER* 32 (January 1905): 100.

111. William Stang, "Socialism II: Not Socialism, but Social Reform," *AER* 29 (October 1903): 374. See also Stang, "Socialism—Its Character and Its Aims," *AER* 29 (September 1903): 226–38; and Stang, *Socialism and Christianity* (New York: Benziger, 1905).

112. Stang, "Socialism II," 375.

113. Ibid., 376–79.

114. Ibid., 378–88.

115. Stang, "The Catholic Movement in Behalf of Social Reform," *AER* 30 (March 1904): 258–59, 268–70.

116. Joseph Selinger, "Is Social Reform Work a Duty of the Parish Clergy?" *AER* 42 (March 1910): 452–58.

117. Unsigned review of Ryan, *A Living Wage*, *AER* 36 (April 1907): 465–67. Other treatments of wages appearing in American Catholic periodicals during the period include Rev. Michael M. O'Kane, O.P., "Wages and the Principle of Justice," *ACQR* 24 (April 1899): 172–83; and E. C. Fortey, "The Living Wage—An English View," *ACQR* 37 (October 1912): 728–36.

118. R. J. Holaind, S.J., "Cardinal Zigliara and the Wage Question," *AER* 8 (June 1893): 401–7.

119. Ibid., 407–11.

120. Quoted in Broderick, *Right Reverend*, 43.

121. T. Slater, S.J., "The Moral Aspect of Commercial 'Stockwatering,'" *AER* 39 (October 1908): 367–79; Ryan, "The Moral Aspect of Stockwatering," *AER* 40 (February 1909): 157–75; Slater, "Dr. Ryan and the Moral Aspect of Stockwatering," *AER* 40 (April 1909): 479–89; Ryan, "Father Slater's Rejoinder on Stockwatering," *AER* 40 (June 1909): 746–57. Quotation is from Slater, "Dr. Ryan," 487. On the broader debate over stockwatering, see Saul Engelbourg, *Power and Morality: American Business Ethics, 1840–1914* (Westport, Conn.: Greenwood Press, 1980), 37–41, 80–85, 120–23.

122. J. A. Dewe, *History of Economics* (New York: Benziger Brothers, 1908), 5; Dewe, "The 'Tractatus de Jure' and the Stock Exchange," *AER* 50 (January 1914): 29–38. On the field of American history in this period, including historians' efforts to depict their profession as scientific, see Peter Novick, *That Noble Dream: The "Objectivity Question" and the American Historical Profession* (New York: Cambridge University Press, 1988), chaps. 1–3.

123. Dewe, "Stock Exchange," 31, 34–35, 38.

124. Recent scholars, including Christopher Shannon and Eugene McCarraher, have not only sought to recover historically the countercultural Catholic critique of the American capitalist system, but have emphasized its advantages over the more conciliatory approach of progressive Catholics and social gospelers. Eugene McCarraher, *Christian Critics: Religion and the Impasse in Modern American Social Thought* (Ithaca, N.Y.: Cornell University Press, 2000); Christopher Shannon, *Conspicuous Criticism: Tradition, the Individual, and Culture in American Social Thought, from Veblen to Mills* (Baltimore: Johns Hopkins University Press, 1996). "While the Vatican's strictures [against modernism, Americanism] paralyzed dogmatic theology for sixty years," McCarraher has written, "they also decisively forced Catholic Progressivism into the ambit of neomedievalism and thus ensured that American Catholics would engage American modernity from a potentially more creative critical location than that occupied by their liberal Protestant counterparts" (26).

125. Philip Gleason, *The Conservative Reformers: German American Catholics and the Social Order* (Notre Dame, Ind.: University of Notre Dame Press, 1968).

126. Ibid., 45, 68, 87.

127. Ibid., 104–5, 111, 205.

128. Ibid., 128ff. On Ketteler, see Paul Misner, *Social Catholicism in Europe: From the Onset of Industrialization to the First World War* (London: Darton, Longman and Todd, 1991), 90ff.

129. Quoted in Gleason, *Conservative Reformers*, 127.

130. T. J. Jackson Lears, *No Place of Grace: Antimodernism and the Transformation of American Culture, 1880–1920* (New York: Pantheon, 1981).

131. Ibid., 64ff., xiii.

132. Ibid., xiv.

133. Ibid., chap. 6; Brooks quoted on 251.

134. Ibid., 283–84. See also Henry Adams, *The Education of Henry Adams* (New York: Vintage Books, 1990 [1907]). On the general American nostalgia for the mystical elements of medieval culture, see Lears, *No Place*, 142ff.

135. Lears, *No Place*, 209.

136. Cram, *My Life in Architecture* (Boston: Little, Brown, 1936), in *The Superfluous Men: Conservative Critics of American Culture, 1900–1945*, ed. Robert M. Crunden (Austin: University of Texas Press, 1977), 24–26.

137. Crunden, *Superfluous Men*, 92.

138. Ibid., 184–85, xiv.

139. Higham, *Strangers*, chap. 6, 222–23. The anti-Catholic newspaper, *The Menace*, reached its highpoint in 1915, with a circulation of 1.5 million (184). Higham notes the irony of anti-German nativism, considering that Germans had been thought to be the most assimilated of the immigrant groups, but offers the interesting explanation that this very assimilation had induced German-Americans to be less circumspect about their public statements concerning patriotism and war (196ff.).

140. John O'Grady, "Aims and Methods in Social Insurance," *CW* 106 (October 1917): 91–101; Unsigned review of James J. Finn, *Operative Ownership* (Chicago: Langdon), *CW* 106 (October 1917): 102–4. The reviewer may have been editor Augustine Hewitt.

141. J. W. R. Maguire, C.S.V., "Priests and the Reform of Industrial Conditions," *AER* 59 (July 1918): 34–41.

142. On the organization of the NCWC, including the CSWA, see Elizabeth Mc-Keown, *War and Welfare: American Catholics and World War I* (New York: Garland, 1988), chap. 3; on the formation of the departments such as the SAD, see 179–80.

143. All quotations from the program are taken from "Program of Social Reconstruction," February 12, 1919, issued by the Administrative Committee of the National Catholic War Council, in *Pastoral Letters of the United States Catholic Bishops*, v. 1 1792–1940, ed. Hugh J. Nolan (Washington, D.C.: United States Catholic Conference, 1984), 265.

144. McShane, *Sufficiently Radical*, 209ff; see also Michael Thomas McCartan, "American Catholic Reception of the Bishops' Program of Social Reconstruction, 1919–1986: The Continuing Conflict between Catholic Social Teaching on Economic Rights and the American Way" (Ph.D. diss., Marquette University, 1994), chap. 3.

145. McShane, *Sufficiently Radical*, 211. See also McCartan, *Reception*, 147–57.

146. Quoted in Gleason, *Conservative Reformers*, 194. There were other Catholic critics, as well, who more polemically accused the NCWC of being dangerously radical and socialistic; see Abell, *American Catholicism*, 205.

147. McShane, *Sufficiently Radical*, 157.

148. Ibid., 190–91.

149. Ibid., 144. See also McKeown, *War and Welfare*, 111–12.

150. McShane, *Sufficiently Radical*, 184ff. McShane, essentially sympathetic to the document's views, nonetheless recognizes the point concerning its authority: "Therefore, whereas the document seemed to bear the stamp of approval of the entire American church and to enunciate a new and unified Catholic stand on social issues, it was actually merely educational and directive, not binding" (182).

The tenuous nature of the NCWC's status as representing the bishops, as well as the shakiness of its very existence, was demonstrated during a 1922 controversy, when it was nearly dissolved. Prompted by the complaints of bishops that the council undermined episcopal authority in their individual sees, Pope Benedict XV had decided to dissolve it. Pope Pius XI confirmed the decision unable to be completed by his predecessor, but he then reconsidered five months later. He issued a clarifying decree that permitted the council but warned that proceedings "have nothing in common with conciliar legislation" and that attendance by bishops was purely voluntary. He also suggested changing the name of the council to reflect this clarification, advice it followed at its next meeting (1923), assuming the title National Catholic Welfare Conference. See Abell, *American Catholicism*, 224; McKeown, *War and Welfare*, 185–94.

151. Quoted in McShane, *Sufficiently Radical*, 229–30.

152. McShane, *Sufficiently Radical*, 248–49. See also Franz H. Mueller, *The Church and the Social Question* (Washington, D.C.: American Enterprise Institute, 1984 [1963]), 108–10. Mueller argues that the program can reasonably be assumed to have represented the bishops' views but also notes the differences in tone and content between the two documents.

153. All quotations from the Pastoral Letter are taken from "Pastoral Letter," September 26, 1919, issued by the Roman Catholic Hierarchy of the United States, 272–333, in *Pastoral Letters*.

3

Catholic Economic Thought in the Twenties: A Survival of American Innocence?

The Problem of American Innocence

Historian Henry May famously described the years leading up to 1920 as the "end of American innocence." In May's account, the tenets comprising the national credo through the nineteenth century and the first decade of the twentieth were belief in the reality, certainty, and eternity of moral values; belief in progress; and belief in culture. These articles of faith, however, were subjected to unprecedented skepticism in the following decade. The experience of the First World War, in particular, led to a "complete disintegration of the old order." The 1920s, then, to continue May's account, were not a time of reaction or a return to an earlier America. The old credo had disappeared; the twenties represented the triumph of "the ultra-practical, anti-intellectual, pseudoidealistic gospel of Prosperity First."[1]

Many questions have been raised with respect to May's claim: How widespread were the ideas he treated? Were the figures he examined representative or idiosyncratic? Were not intellectuals of every era equally contentious vis-à-vis the reigning attitudes of their day?[2] These are important questions, which call into question May's broader project. It seems clear, however, that May described accurately and astutely the thinkers whom he did investigate and drew valid lines of commonality among the characters in the group. There is historical consensus regarding the transformative effect of World War I on American society—in its outlines if not in its details—and May's analysis can be seen to fit into this larger context.

59

The dominant view of Catholic intellectual life in the 1920s takes May's interpretation as its starting point. William Halsey's seminal book, *The Survival of American Innocence*, is the most influential characterization of Catholic thought during the period. Halsey's argument is that Catholics were, in general, "fifty years behind" American intellectual life. As disillusionment set in among the American elite, Catholics picked up the banner of Enlightenment faith in the troika of reason, progress, and an objective natural moral order.[3]

The deep irony in Halsey's story is that Catholics had once proudly opposed the progressive optimism of modernism, an opposition symbolized by Pius IX's *Syllabus of Errors* (1864) and Pius X's condemnation of modernism in *Pascendi Dominici Gregis* (1907). In the American context, though, Catholics at last succumbed to the old American credo, embracing the optimistic outlook of American innocence. Halsey cites a telling statement from New York's Archbishop Michael Corrigan to the First National Social Action Conference, in which Corrigan articulated the obligation of "re-Americanizing America."[4]

A corollary to Halsey's argument with respect to the Catholic preservation of American innocence is his characterization of innocence as a peculiarly American phenomenon. In his view, then, as the "New World" became more like the "Old World" (as Americans generally grew pessimistic, skeptical, disenchanted), the most Old World aspect of the New World (American Catholics) became more like the New World.[5] Halsey's argument begs a question, however, by assuming that the coterie of ideas designated as *innocence* was itself not "Old World."

It is true that Catholic apologists in the early twentieth century at times overstated the case that the American experiment derived directly from medieval (European) intellectual sources. Halsey and other commentators may overstate the case, however, in criticizing the apologists. There is at least a strong argument for the position that the ideas of American innocence were rooted in European Christianity, including Catholicism. Belief in the ability of reason to discern an objective moral order (natural law), for instance, is hardly a peculiarly American characteristic; it is an idea at the core of the Christian intellectual tradition.[6]

One can grant, then, more plausibility to the arguments of the early twentieth-century champions of an American-Catholic synthesis than do Halsey and other critics. In this way, their project can be viewed not as naively promoting the wedding of Catholicism with American innocence; instead, they can be seen as upholding traditional Catholicism through a defense of so-called "American" ideas (which is what they claimed to be doing).

This presentation of Catholic economic thought in the 1920s will not fundamentally question the May and Halsey theses, but it will suggest that the lines are less defined than May and Halsey imply. In the words of one May critic: "The absence of guilt, doubt, and complexity (what May terms 'innocence') simply did not end for many Americans either between 1912 and 1917, or in the

1920s, or since."[7] If many American intellectuals, including social thinkers, continued to adhere to the tenets of American innocence, then Catholics who shared those beliefs (at least to some degree) were not really "behind" their non-Catholic counterparts at all. They simply tended to agree more with certain positions than with others.

Most Catholic thinkers of the time, moreover, should not be so easily categorized as innocent.[8] In the area of economics, in particular, the lines of division were more complicated than the paradigm of innocence allows. Many Catholics who viewed the American project as compatible with Catholic tradition nonetheless remained highly skeptical of the competitive market system that had developed within the nation they admired.

Protestantism in the Twenties

One powerful force confronting Catholics in the 1920s was the resurgence of nativism. As with nativisms before and since, viewing the manifestation of nativism in the "Tribal Twenties" as exclusively religious in motivation is overly simplistic. It might be more accurate, in fact, to place ethnicity, and even more, race, at the center of any explanation of the 1920s phenomenon.[9]

Religion was tied up with ethnicity, however. From the perspective of Catholics, it was not easy to differentiate the two, and Catholics from old American families were as offended by anti-Catholic slurs as were the first-generation Polish- and Italian-Americans who were their primary target. Among non-Catholic Christians, ethnic prejudice and racialism merged with theological animus against Catholics. The theological concerns, in turn, were connected to political fears concerning church and state issues that reached back ultimately to the religious wars of the seventeenth century. This aspect of anti-Catholicism had its culmination in the reaction to Al Smith's campaign for president in 1928.[10]

There were several varieties of nativism in the 1920s. Frances Kellor's "Americanization" movement was relatively benign, but the economic depression of the early twenties provoked a shift to a more virulent strain aimed at keeping immigrants away. Factors exacerbating the anti-immigrant sentiment were the resumption of significant immigration following the war and the association of immigrants with a crime wave and growing sense of lawlessness, stemming from the problems of Prohibition. In this context, the Ku Klux Klan underwent its twentieth-century revival, with significant expansion beginning in 1920. This development was particularly troubling for Catholics, because the revitalized Klan exhibited a new focus on anti-Catholicism and gained new strength in the more Catholic states of the North. The Klan reached its apex in 1923 when it counted three million members, its greatest concentrations being in Indiana and Ohio.[11]

Big business continued to oppose immigration restriction into the twenties, but even within that segment some concessions were made. The immigration legislation of 1921 set the precedent for all subsequent restrictions by imposing for the first time numerical limits on European immigration and by basing limits on the current ethnic makeup of the country. Immigration restriction climaxed with the Johnson-Reed Act of 1924, and the remainder of the decade saw the "ebb tide" of nativism.[12]

Even leaving aside the complex combination of factors comprising the nativist impulse, there were other reasons Catholics did not find willing allies among other American Christians. In the 1920s, Protestants were internally focused, embroiled in the most serious internal debate since at least the Unitarian controversy of the early nineteenth century.[13] The significance of the debate goes beyond the simple fact that Protestants were too busy disputing theology to worry about being amicable with Catholics. The fundamentalist/modernist controversy is also important because it indicates the dominant trends in twentieth-century Protestant Christianity, trends that had implications for the possibility of alliance with Catholics.

Outside of the churches, the split in Protestantism had the effect of "erod[ing] the general influence of Protestantism in American life. The white Protestant phalanx, which had exerted a shaping national influence for much of American history, was no more."[14] This effect was an ambivalent one for Catholics, and they viewed it as such. On the one hand, the decline of Protestant hegemony allowed other forces, including Catholicism, to exert influence on American life. On the other hand, there was a possibility that those other forces could include some—such as secularism—that were much worse than the Protestantism now in decline.[15]

Within the churches, historian Mark Noll has observed, the effect of the controversy was distorting and lasting. Fundamentalists would henceforth lean toward sectarianism and anti-intellectualism, so as to avoid the plague of "modernism." Modernists would lean toward inclusivism to the point of articulating a theology barely recognizable as Christian, so as to avoid the taint of "fundamentalism." In short, the new polarity discouraged the healthy development of an intellectually rigorous, culture-engaging, orthodox-Christian form of Protestantism.[16]

The controversy also affected social Christianity. As was noted in chapter 2, prior to 1915, Christians of various theological stripes were united in social concern. This alliance broke down in the late teens and early twenties as theological differences came to the fore. Gary Scott Smith places most of the blame on the liberal contingent who, beginning in the second decade of the century, began articulating more vigorously the theological foundations of their social attitudes. The result was that, among both social Christians and outside observers, concern with social reform became linked to theological liberalism. As this understanding became entrenched, it naturally became more difficult for evangelicals or other orthodox Christians to cooperate with more liberal groups at the level of social action. In Smith's words, the efforts of theological liberals on this score "drove a wedge" between liberals and other Christians who had previously cooperated. This wedge provided fuel for a conservative evangelical critique of social Christianity, which had been simmering all along. This critique would contribute to the polarization of the fundamentalist/modernist controversy of the later twenties.[17]

Smith thus agrees that there was a precipitous decline in social action among evangelicals in the 1920s, a phenomenon memorably termed the "great reversal." Smith argues, however, that this decline did not represent the continuation of a trend long recognizable and rooted in orthodox theology. It was, instead, a radical departure from the longstanding commitment of the churches, evangelical and others, to dynamic engagement of social problems.[18] The perceived antagonism between an evangelical Christianity aimed at religious conversion and a liberal social Christianity aimed at addressing social problems was a result, in this view, of an accidental historical development. John Bennett observed and decried the development as early as 1935: "It is one of the curious perversions of a great faith that there ever arose the confusing division between personal and social Christianity."[19]

In any case, the conservative fight against a common foe—the "modernist impulse"—led to interesting alliances. In addition to neoorthodox theologians joining forces with fundamentalists, the opposition was sometimes joined by nonbelieving intellectuals such as Joseph Wood Krutch, Walter Lippman, John Crowe Ransom, and Clarence Ayres. These humanists argued that, as a matter of intellectual consistency, the only tenable options seemed to be orthodox Christianity or no Christianity. Liberal Christians, they averred, attempted to effect a compromise that was not possible.[20]

Ultimately, the character of the social gospel movement required it to adapt or disintegrate in the face of economic reality. Smith has aptly observed the errors in the liberal wing of the movement, deriving from its lack of a sound theological foundation: "Their exuberant optimism, utopian tendencies, and belief in linear universal human progress prevented some of them from seeing how deeply rooted sin is in both the human heart and in social structures." On some counts, Smith's criticism extends as well to conservative social gospelers, who, in his view, shared the liberals' tendency to overestimate the efficacy of love and education in the amelioration of social ills. Their assumption of the possibility of a cooperative commonwealth, as opposed to a political regime of conflicting interests, colored their hopes with naivete.[21]

These were precisely the points at which the social gospel was vulnerable to criticism at the time, and the Niebuhr brothers made the most of it in their reassertion of the doctrine of original sin and insistence on the intractability of power struggle as an element of human affairs.[22] Among Catholics, William Kerby joined in the criticism of the social work to which many social gospelers had devoted themselves. Kerby did not reject the modernization of welfare provision with its greater focus on institutional problems: "We have deeper insight into the organic nature of poverty as a product of our social organization." He did continue to stress the spiritual dimension of such work, however, and insisted that, insofar as modern social work exhibited a tendency to secularization, Catholic social work "is a protest against this tendency."[23]

Eugene McCarraher has summarized the divergent paths taken by socially concerned Christians in the twenties:

> Loyal to the shibboleths of personality, industrial democracy, and beloved community, many social gospelers preserved the hopes of prewar progressivism more steadfastly than their secular brethren. Some brought the social gospel more closely in line with the protocols of an aggressively and thoroughly secularized intelligentsia that was itself claiming clerical status in American culture. Others—often Protestant and Catholic champions of some "new medievalism" or medievalist modernism—reasserted the centrality of theology and church to the social gospel.[24]

As will be seen, Catholics were located among those occupying each of these categories. While many fit into the last (medievalist) camp, others, such as John Ryan, might be located in one of the first two.

Catholics and Conservative Social Movements

Antiliberal Protestantism

Although conservative Protestants shared much in common with many American Catholics, the two groups failed to ally significantly during the 1920s. Outright antagonism between Catholic and Protestant seemed to be diminishing over the course of the decade, but major obstacles to cooperation remained.

The situation is illustrated by the case of J. Gresham Machen (1881–1937). Machen taught at Princeton Seminary and later founded Westminster Seminary in Philadelphia. He became known as the most articulate defender of orthodox Presbyterianism against modernizing trends in theology that threatened, in his view, to distort essentially the Christian religion.

On many counts, Catholics would have found Machen a congenial ally. He vigorously attacked theological modernism, voted for Al Smith and disliked Prohibition, and criticized the Oregon law forbidding private schooling. He shared with many Catholics an opposition to the child labor amendment and the creation of a federal department of education on the grounds that such measures lodged too much power in the national government. He deplored the use of religion as a tool for Americanizing immigrants.[25]

Yet the opportunity for cooperation between Machen and Catholics seemed never to occur to either party. Machen's comments on Catholicism and liberal Christianity indicate at once the development of changing alliances and the persistence of older positions. Catholicism, Machen insinuated, was a more "Christian" form of religion than liberal Christianity. While Catholicism was a "perversion" of Christianity, he observed, "naturalistic liberalism is not Christianity at all."[26] Machen perceived the drawing together of Catholicism and conservative Protestantism against common enemies, but the language of "perversion" would not foster an intimate alliance.

Reinhold Niebuhr (1892–1971), perhaps the most significant American theologian of the twentieth century, saw value in the Catholic Church's appreciation for the working class and its "vast institutional charities," which rested upon "a religiously inspired sense of social solidarity and mutual responsibility." He also objected strongly to aspects of Catholicism. Besides highlighting the obvious theological differences between his Calvinism and the Catholic position on issues such as grace, Niebuhr criticized the Catholic interpretation of natural law. As for most Protestants and Catholics alike, for Niebuhr the sources of contention seemed to outweigh the potential for concerted action in the 1920s.[27]

New Humanists

Catholics paid more attention to the development of the movement that came to be known as "New Humanism." An important principle uniting the New Humanists was a belief in the "dualistic" quality of human nature; that is, human beings consist of both spiritual and material aspects and theories ignoring the spiritual were defective.[28]

Irving Babbitt (1865–1933), for instance, perceiving that the contemporary situation obligated humanists to take a stand on the side of either naturalists or supernaturalists, insisted, "For my part, I range myself unhesitatingly on the side of the supernaturalists." Babbitt thought humanism did not require religion necessarily, but allowed that it "gains immensely in effectiveness when it has a background of religious insight." With respect to Catholics, specifically, Babbitt saw potential for cooperation "on the humanistic level." Catholicism entailed much more than humanism, he understood, but he believed that it shared the humanistic reasonableness of the philosophical tradition dating to Aristotle.[29]

Babbitt thought that immense individual wealth was harmful, but he defended competition and private property. He argued that the remedy for excessive concentration of wealth was voluntary limitation, not forcible redistribution. Such redistribution (a "substitution," he wrote, of "some phantasmagoria of social justice" for "real justice") would be "an attack on the institution of private property itself; and a war on capital will speedily degenerate . . . into a war on thrift and industry in favor of laziness and incompetence."[30]

Economic issues were not Babbitt's main concern, however, a fact at least partially due to his belief that economic problems were simply superficial manifestations of deeper errors. "When studied with any degree of thoroughness," he explained, "the economic problem will be found to run into the political problem, and the political problem in turn into the philosophical problem, and philosophical problem itself to be almost indissolubly bound up at last with the religious problem."[31] In this analysis, Babbitt seemed to be close to the position expounded by Catholic social thinkers.

Paul Elmer More (1864–1937) was similarly ambivalent—friendly, but not without qualification—toward religion. He once published a forceful denunciation of many points of Catholic doctrine. But he also reported that Babbitt once asked him in exasperation: "Are you a Jesuit in disguise?" and that he had "never been able to answer the question satisfactorily." While the exact character of More's beliefs remains in question, he was concerned, at least in later writings, to defend theistic religion.[32]

In the Catholic reading, New Humanism's prominent figures, such as Babbitt and More, were sojourners on an intellectual odyssey that had moved beyond Protestantism into agnostic relativism. There they experienced the fruitlessness of that Weltanschauung, and they were seeking, once again, philosophical grounds for objective truth and moral standards. Georgetown historian William Franklin Sands, who provided this interpretation, urged Catholics to engage the New Humanists in their search for objective truth and meaning.[33] Thomas Woodlock (1866–1945), a prominent Catholic and contributing editor of the *Wall Street Journal*, joined this enthusiastic assessment, regarding Babbitt and More as "authentic prophets who have come at a time when the need for their doctrine is greatest."[34] Ross Hoffman (1902–1979), a Catholic convert and Fordham University historian contributed to the New Humanists' main organ, the *American Review*.[35]

Southern Agrarians

The *American Review* shifted its focus during the 1930s to include a number of intellectual strands other than New Humanism, including southern agrarianism and English distributism. The Southern Agrarians, formed during the 1920s, were a group of writers affiliated with Vanderbilt University. Their major statement of literary, cultural, and political criticism appeared in 1930, a collection of essays titled *I'll Take My Stand*.[36]

As with the New Humanists, the agrarians promoted ideas that many Catholics would find congenial, but the agrarians' relationship to Catholic theology was sketchy. The poet Allen Tate was perhaps the agrarian most favorable toward Catholicism, a judgment substantiated by Tate's conversion to the Catholic faith in 1950.[37]

Tate criticized the New Humanists for their failure to consider adequately the connection between religion and the ideas that they advocated. Without religion, he thought, humanism lacked a sure foundation. "Humanism is obscure in its sources," he wrote in critique of Babbitt and More, "It is even more ambiguous as to the kind of authority to which it appeals." He viewed More's religious ideas as eclectic rather than traditionally Christian. At the root of humanism's concept of religion, in Tate's analysis, was its belief that religion and reason operated on separate planes. Tate understood the possibilities for cooperation between humanists and religious thinkers "on the humanistic level," as Babbitt had put it, but Tate thought that humanism itself appeared as an arbitrary allegiance unless its commitments were founded on the solid ground of religious authority.[38]

That Tate found common ground with Catholics seems clear from his decision to join their ranks. Other agrarians were less interested in religion, and Tate criticized his colleagues on this score. Agrarians, he explained, were "trying to make a political creed do the work of religion" and restore a proudly insular community of values.[39] True community, Tate implied, could come about only through the unity offered by religious belief.

Agrarians such as Donald Davidson and Frank Owsley did not embrace religion so forthrightly, but they did voice ideas that would have resonated with Catholic audiences. "The evil of industrial economics," Davidson wrote, "was that it squeezed all human motives into one narrow channel and then looked for humanitarian means to repair the injury." In contrast, he observed, the southern agrarian tradition "mixed up a great many motives with the economic motive, thus enriching it and reducing it to a proper subordination."[40] Davidson was skeptical of the idea of progress and its economic implications, of ever increasing technological change, higher living standards, and consumption.[41] In other respects Davidson demonstrated the difficulty of Catholics engaging some segments of American conservatism, however: He clung to segregation as his main cause into the 1950s.[42]

Owsley found common cause with English Distributists, who had a following among American Catholics, as well. Owsley called explicitly for the de-urbanization of populations, a call for which some Catholic thinkers had sympathy, but which was considered unrealistic by most observers, Catholic or not. Owsley's excoriation of the Constitution as a tool of capitalists probably went beyond what most Catholics would countenance.[43]

Although conservative social critics represented potential allies with American Catholics, contact and cooperation between the two groups remained sporadic. At the same time, the possibility of convergent interests was recognized by some Catholics and was indicated by Allen Tate's conversion. What is clear, irrespective of the issue of active alliance, is that most of the positions concerning the socioeconomic sphere articulated by the conservatives were also represented by some group of American Catholics. Machen's antistatism, Babbitt's defense of property, and the agrarians' anticapitalism and antiprogressivism were all represented in Catholic circles as well. As was the case among Catholics, these "conservative" positions (some of which were at odds with each other) seemed to be in no necessary relation to their expounders' religious views.

"Agreeing Pretty Generally": Kenkel, Ryan, and the NCWC

Differences in the interpretation of Catholic social teaching in the American context continued to be evident in the approaches of John Ryan and Frederick Kenkel. While Ryan continued to articulate a program of reform that rested on progressive economic foundations, Kenkel and the Catholic Central Verein (CCV) advocated social reform along the lines suggested by the corporatism of European (especially German) social thought.

Kenkel's concern with state centralization colored his application of Catholic teaching to every issue. While one might infer from Kenkel's criticisms of a strong federal government that he would be friendlier toward Republican administrations, Kenkel remained disconnected from both major political parties. A more searching look at Kenkel's writings reveals the reasons: Kenkel's explicit adherence to papal teaching (a position not admissible to political discourse in the 1920s) and his principled stand on decentralized power. For, some misinterpretation of the Republican administrations of the 1920s notwithstanding, the underlying trend toward centralization of power in the national government continued apace during the presidencies of Coolidge, Harding, and, particularly, Hoover.[44]

The "conservative reformers"—German-Americans such as Kenkel, affiliated with the Central Verein—have generally been seen as fundamentally alienated from American politics, offering nothing but a marginal critique of American social order based on the obscure principles of corporatism as expounded by a handful of Germans and other European Catholics. Kenkel's perspective, then, is essentially European and thereby doomed to failure in the American context. In Philip Gleason's words, "It would hardly be too much to say that Kenkel approached the social question in the spirit of a latter-day German romantic. . . ." Kenkel admired the German corporatist Kurt von Vogelsgang, who vehemently rejected the direction of the modern world since the Middle Ages, and Kenkel's views in many ways depended on his reading of historical developments in Germany.[45]

The Central Verein did at times suffer from its failure to engage a broader American audience, its apathy toward forming alliances with non-Catholic Americans, and its contentious stance toward modernity—all due in part to the group's uncompromising commitment to corporatism. Kenkel considered himself an agrarian, thought that medieval society was far superior to the "crass individualism [that had] developed since the eighteenth century," and once declared the need for Catholics to realize that "we are living in a pagan world, the very breath of whose nostrils emit a poison-gas as deadly for our spiritual and intellectual life as monoxide-gas is for physical man."[46] Yet, as Gleason intimates in places, the view of Kenkel as detached from American life misses something crucial.[47] It does not see the ways in which the positions of the Central Verein dovetailed with venerable American political traditions. This fact, moreover, was not lost on Frederick Kenkel; he explicitly recognized it.

Kenkel's complicity with American political philosophy was demonstrated in the course of debates on education. Efforts to create a national department of education in the 1920s provoked what the *New York Times* called "a controversial discussion that spread in an accelerating wave over the whole country, until every village is lined up pro or con." The debate created odd coalitions on either side: The National Education Association, Chamber of Commerce, Ku Klux Klan, Masons, and Daughters of the American Revolution supported the bills.

An antistatist alliance, including states' rights politicians, the Sentinels of the Republic, and the Catholic Church, formed to oppose the proposal.[48]

In a letter to CCV members concerning one of the bills, Kenkel outlined the rationale for his position:

> Our opposition . . . should be based primarily on our objection to centralization of power which, in the end, leads to bureaucracy, and even autocracy, and on our policy, based on sound civic theory and the experience of history, to uphold the rights of the family, communities, and the States, to regulate their internal affairs in accordance with the natural law and the guarantees of the Federal Constitution.[49]

Kenkel proceeded to quote approvingly Thomas Jefferson on the need for division of the nation into states, "'that each might better do for itself what concerns itself directly, and what it can so much better do than a distant authority.'"[50] The CCV's political stand in this case, then, was presented not as an outcropping of Catholic doctrine, but as an alignment with the Jeffersonian tradition of decentralization or, more broadly, the American tradition of federalism.[51]

While many Catholics, including some priests, cast their lots with the labor movement as the most promising vehicle for social reform along Catholic lines, Kenkel remained skeptical of the theoretical foundations of the movement in the United States. Kenkel questioned the participation of Catholic laborers in unions that did not avow Catholic principles, and worried that "the Church and Society will ultimately suffer great harm because of the neglect to bring the Catholic laboring element of our country under ethically sound influence."[52]

Kenkel's criticism of the labor movement in the same letter remained vague, but his conviction that its principles conflicted with what Catholic teaching required was evident: "While [labor editors and labor leaders] eschew what is called 'radicalism' in our country, and while they profess horror for communists, the principles professed by them must ultimately lead to the very thing they now condemn."[53]

The issue of labor unions upset Kenkel's correspondent, Jesuit William Engelen. Engelen criticized his fellow Jesuit social thinker Joseph Husslein for ignoring the matter of Catholic labor unions, and linked him with John Ryan on this count. Dismissive of Ryan, Engelen scoffed at Husslein for being a popularizer.[54] The rift portrayed by Engelen between the CCV and thinkers such as Ryan and Husslein was due at least in part to Engelen's perception that the CCV was given less attention than it deserved.[55] Relations between the CCV and the National Catholic Welfare Conference (NCWC), while sometime friendly, were often strained. The differences, Philip Gleason explains, "arose from matters of personality, from organizational fears, and from ideological difference; these three causes were often intertwined, and the factor of ethnic sensitivity cut across all of them."[56]

At the same time, the statements of the NCWC itself sometimes sounded more like Frederick Kenkel than John Ryan. "The growth of bureaucracy in the United States," warned a 1922 statement, "is one of the most significant aftereffects of the war. This growth must be resolutely checked." For the administrative committee of the NCWC, as for Kenkel, a dangerous tendency to centralization of power in the national government predated the New Deal and crossed party lines. "The forward-looking forces in our national life," the statement continued, "must resolutely stand against further encroachments on individual and state liberty."[57]

Husslein and Ryan, for their part, viewed the CCV as allies in the effort to bring Catholic social principles to bear on America. There were some differences in language, they admitted, but the goal was the same. "I see you are still holding onto the word 'solidarism,'" Husslein wrote to Kenkel. "We all say the same thing, but have no common word by which to call it." Husslein, more concerned with appealing to his American audience, observed that the term solidarism "is too heavy and will hardly become popular."[58]

Ryan, too, saw Kenkel as an ally, not a competitor. In a letter to the editor of a paper that had published an opinion piece calling attention to the differences between Kenkel and Ryan, Ryan sought to correct what he saw as a mistaken interpretation. "Mr. Kenkel and I have worked in harmony for a great many years in the field of social action," he began, "It has never occurred to me that there was enough difference in our 'methods' to deserve mention, much less emphasis." Ryan did not deny outright the possibility that he and Kenkel approached social issues from different theoretical perspectives—"If Mr. Kenkel and I are head of different schools of thought, as your editorial implies"—but insisted that "our speculative views [do not] prevent us from agreeing pretty generally on practical programs."[59]

The Child Labor Amendment

On one issue, Ryan admitted, he did recall a difference of opinion with Kenkel: the child labor amendment (CLA). An amendment to the national Constitution for the purpose of outlawing child wage labor was proposed in the 1920s and again as part of the New Deal. Some historians have mistakenly portrayed the Church as monolithically opposed to the CLA.[60] In 1924, Ryan had provoked controversy by promoting the amendment in Boston, under the nose of Cardinal William O'Connell, who had already made public his strident opposition to the CLA. O'Connell bridled at Ryan's opposition: "It is made to appear that we Catholics who oppose this soviet legislation are incapable of reading plain English and making correct logical conclusions—a thing which it would appear is the special privilege of J. A. Ryan, Jane Addams and a few more socialistic teachers and writers."[61]

In 1925, Ryan and Kenkel, at a meeting of the Catholic Conference on Industrial Relations, went head to head over the amendment. In this venue, Ryan presented his case irenically, allowing that men of goodwill could reach different conclusions with respect to the prudence of enacting the proposed twentieth amendment. Americans were faced with a "choice between two evils," Ryan claimed: "Is the evil of centralized control greater or less than the evil of inadequate regulation by the states?" While Ryan's progressive assumptions rendered him more optimistic about the state's involvement, he conceded that "a person may be at once intelligent and honest and answer in the affirmative or the negative, according to his estimate of all the considerations involved."[62]

Kenkel's remarks on the CLA reveal his differing estimate of the considerations. He began by insisting that the CCV is not opposed to legislation concerning child labor, nor even, necessarily, to federal action on the matter. There had been much progress in the states over the course of the preceding decade, Kenkel observed, and social activists should not be impatient by pushing for federal power.[63]

The fear driving Kenkel's caution in this respect was the one that Ryan identified: centralization. The danger in centralization, he argued, was its debilitating effect on self-government. "Self-government," he wrote, "is founded on the willingness of the people to take care of their own affairs, and the absence of that disposition which looks to the general government for everything." In Kenkel's judgment, "the willingness for self-government [has] suffered during the last decades and would not wish anything to further undermine or weaken it, since we believe it to be the corollary of liberty."[64] Once again, Kenkel was invoking themes that, if not peculiarly American, sound quite familiar to students of American political thought.

There is no reason to believe that Kenkel was enlisting the rhetoric of American politics to justify positions that were arrived at surreptitiously on the basis of philosophies alien to the American experience. Kenkel was in this instance speaking to what was presumably an almost exclusively Catholic audience and did not need to be concerned with being branded "un-American." Yet, the thrust of Kenkel's argument against the CLA was provided not by papal encyclicals but by the idea of federalism. "Federalism is that self-determination," he explained, "which, beginning with the family, the community, the district, then the historically concluded state, is guaranteed to every territorial entity, and which relinquishes only those tasks, the limited units are not able to accomplish, to each higher one, and in the end to the nation."[65]

Kenkel's articulation of federalism sounds remarkably like Pius XI's exposition of the principle of subsidiarity, which would appear six years later in *Quadragesimo Anno*. Perhaps, had Kenkel had subsidiarity in his arsenal, he would have been as willing to use it as he was federalism. Kenkel's comments on federalism went beyond his employment of the idea against the amendment, however. He expressed satisfaction that the federalists (e.g., Madison) had prevailed against the nationalists (e.g., Hamilton) in formulating the Constitution, and he went on to invoke again the notion of liberty: "The cause of religion and the Church are always affected adversely when liberty suffers. Let us beware, therefore, both for the sake of our country and our Church, of those apothecaries whose drugs are popular because they are powerful and quick. . . . Let us see to it that institutional self-government will not come to harm."[66] He was careful, as always, to define what he meant by liberty and to distinguish it from individualism, but one is struck, nonetheless, by the impression that this representative of the "conservative" German immigrants sounds more like Lord Acton than Pius IX. He went on to quote, not Acton, but Daniel Webster, on liberty and the need for the division of power.

Ryan's allies at the Social Action Department (SAD), meanwhile, viewed the antistatism of Kenkel and other Catholics as unhelpful. J. W. R. Maguire summed up the conventional Catholic view on social issues of the last "ten or fifteen years" as comprising three elements: distrust of federal legislation and bias toward states' rights, fear of "distantly possible results" from new legislation or constitutional amendments, and confidence in the Supreme Court as a protector of minority rights. Maguire allowed that each of these could be defended to some degree, but he warned that "the element of error in all of them may lead to very erroneous conclusions."[67]

The thrust of Maguire's argument was his exhortation that "Catholics cannot afford to take an obstructionist attitude toward new social legislation, but should instead make constructive contributions to the solution of social problems." Specifically, Maguire cited the federal education bills and the child labor amendment as two examples of cases in which, even if such initiatives were imperfect, Catholics must do more than simply oppose them. They must also offer alternative solutions to the real problems these measures sought to address.[68]

The Catholic Conference on Industrial Problems

The varying opinions among Catholics concerned with social issues were manifested in the meetings of the Catholic Conference on Industrial Problems (CCIP). The brainchild of Father Raymond McGowan, assistant director of the Social Action Department, the CCIP conducted its first meeting in Milwaukee in 1923. The meetings were unique because they brought together a diverse group of Catholics, including both academics and businessmen.

The need to apply Church teaching to modern business practice was gaining some attention among Catholics in the 1920s. In the *Catholic World*, a Belgian Jesuit school of commerce and finance was presented as a "stimulus" and a "suggestion" for imitation in the United States. The school's method consisted of "recording and crystallizing the experiences of thousands of successful business men and financiers" and imparting "a training, direct, scientific, and economic. . . ." This venture, the author wrote, merited the "admiration and emulation of the Catholic world at large for having shown that, whatever people say to the contrary, Catholic principles may hold good even in highly efficient business life."[69]

The CCIP, for its part, was not uniformly successful. Historian Aaron Abell claimed that the conferences "were more instrumental than any other agency in acquainting the Catholic and non-Catholic public with the Church's social doctrine." Abell also observed, however, that employers were distinctly in the minority and that this fact gave rise to an anti-employer bias.[70]

At the same time, some business leaders did attend the conferences, and the proceedings are thereby illuminative of a phenomenon characteristic of Catholic opinion during the period. By and large, religious professionals and academics lined up on one side of an economic issue, while those involved professionally in business lined up on the other.

It might be tempting to offer one of two easy explanations for this phenomenon: Academics simply did not understand the actual workings of the economy and, therefore, could not comment intelligently on it, or, alternatively, businessmen did not think deeply or clearly about the moral ramifications of their actions or perhaps were even ignorant of the Church's social teaching. There is probably some truth in both of these assertions. Some of the theologians did not appreciate the workings of a market economy and naively applied Church social teaching in unrealistic ways. Some business leaders were ill-informed with respect to the teachings of their Church.

In general, however—and this applies to the majority of the participants in the Catholic Conferences on Industrial Problems—the theologians did have an understanding of the economy and the professionals did know the encyclicals. Why, then, did the two groups usually come to different conclusions about specific policy issues? As has been stated, the social teaching of the Church does not stipulate particular policy stands. It is not surprising, therefore, that Catholics with different backgrounds and different political and social beliefs and allegiances would come to different positions.

Stephen DuBrul's address to the 1926 meeting is a good example of this diversity. As has been noted, there was significant support among Catholic social thinkers for the formation of a corporatist system reflective of the medieval guild system. Among businessmen, the idea was less popular. DuBrul, manager of an Ohio firm, argued against simplistic recourse to institutions that had been appropriate in the past. "As long as the Guilds were free, unselfish, economic institutions with competition between their members, they succeeded," DuBrul observed. The guilds failed, he contended, because they became monopolies with strict rules limiting membership and production, could not compete with "outsiders," and finally had lost their spiritual purpose and therefore the ability to reform themselves. DuBrul questioned the theory that the Reformation killed the guilds, insisting that the guilds "were dying long before that."[71]

In any case, the realities of modern society made the guilds impossible, DuBrul argued. They had been possible when society was so unified religiously as to submit to the direction and authority of the Church. At present, "the only

system which will function is that which appeals to the one trait common to practically all of us, the desire for gain." Anyone wishing to base an economic system on a motive higher than the profit motive, DuBrul cautioned, "is faced with
a fact which cannot be presented too strongly. Human nature is base."[72]

DuBrul was not a proponent of laissez-faire. He advocated the development,
"alongside of our present economic system, [of] a social organization for dealing
with situations incompatible with our sense of fairness." He was not opposed to
taxing industry, moreover, for the purpose of building such an organization if it
were not forthcoming privately. He considered the tax for Industrial Compensation Insurance "a great step, one of the most forward steps a state ever took."[73]
Informed in Catholic social teaching, DuBrul nevertheless did not advocate a
wholesale reconstruction of the American economic system, but thought amelio-
rative measures more helpful for achieving the desired ends.

The CCIP's failures demonstrated the limitations of the project. Opposition
and refusal to participate came from the more intransigent among both labor and
business. Dissatisfaction with the "truculence toward employers" that dominated
the conferences led one of its own vice presidents to recommend its dissolution
in 1937.[74] The CCIP did accomplish much, however, in the way of spreading the
Church's social teaching and in bringing labor, clergy, and businessmen into
interaction. It provided a forum for each of these groups to confront perspectives
on the application of social teaching to the American economy that they were not
likely to encounter in their conventional social circles.

Academic Economics in the Twenties

Academic economics in the 1920s looked much as it had in the past. Dominated
by orthodox economists, there existed at the same time significant heterodox
movements that offered critiques of the mainstream at various points.[75]

The vitality of heterodox economics was threatened, however, by the rise of
a new emphasis on "science" across the social sciences. By the end of the decade,
the social sciences, economics included, had to a large extent come to model
themselves on the natural sciences. Economists became less concerned with
accounting for the contingencies of human behavior and more concerned with
the universal laws that governed and explained economic activity. The collection
of data and its organization into a predictive model became the normative purpose of the profession.[76]

Financial motives had a role in this development. Foundations—especially
the Rockefeller Foundation, which funded the Social Science Research
Council—were interested in the information that a scientific, not a humanistic,
discipline could provide. The importance of nonprofit funding sources exploded
during the 1920s, moreover. Foundations provided $180,000 for social science
research in 1921; by 1927 the figure was $8,000,000.[77]

Institutional economists, meanwhile, continued to question the assumptions of the mainstream. Different forms of institutionalism developed among the disciples of Thorstein Veblen and around the work of J. M. Clark, Wesley Mitchell, and John R. Commons. Clark and Mitchell adopted a less radical approach, perceiving that the insights of institutionalism could to some degree be integrated with the orthodox position.[78]

In addition, there remained undercurrents of dissent that would be felt more strongly with the onset of economic crisis at the end of the decade. English economist John A. Hobson's theory of underconsumption, cited in chapter 2 in reference to Richard Ely, held that Say's law was a fallacy. If too much revenue were plowed back into firms by capital investment, Hobson's theory went, workers' wages would be insufficient to support the consumption of the goods that the economy was able to produce. While the theory was not widely accepted among mainstream economists in the 1920s, economic historian Joseph Dorfman argues that his ideas were influential in some circles during that decade and thereby "prepared the groundwork for the rapid spread of similar ideas during the Great Depression of the 1930s."[79]

Catholic laymen, such as Arthur Eli Monroe, were active members of the mainstream profession. Monroe was a professor of economics at Harvard and an expert in premodern economic theory. Among clergy, some of the progressive-era concern with economic questions seems to have waned during the twenties. The *Ecclesiastical Review*, for instance, did not review as many books with economic themes, nor did it publish as many articles on the subject. One of the few it did publish was a piece on the "Economics of Aquinas," that demonstrated little in the way of engagement with modern economic thought.[80]

As the 1920s passed, Catholics' views on American economic life remained rooted in their experience and their political and economic ideas. Still at odds in some ways with American culture and smarting from Al Smith's defeat in 1928, Catholics social thinkers were generally less committed to defending wholeheartedly the American economic system when it came crashing down in 1929. The subsequent experience of depression would have an impact on Catholic views, but for most, previous intellectual commitments would also determine to a large extent the way in which they interpreted that event. John Ryan had already joined heterodox economists in accepting the theory of underconsumption; Frederick Kenkel's antistatist stance would provide the basis for his assessment of the New Deal. With other Americans, Catholics would suffer through the depression and struggle to understand its economic lessons.

Notes

1. Henry F. May, *The End of American Innocence: A Study of the First Years of Our Own Time, 1912–1917* (New York: Alfred A. Knopf, 1969 [1959]), chaps. 2–4, 393–94. Culture, in May's definition, was "a particular part of the heritage from the European past, including polite manners, respect for traditional learning, appreciation of the arts, and above all an informed and devoted love of standard literature" (30).

2. Roderick Nash, for instance, questions this interpretation of the period, arguing that the conventional view of the 1920s as depicted by intellectual historians such as May and Morton White (*Revolt of Formalism*), really only describes a handful of intellectuals. Most people (and many intellectuals) remained rooted in the ideas of the nineteenth century—or continued to grope for the certainty these ideas provided. Roderick Nash, *The Nervous Generation: American Thought, 1917–1930* (Chicago: Rand McNally, 1970), chap. 1.

Robert Dorman, meanwhile, has documented continued resistance to the dominance of capitalism in the 1920s in the form of regionalist movements. Robert L. Dorman, *Revolt of the Provinces: The Regionalist Movement in America, 1920–1945* (Chapel Hill: University of North Carolina Press, 1993), xi–xii.

3. William M. Halsey, *The Survival of American Innocence: Catholicism in an Era of Disillusionment, 1920–1940* (Notre Dame, Ind.: University of Notre Dame Press, 1980). Many historians share Halsey's view of the period. Mel Piehl, for instance, observes that early twentieth-century American Catholics "observed Protestant and secular intellectual struggles from a safe distance." Mel Piehl, *Breaking Bread: The Catholic Worker and the Origin of Catholic Radicalism in America* (Philadelphia: Temple University Press, 1982), 49.

4. Halsey, *Survival of Innocence*, 10–11, 50.

5. Ibid., 169.

6. Halsey concedes early in the book that "there is nothing inherently debilitating in a confident approach to reality, nor in believing that in life there dwells a structure of morality necessary for the common interests of humankind" (7). The thrust of his argument throughout the book, however, seems to be to belittle the ideas of "innocence." Robert Cross, while accepting Halsey's portrayal of Catholics as disconnected from American intellectual life, similarly thinks that Halsey "would have written a better book if he had not so obviously and deeply deplored" the character of Catholic intellectual life in this period. Robert D. Cross, Review of Halsey, *Survival, Journal of American History* 67 (September 1980): 444.

On the early twentieth-century Catholic historiography on the Founding, see Kevin Schmiesing, *American Catholic Intellectuals and the Dilemma of Dual Identities* (Lewiston, N.Y.: Edwin Mellen Press, 2002), chap. 2.

7. Nash, *Nervous Generation*, 24. See also Joan Shelley Rubin, "Henry F. May's *The End of American Innocence*," *Reviews in American History* 18 (March 1990): 142–49.

8. The problem may be traced to Halsey's tendency to portray ideas in an overly dichotomous fashion. He implies, for instance, that "diversity, mystery, and experience," are irreconcilable with "universal and absolute principles." *Survival of Innocence*, 161. With this dichotomy in place, he characterizes most of the thinkers he treats as coming down definitively on one side or the other. But most Catholics of the period would have combined an appreciation of mystery with the assertion that universal moral principles can be known by human reason. For a discussion by a neo-Thomist of the 1920s that

belies the characterization of neo-Thomism as rigid, ahistorical, and rationalistic, see John
S. Zybura "Translator's Introduction," in Gerardo Bruni, *Progressive Scholasticism*, trans.
Zybura (St. Louis: B. Herder, 1929), iv–xxxv.

9. Alan Dawley, *Struggles for Justice: Social Responsibility and the Liberal State*
(Cambridge, Mass.: Belknap, 1991), 254–68.

10. Robert Moats Miller makes the case that, while some Protestants were anti-
Catholic, most opposed Smith for other reasons, such as his opposition to Prohibition. See
Robert Moats Miller, *American Protestantism and Social Issues, 1919–1939* (Chapel Hill:
University of North Carolina Press, 1958), chap. 4. That a large number of both Protestants
and Catholics tied their positions on liquor consumption to their faiths, however, meant
that the distinction between being anti-wet and anti-Catholic was not an obvious one.

11. John Higham, *Strangers in the Land: Patterns of American Nativism, 1860–
1925* (New Brunswick, N.J.: Rutgers University Press, 1955), 257–67, 286–97.

12. Ibid., 303, 311, 323–30.

13. For a treatment of the fundamentalist/modernist controversy, see Robert Moats
Miller, *American Protestantism and Social Issues, 1919–1939* (Chapel Hill: University of
North Carolina Press, 1958), chap. 11.

14. Mark A. Noll, *A History of Christianity in the United States and Canada* (Grand
Rapids, Mich.: William B. Eerdmans, 1992), 385.

15. See, for instance, William Franklin Sands, "Catholics and the New Humanism,"
Thought 5 (June 1930): 5–21.

16. Noll, *History of Christianity*, 385–86.

17. Gary Scott Smith, *The Search for Social Salvation: Social Christianity and
America, 1880–1925* (Lanham, Md.: Lexington Books, 2000), 45–46, 350.

18. Smith, *Social Salvation*, 384, chap. 9; David Moberg, *The Great Reversal:
Evangelism Versus Social Concern* (New York: J. B. Lippincott Company, 1972).

19. John Bennett, *Social Salvation* (New York: Charles Scribner's Sons, 1935), 65.
Quoted in William McGuire King, "An Enthusiasm for Humanity: The Social Emphasis
in Religion and Its Accommodation in Protestant Theology," in *Religion and Twentieth-
Century American Intellectual Life*, ed. Michael J. Lacey, 77. For one explanation of the
dissipation of the social gospel impulse in the 1920s, see Paul A. Carter, *The Decline and
Revival of the Social Gospel: Social and Political Liberalism in American Protestant
Churches, 1920–1940* (Ithaca, N.Y.: Cornell University Press, 1954).

The retreat from the social sphere by evangelicals and the concomitant decline of the
social gospel movement has led to the impression that American Christianity became
something of a chaplain to capitalism in the 1920s. Robert Moats Miller has admitted that
there is some truth to the generalization that churches were overly deferential to capitalism
in the 1920s, but that the situation was more complicated than the generalization. He concedes that there was a "partial deadening of social Christianity," but also presents evidence that the social impulse in Christianity was still notable during the decade. In Miller's
view, the fundamentalist/modernist controversy did play a role, but the most compelling
reason was that, "there seemed precious little in American society that required reformation." Miller, *American Protestantism*, chaps. 2, 3 (quotes on 18, 21).

20. William R. Hutchison, *The Modernist Impulse in American Protestantism*
(Cambridge, Mass.: Harvard University Press, 1976), chap. 8.

21. Smith, *Social Salvation*, 410–11.

22. While he shares some of their perspective, Smith argues that the Niebuhrs' critique was overdone. Most of the social gospelers, he observes, did recognize the reality of
sin and the limits of progress. *Social Salvation*, 412.

23. William J. Kerby, "The Spiritual Quality of Social Work," *AER* 78 (April 1928): 376–90.

24. Eugene McCarraher, *Christian Critics: Religion and the Impasse in Modern American Social Thought* (Ithaca, N.Y.: Cornell University Press, 2000), 35.

25. D. G. Hart, *Defending the Faith: J. Gresham Machen and the Crisis of Conservative Protestantism in Modern America* (Baltimore: Johns Hopkins University Press, 1994), 135ff; J. Gresham Machen, *Christianity and Liberalism* (New York: Macmillan, 1923), 12–13, 149. Machen's politics were probably too libertarian for most Catholics; his overriding fear of the faith being distorted by being used politically led him to denounce any connection betwen Christianity and the state and to deny categorically the ability of government to promote virtue. See Hart, *Defending*, 75–76, and Machen, "The Responsibility of the Church in Our New Age," *Annals of the American Academy of Political and Social Science* 65 (1933): 38–47.

26. Hart, *Defending*, 69.

27. Reinhold Niebuhr, "Is Protestantism Self-Deceived?" *Christian Century*, December 25, 1924, 166f; Niebuhr, *The Contribution of Religion to Social Work* (New York: Columbia University Press, 1932), 8f. Quoted in James Leo Garrett Jr., *Reinhold Niebuhr on Roman Catholicism* (Lousville, Ky.: Seminary Baptist Book Store, 1972), 3–4. For a thorough treatment of Niebuhr's life and work, see Richard Wightman Fox, *Reinhold Niebuhr: A Biography* (San Francisco: Harper & Row, 1985).

28. See J. David Hoeveler Jr., *The New Humanism: A Critique of Modern America, 1900–1940* (Charlottesville: University Press of Virginia, 1977), chap. 3.

29. Irving Babbitt, "Humanism: An Essay at Definition," in *Humanism and America: Essays on the Outlook of Modern Civilisation*, ed. Norman Foerster (New York: Farrar and Rinehart, 1930), 39, 44. On Babbitt's views on religion, see also Paul Elmer More, "Irving Babbitt," *University of Toronto Quarterly* 3 (1933–1934), in *The Superfluous Men: Conservative Critics of American Culture, 1900–1945*, ed. Robert M. Crunden (Austin: University of Texas Press, 1977), 142–43.

30. Babbitt, *Democracy and Leadership* (Boston: Houghton Mifflin, 1924), in *Superfluous Men*, 219.

31. Ibid., 212.

32. J. David Hoeveler Jr., *The New Humanism: A Critique of Modern America, 1900–1940* (Charlottesville: University Press of Virginia, 1977), 174–76. See chapter 7 on New Humanists and religion in general; More, "Irving Babbitt," 137, 141–42; and *The Skeptical Approach to Religion* (Princeton, N.J.: Princeton University Press, 1934), in *Superfluous Men*, 251.

33. William Franklin Sands, "Catholics and the New Humanism," *Thought* 5 (June 1930): 12–14 and passim. For a discussion of Catholic attraction to New Humanism, see Halsey, *Survival*, 116–17.

34. Woodlock to Louis Mercier, March 21, 1933, LMP, box 12, folder 25.

35. Patrick Allitt, *Catholic Intellectuals and Conservative Politics in America, 1950–1985* (Ithaca, N.Y.: Cornell University Press, 1993), 51–52. See also Albert E. Stone Jr., "Seward Collins and the American Review: Experiment in Pro-Fascism, 1933–1937," *American Quarterly* 12 (Spring 1960): 3–19.

36. Twelve Southerners, *I'll Take My Stand: The South and the Agrarian Tradition* (Baton Rouge: Louisiana State University Press, 1991 [1930]). For an introduction to the agrarians, see John L. Stewart, *The Burden of Time: The Fugitives and Agrarians* (Princeton, N.J.: Princeton University Press, 1965). On the *American Review* and its con-

nection to New Humanism and Southern Agrarianism, see Patrick Allitt, *Catholic Intellectuals and Conservative Politics in America, 1950–1985* (Ithaca, N.Y.: Cornell University Press, 1993), 52.

37. On Tate and Catholicism, see Peter A. Huff, *Allen Tate and the Catholic Revival: Trace of the Fugitive Gods* (New York: Paulist Press, 1996).

38. Allen Tate, "The Fallacy of Humanism," in *The Critique of Humanism: A Symposium*, ed. C. Hartley Grattan (New York: Brewer and Warren, 1930), 131, 148–60.

39. Quoted in Dorman, *Revolt*, 50.

40. Davidson, "I'll Take My Stand: A History," *American Review* 5 (Summer 1935), in *Superfluous Men*, 201.

41. Davidson, "The World as Ford Factory," *Nashville Tennessean*, November 9, 1930, in *Superfluous Men*, 82–83.

42. Dorman, *Revolt*, 309–10.

43. Frank L. Owsley, "The Pillars of Agrarianism," *American Review* 4 (March 1935), in *Superfluous Men*, 186.

44. On Hoover's policies vis-à-vis Roosevelt, see Dawley, *Struggles for Justice*, 343–51; and Murray N. Rothbard, *America's Great Depression* (Los Angeles: Nash, 1972 [1963]), chap. 7.

45. Gleason, *Conservative Reformers*, 102, 192–98.

46. Kenkel to Rev. Frank Moellering, S.J., CCCV, 3/2; Kenkel, *The Church, Patron of a Christian Social Order* (St. Louis: Central Bureau Press, 1944), 15; Kenkel to Rev. Jac. Wm. Post, April 8, 1936, CCCV, 3/20.

47. Gleason highlights the similarity of Kenkel's views, in certain ways, with those of, for instance, American businessmen (antistatism), Sinclair Lewis and H. L. Mencken (critique of philistinism and materialism), and Ralph Adams Cram (admiration for Middle Ages). *Conservative Reformers*, 199–201.

48. Lynn Dumenil, "'The Insatiable Maw of Bureaucracy': Antistatism and Education Reform in the 1920s," *Journal of American History* 77 (September 1990): 499–524, *Times* quoted on 499. Opposition to the federalization of education was one of the initial causes of the NCWC. Elizabeth McKeown, *War and Welfare: American Catholics and World War I* (New York: Garland, 1988), 180–82.

49. Kenkel to CCV Members, January 4, 1926, CCCV, 2/7. See also Kenkel to Members of the Major Executive Committee of the CCV, May 6, 1930, CCCV, 1/28: "Central Bureau Correspondence."

50. Kenkel to CCV Members, January 4, 1926, CCCV, 2/7.

51. Kenkel was not alone in identifying a central principle of the Catholic social tradition (the principle that came to be called *subsidiarity* following Pius XI's 1931 encyclical, *Quadragesimo Anno*) with concepts prominent in the American political tradition. German Jesuit Oswald von Nell-Breuning, a major influence on *Quadragesimo*, noted in a 1969 article the correspondence of the principle of subsidiarity with the idea articulated by Abraham Lincoln in the following quotation: "The legitimate object of government is to do for a community of people whatever they need to have done but cannot do for themselves in their separate and individual capacities. In all that people can individually do for themselves government ought not to interfere" (July 1, 1854). Nell-Breuning, "Subsidiarity," in *Sacramentum Mundi* vol. 6 (New York: Herder and Herder), 115. Cited in John J. Kelley, S.M., *Freedom in the Church: A Documented History of the Principle of Subsidiary Function* (Dayton, Ohio: Peter Li, 2000), 18.

52. Kenkel to Rev. William Engelen, S.J., August 9, 1928, CCCV, 2/5.

53. Ibid.

54. "Aber auch kein Wort ueber Kath. Arbeitervereine. Ganz a la Ryan. . . . Of late I talked to a number of union men. They laugh at Dr. Ryan's ideas." Engelen to Kenkel, December 29, 1920, CCCV, 4/13. On Husslein as a popularizer, see Engelen to Kenkel, January 24, 1921, CCCV 4/13. Engelen did not see any room for cooperation with Ryan, whom he saw as intellectually committed to American liberalism; see Engelen to Kenkel, November 29, 1922, CCCV, 4/18. On Engelen's social thought, see Charles E. Curran, *American Catholic Social Ethics: Twentieth-Century Approaches* (Notre Dame, Ind.: University of Notre Dame Press, 1982), chap. 3.

55. This was a frequent complaint lodged by Engelen during the 1920s. See, for instance, Engelen to Kenkel, October 5, 1920, CCCV, 4/12; and Engelen to Kenkel, April 4, 1921, CCCV, 4/14. Inconsistently, Engelen criticizes Husslein's ideas in one place, then in another complains that Husslein copied his ideas from Engelen without attributing their source. See also Gleason's discussion of Engelen, Kenkel, and the NCWC in *Conservative Reformers*, 191–94.

56. Gleason, *Conservative Reformers*, 191. The Central Bureau had sponsored talks by William Kerby and John Ryan in 1910, indicating the initial spirit of cooperation between the CCV and the men involved in the organization of the NCWC. *Conservative Reformers*, 119.

57. "Statement on Federalization and Bureacracy," Issued by the Administrative Committee of the National Catholic Welfare Conference, January 26, 1922, in *Pastoral Letters of the United States Catholic Bishops*, vol. 1, 1792–1940, ed. Hugh J. Nolan (Washington, D.C.: United States Catholic Conference, 1984), 334.

58. Husslein to Kenkel, CCCV, 4/15. Husslein's views on social questions do seem similar to those expressed by Kenkel and the CCV. Husslein focused on the role of personal conversion in social reform and supported a transition to a corporatist form of economic life mirroring the medieval guild system. See his magnum opus, *The Christian Social Manifesto* (Milwaukee: Bruce, 1931). For an overview of Husslein's life and thought, see Stephen A. Werner, *Prophet of the Christian Social Manifesto: Joseph Husslein, S.J.* (Milwaukee: Marquette University Press, 2001).

59. Ryan to Editor, *Dubuque Daily American Tribune*, November 25, 1927, copy in CCCV, 4/26. On Ryan and Kenkel, see also Franz H. Mueller, *The Church and the Social Question* (Washington, D.C.: American Enterprise Institute, 1984 [1963]), 95–97.

60. See, for example, Dawley, *Struggles for Justice*, 282–83. Dawley's presentation is technically accurate, since he restricts his claim to the position of the "Catholic hierarchy," but the implication of the passage is that there was no Catholic support for the amendment. Ironically, Dawley cites John Ryan (who vocally supported the amendment) in a footnote immediately preceding this passage (282n59).

61. O'Connell to Archbishop Michael Curley, November 2, 1924. Quoted in Francis L. Broderick, *Right Reverend New Dealer: John A. Ryan* (New York: Macmillan, 1963), 158. The event prompted O'Connell to lead an effort (joined by Cardinal Dougherty of Philadelphia and Bishop Keane of Dubuque), to shut down the NCWC and its Social Action Department. Joseph M. McShane, S.J., *"Sufficiently Radical": Catholicism, Progressivism, and the Bishops' Program of 1919* (Washington, D.C.: Catholic University, 1986), 269–70. For a summary of the debate over the CLA among Catholics, see George Q. Flynn, *American Catholics and the Roosevelt Presidency, 1932–1936* (Lexington: University of Kentucky Press, 1968), 108–17.

62. John A. Ryan, "For the Amendment," *Third Annual Meeting of the Catholic Conference on Industrial Relations, June 24–25, 1925, Chicago* (Washington, D.C.: National Headquarters), 7, in PKNA 1/18 "Catholic Conference on Industrial Problems, 1925–1926." Kenkel similarly differed from Ryan on the related Sheppard-Towner bill (Maternity and Infancy Act). A letter to Kenkel referring to his opposition to the Sheppard-Towner bill also notes the approval of that bill by John Ryan and John O'Grady, president of National Catholic Charities. J. J. Cochran to Kenkel, December 6, 1921, CCCV, 2/7.

63. Frederick P. Kenkel, "Against the Amendment," *Third Annual Meeting*, 8–9.

64. Ibid., 10.

65. Ibid., 11.

66. Ibid., 11–12, 15.

67. J. W. R. Maguire, "Catholic Opinion and Social Reform," *CW* 123 (August 1926): 634. Maguire was on the executive committee of the SAD.

68. Ibid., 637–38.

69. J. Theyskens, S.J., "A Jesuit Higher School of Commerce and Finance," *CW* 114 (January 1922): 533, 535.

70. Aaron I. Abell, *American Catholicism and Social Action: A Search for Social Justice, 1865–1950* (Garden City, N.Y.: Hanover, 1960), 215–16. Thomas Greene's more recent treatment of the CCIP substantiates this observation. Thomas R. Greene, "The Catholic Conference on Industrial Problems in Normalcy and Depression," *CHR* 77 (July 1991), 442 and passim.

71. Stephen DuBrul, "The Wage Question," *Proceedings of Catholic Congress on Industrial Problems*, 1926, PKNA/"Catholic Conference on Industrial Problems," 14.

72. Ibid., 14–15.

73. Ibid., 15.

74. Greene, "Catholic Conference," 453–54, 468.

75. For a survey of academic economics in the 1920s, see Joseph Dorfman, *The Economic Mind in American Civilization*, 5 vols. (New York: Viking Press, 1959 [1949]), vol. 4, chaps. 8–10; and vol. 5, pt. I.

76. Dorothy Ross, *The Origins of American Social Science* (New York: Cambridge University Press, 1991), xiv., chap. 10. Edward A. Purcell Jr., *The Crisis of Democratic Theory: Scientific Naturalism and the Problem of Value* (Lexington: University Press of Kentucky, 1973), 31ff.

77. Ross, *Origins*, 400–403; Purcell, *Crisis*, 28.

78. Dorfman, *Economic Mind*, vol. 4, chap. 13; Ross, *Origins*, 414–15. Ross depicts the 1920s as the triumph of the natural/liberal over the historicist approach, and portrays Clark and Mitchell as having capitulated to neoclassicism. She probably overstates the case, however. That Clark and Mitchell did not reject the neoclassical approach in toto does not mean that they did not retain a critical stance from an institutional perspective.

79. Dorfman, *Economic Mind*, vol. 4, 175. For a discussion of early underconsumption/overproduction theories (1880s), see vol. 3, 130–36. See also *Two Hundred Years of Say's Law: Essays on Economic Theory's Most Controversial Principle*, ed. Steven Kates (Cheltenham, U.K.: Edward Elgar, 2003).

80. Edward F. Murphy, S.S.J., "Economics of Aquinas," *AER* 69 (July 1923): 64–69. Monroe's books included *Early Economic Thought* (Cambridge, Mass.: Harvard University Press, 1924), and *Monetary Theory Before Adam Smith* (New York: Sentry Press, 1923).

4

Catholics and the New Deal

The Intellectual Sources of New Deal Reform

The New Deal was at once in the tradition of but also a departure from progressivism. New Dealers were worried less than progressives about the bigness of business and more about its conduct. They were not as concerned with political-machine reform as had been their predecessors, but they were willing to call into question more fundamentally the capitalist economy. In sum, the reformers of the thirties were faced with an economic crisis and their main goal was recovery, not gentle reform of an already effective economic system.[1] Robert Crunden, viewing the progressive impulse as fundamentally opposed to the centralization of government power, claims, "Progressives were not collectivists of the New Deal variety. If they lived into the 1930s, they either changed significantly in order to support the measures of the New Deal, or they flatly opposed those measures as being contrary to the reform spirit as they understood it."[2]

At the same time, the New Deal was not as radical a break with the policy of previous administrations as it has sometimes been viewed. Roosevelt's policies, in many ways, can be seen as the culmination of a longstanding trend toward centralization of economic functions in the federal government. Alan Dawley, for instance, observes that it was Herbert Hoover who took the first major steps down the road of corporatist organization and state intervention. Roosevelt's goal was security for farmers, business, and workers, but he did not intend to restructure radically the American economy.[3]

Third, the New Deal was driven not by a single ideology; instead, its intellectual sources were multifarious. In Alan Brinkley's words, "the early New Deal was awash in ideas—ideas of significant range and diversity . . . but ones

83

that somehow managed for a time to coexist." Terry Cooney has argued similarly that the "psychological success" of the New Deal, its generation of popular support and hope, was the result of and not in tension with its "failures" in terms of ideological consistency. "In their collective tolerance for inconsistency," Cooney writes, "in their efforts to balance competing values, claims, and ideas, New Deal programs created channels of political expression for the thought and culture of the decade that earned them their 'psychological success.'"[4]

Cooney's terminology of *psychological success* points to another important point to be made concerning New Deal reform, especially as it relates to Catholic views to be analyzed later in this chapter. Alan Brinkley has argued compellingly that Roosevelt and his liberal allies misinterpreted the mandate they received in the election of 1936. Their overwhelming electoral support did not mean popular support for expansion and centralization of government power, in principle. "As on other occasions both before and after the Great Depression," Brinkley notes, "much of the American electorate welcomed (even expected) assistance from government in solving their own problems but nonetheless remained skeptical of state power and particularly of efforts to expand and concentrate it."[5]

A similar kind of ambivalence marked Catholic thought on the New Deal. Catholic thinkers were not deeply committed to the American system of capitalism and were, therefore, open to reform. At the same time, most were keenly aware of the dangers of centralizing power in the national government, a direction in which many New Deal programs tended.

Catholic Response to the New Deal

The ability of the New Deal to draw on diverse sources for its reform program meant that the ideas that had been percolating in Catholic social reform circles could also be seen to be one of the New Deal's sources. Catholics were generally quick to perceive the consonance of New Deal proposals with their own ideas concerning social reform. The matter was not simply one of perception, moreover; Catholics came to assume more positions of influence during the Roosevelt administration than they had during any previous regime. These factors contributed to the fact that, initially at least, Catholic commentators greeted the New Deal with "nearly universal enthusiasm."[6]

Their perception of having gained the ear of the president helped Catholics to overcome the ostracism that they had experienced following the defeat of Al Smith in 1928. As the experience of the Great Depression pushed American sentiment to the left and criticism of capitalism became more frequent and increasingly severe, Protestant and Catholic clergy alike grew more open to government intervention in the economy.[7] Catholics as a body, the bulk of whom were first or second generation immigrants and of relatively low economic status, may have been less attached to American capitalism and, therefore, more inclined to countenance its reform.[8]

There was less polarization in general between Catholic and Protestant Americans during the 1930s than there had been in the 1920s, and at the end of the decade Catholics joined other religious people in celebrating a sense of religion's return to prominence in American public life. There also appeared important points of contact between Catholic thought and major figures in secular American intellectual life, such as the University of Chicago's Robert Maynard Hutchins and Mortimer Adler.[9] The rise of totalitarianism abroad, in addition, provided an issue that could serve as a unifying force for its opposition, among whom American Catholics counted themselves. The tortuous matter of the Spanish Civil War delayed the realization of that potential, but the end of Nazism and the focus on Communism in the late 1940s would bring it to fruition.

John Ryan

Situated within the context of Catholicism's coming to prominence in American life, the early years of the New Deal were a high point for John Ryan. Catholic clergy and laity alike were strongly supportive of Roosevelt's initiatives, and some Catholics, like Ryan's ally and fellow priest Francis Haas, assumed important positions in the administration of the president's social programs.[10] Ryan's mentor and colleague, William Kerby, won over to the prospects of a governmental solution of the social question during World War I, welcomed the New Deal enthusiastically. "The function of the State," he argued, "must expand under the imperial orders of truth, morality, and justice, until the facts of historical democracy are corrected and life enters upon the pathway towards democracy in fact." Kerby unambiguously endorsed Roosevelt's efforts: "We have less occasion to fear codes, even planned production, State paternalism, and a diminishing return on capital than we have to fear economic slavery, broken health, constant worry, broken homes, massive poverty and insecurity. . . ."[11]

In Pius XI's *Quadragesimo Anno* of 1931, commemorating Leo's earlier social encyclical, Ryan found ample support for his (and Roosevelt's) social programs. "I derived great comfort," Ryan reflected later, "from the implicit approval which the Holy Father's pronouncement gave to the socio-ethical doctrines which I had been defending for almost forty years." Others saw it the same way. Bishop Thomas Shahan exclaimed of *Quadragesimo*, "Well, this is a great vindication for John Ryan."[12]

While he did not occupy the highest appointed position of any Catholic in Roosevelt's administration, Ryan was the most important Catholic spokesman for Roosevelt. Ryan held posts in government agencies in the 1930s, including a National Recovery Act (NRA) industrial appeals board (1934–1935) and the Committee on Farm Tenancy. More importantly, Ryan articulated the relationship between Roosevelt's reforms and Catholic social teaching for an intellectual and middlebrow audience. Ryan seldom saw tension between the programs of New Deal reform and Catholic teaching, and his conviction as to their compatibility seemed to intensify over the course of the 1930s. His identification with Roosevelt led the radio priest Charles Coughlin to call him "the Right Reverend New Dealer."

For Ryan, the Great Depression confirmed the economic theories that he had embraced for decades. Like many critics of orthodox economics, Ryan was skeptical of Say's law; in Ryan's case, he drew on the alternative underconsumption theory of English economist John Hobson. The theory of underconsumption was one of the intellectual influences of the New Deal. It would only come to have predominant influence later in the administration, after the recession of 1937 forced some rethinking among Roosevelt and his top advisors, who feared that Roosevelt's presidency might "end like Hoover's."[13] As they came to accept the theory, the advisors began to adopt the argument that deficit spending by government was necessary to provide purchasing power.

The initiatives put forth by Roosevelt in the spring of 1938 showed that the president had at least partially accepted the argument as well. "In the past," Alan Brinkley explains, "the President had generally justified spending programs as ways to deal with particular social problems: helping the unemployed, subsidizing farmers or homeowners or troubled industries, building the national infrastructure. Now he described such programs as vehicles for bringing the economy as a whole back to health."[14]

The openness of Roosevelt and his advisers to previously marginal theories such as underconsumption and the effectiveness of "pump priming" (through public works) was reflective of a broader development in the economics profession during the course of the thirties. Economists as a group were as puzzled by the onset and severity of the depression as were other Americans. Many had begun to believe that increasing knowledge of the nature of business cycles had come to a point at which serious downturns would no longer occur. The experience of the depression pushed them in new directions.[15]

In the face of depression, economists offered various schemes to rejuvenate the economy. Unsurprisingly, the proposals tended to follow the proclivities of their authors. Richard Ely, for instance, proposed one of the more radical ideas: a vast peacetime army to absorb the unemployed while promoting the values of military service. At the same time, economists of diverse leanings found common ground in advocating moves such as federal easy money policies and expanded public works. John Ryan signed on to one petition urging credit and money expansion.[16]

One result of economists' grappling with the problem of the depression was more widespread acceptance within the profession of ideas such as Hobson's underconsumption theory. The fact was not lost on a longtime devotee, John Ryan. Hobson's theory, Ryan observed in 1931, "has not been generally adopted by economists until rather recently, but now, if you notice, a great many economists have adopted it."[17]

The deflation and unemployment rampant from 1929 on was evidence, in Ryan's view, that Hobson's thesis was correct. The source of the depression,

Ryan argued in 1935, was irrational distribution—excessive spending on capital goods, excessive production, and insufficient consumption (low wages).[18]

This underlying interpretation of the economics of the depression a fortiori influenced Ryan's judgments regarding the efficacy of New Deal measures to counteract it. The Agricultural Adjustment Act (1933), for instance, passed muster as a step in the direction of social justice because it circumvented the price mechanism of the market in favor of enforced production limits. The reason such a step was necessary was that insufficient purchasing power on the part of consumers made it impossible for them to buy all the farm products they actually desired.[19]

Ryan's denial of Say's law was not at the heart of what separated him from many other Catholic thinkers, however. More striking was his dismissal of the constitutional scruples many raised with respect to New Deal programs. In the context of the Great Depression, Ryan was willing to set aside whatever constitutional qualms he may have shared with New Deal critics in his conviction that the amelioration of economic hardship was more immediately important. In *A Better Economic Order*, Ryan stated explicitly that he desired a government unencumbered by constitutional limitations so as to permit it to pursue most effectively the end of better economic distribution. Most fellow Catholics were considerably more cautious about allowing government to take on functions that had previously been considered constitutionally off limits.[20]

It is important to note that Ryan did remain aware of the fact that Roosevelt's measures did not represent a perfect transference of Catholic social principles into American politics. In his 1935 book on New Deal reform he observed that the National Recovery Administration did not include labor, consumers, or small business owners in its decision-making—a stipulation required by the reform articulated by Pius XI—and called it a "vital difference" and a "fundamental defect."[21] Ryan was not optimistic, moreover, that the current system would develop into the cooperative arrangement that Pius envisioned.[22]

For the most part, though, Ryan continued to endorse Roosevelt's initiatives, a stand he presented as the one most consistent with economic theory and Catholic teaching. As will be seen, others disagreed. David O'Brien described well American Catholic social thought in the thirties when he wrote that it was "characterized by unanimous and enthusiastic approval of official Church teachings and wide, often bitter, disagreement over their meaning and application."[23]

Apolitical Catholics in the Thirties

Among Catholics less enthusiastic about the New Deal than Ryan were those who believed that spirituality and culture were more important sources of economic well-being than was politics. For Virgil Michel and the Catholic Workers, the key to justice in the economic sphere could be found not in politics but in personal spiritual reform and social action.

Virgil Michel

A social thinker who shared some of the traits of the conservative reformers was Benedictine monk Virgil Michel (1890–1938).[24] Michel was the most respected figure in the liturgical reform movement in the United States during the 1920s and thirties.[25] He was also a social critic. Working from rural Minnesota, Michel fashioned a critique of American individualism and industrialism that resembled the views of other American agrarians.

Born George Michel in St. Paul, Minnesota, in 1890, he professed solemn vows in the Benedictine order in 1913.[26] The Rule of Saint Benedict, with its maxim *ora et labora* (pray and work), can be seen as the inspiring ideal of Michel's life and thought. Perhaps Michel's most insistent message, throughout the course of his copious writings, was the idea that the prayer life of the Church, specifically the liturgy, served as the principle by which the practical life of the Church was ordered and promoted. In short, there was a symbiotic relationship between prayer and work. Michel was not content to stress the individual benefits of contemplation and prayer; the liturgy also had profound social implications. By exploring this connection, Michel became one of the most outstanding proponents of Catholic social teaching in the early decades of the twentieth century.[27]

Michel deplored the dualism he saw as characteristic of the modern world. "Modern man" ignored the spiritual, he argued, while modern Christian man ignored the temporal. This was not an authentically Catholic view of things. Instead, Michel called for "engagement" of the modern world, with the realities of spiritual and temporal being everywhere recognized and ordered as part of an organic whole. This engagement implied an emphasis on "action."[28] Catholic education, properly delivered, would prompt not only right thinking but right doing as well. Catholic thought, for Virgil Michel, must have social impact.

Michel, like most Catholic intellectuals of the period, thus demonstrated an ambivalent relationship with the American society that surrounded him. By calling for a more comprehensive religious (specifically Catholic) influence on American life, Michel displayed a hope both naive and noble. He decried the separation of Church life from public life, but he was confronted with the fact that most Catholics believed that, given their minority status, it was not prudent to brandish one's religious identity before a public audience. The election of 1928 abetted this view.

Characteristic of his detached approach to American life, Virgil Michel did not comment on Roosevelt or his programs directly. His commentary, instead, continued to advocate a third way between individualist capitalism and collectivist socialism without passing judgment specifically on contemporary politics. "It takes but a moment's glance," he wrote in 1936, "to see that both the totalitarian State and the amorphous mass-rabble aggregate that individualism has made of democracy are quite out of harmony with the Christian concept of society as reflected in the mystical body of Christ."[29] While the rise of fascism and communism in Europe provided easy targets for Catholic commentators in the 1930s, democratic America, in Michel's view, was not a paragon of Catholic social practice either. Mired in depression, the United States displayed the negative effects of rampant individualism.

Michel warmly recommended Dorothy Day's Catholic Worker movement and lauded the "toiling masses," concurrently criticizing the majority of Catholics for ignoring their church's social teaching.[30] He also criticized the "bourgeois mind" for whom profit was the "supreme guiding notion." The bourgeois American, for Michel, violated most brazenly the ideal of the good citizen. For the wealthy man who avoided paying taxes "circumvents both admonitions of the saying of Christ: 'Render to Caesar what is Caesar's and to God what is God's.'"[31] Yet, Michel did not extol Roosevelt's programs as the instantiation of Catholic social thought in American governmental policy.

The reason for Michel's reticence on this score may have been his unwillingness to become identified with any specific political program or party. In fact, Michel browbeat Catholics who identified the "eternal Church with the fortunes of a particular political set-up." He had in mind here not so much political theorists like Ryan, but the "wire pullers" and "pressure agents" of the Church, political bosses and ward heelers. Michel was not above offering specific criticism or advice on political affairs, then; he simply thought that Catholic ideals, though requiring practical implementation, at the same time transcended particular political persons and parties. Michel was more interested in fundamentally transforming the economy through movements such as consumers' cooperatives than in Ryan's moderate legislative reforms.[32]

Michel's social thought, focused as it was on theological and spiritual ideas, did nonetheless carry practical force. By the testimony of some of the most distinguished social activists of the period, it provided a powerful impetus to social action. Michel's collaboration with Dorothy Day has already been noted. The liturgical reformer also served as inspiration for Ellen Gates Starr, cofounder with Jane Addams of Hull House, and for Catherine De Hueck, founder of Friendship House. De Hueck paid tribute to Michel's emphasis on lay action in the Church and the centrality of the liturgy: "Without him," she once said, "there may not have been a Friendship House movement at all."[33]

Like Ryan and many Catholic social thinkers before and since, Michel conceived of the Church's social teaching as a "middle way" between individualism and collectivism. For Michel, individualism was the explanatory key for all that was wrong with American society. "Economic individualism" was not only the ideology behind the attitudes of laissez-faire advocates who resisted any restriction on economic activity; it was also the inspiration of most political activity, through which occurred the "safeguarding of vested interests." While consumption had been the purpose of production during the Middle Ages, Michel argued, in capitalism the making of profit for further investment replaced consumption as the driving engine of the economic system. "Such is the nature of capitalism as it has developed up to our own day," Michel concluded an essay on the subject: "It is an economic system that is the combined product of the high-powered individualism of the modern world and the supremacy of material ownership above all other human rights."[34]

Michel was not unaware of the work of his counterpart in the field of social justice, Monsignor John Ryan. Indeed, in an article in *Commonweal* in 1936, Michel notes that the only instance he could find of an attempt to define social justice was John Ryan's 1934 article in the same journal. While Michel was not explicitly critical of Ryan, the difference between his piece and that of Ryan indicates the gap that separated their approaches to the social question.

Ryan's article described social justice as rendering to each person in a society his or her due (with special emphasis placed on the working class). Ryan went on to examine the various policy initiatives of the New Deal, including minimum wage legislation and the NRA and concluded that, by his definition, these programs served the principle of social justice.[35]

Michel, meanwhile, posited the following definition of social justice: "that virtue by which individuals and groups contribute their positive share to the maintenance of the common good and moreover regulate all their actions in proper relation to the common good."[36] Michel thereby implied that Ryan's treatment of social justice was insufficient, because it failed to focus on the common good. Ryan stressed the requirements of distributive justice (society's obligations to individuals), while Michel stressed the obligations of individuals and groups to the common good.

Put another way, Ryan emphasized the capacity of legal and political mechanisms to bring about social justice while Michel viewed the issue as one of personal and corporate responsibility that implied a moral and spiritual recognition of the unity of the human family. As one historian of the liturgical movement, Keith Pecklers, has summarized, Michel was "critical of Ryan's stress on material rather than spiritual reform."[37] Ryan, for his part, seemed unwilling to grant status to Michel or the liturgical reform movement. "In fact it is not too much to say," he wrote in 1937, "that the only adequate and effective leadership both in education and in social problems that exists in this country derives from the Catholic University [Ryan's home institution]."[38]

Catholic Worker

Initially sharing more with Michel's approach than with Ryan's, Dorothy Day's and Peter Maurin's Catholic Worker movement aspired to be truly radical and nonpolitical. James Fisher has characterized well the radicalism of Day's intellectual guide, Peter Maurin: "The essential difference between Maurin and the classical model of American selfhood was in his acceptance of poverty as a goal in itself, even as one to be worked toward."[39]

Maurin was an eccentric figure and his views on economics are hard to pin down. It seems correct to assume that he saw more merit in the corporatism of Kenkel than in the liberalism of Ryan, but he also criticized Pius XI's corporatism as not "hold[ing] up the ideal of personal responsibility. . . ."[40] Maurin was in some ways connected to the nostalgic medieval Catholicism of Albert de Mun, but he differed from the de Mun circle in his antimilitarism and philo-Semitism.[41]

In general, Day and Maurin saw their vocation as engaging the social, not the political sphere, though Day did sign the public statement, "Organized Social Justice" (1935), which denounced the Supreme Court's striking down New Deal legislation *(Schechter)* and called for more social reform. While, insofar as it can be conceived politically, the Catholic Worker might be located on the left and while its impulse was explicitly religious, it did not naturally fit into the mainstream Protestant social reform movement. As the social gospel movement moved toward both political engagement and theological liberalism, the prospects of finding common ground with Day and her Catholic Workers dimmed.[42]

The Catholic Worker had connections to broader Catholic intellectual trends, manifested in Day's endorsement of Paul Hanly Furfey's *Fire on the Earth* (1936) as a statement of Catholic Worker principles. Furfey, a sociologist at Catholic University, was an advocate of "supernatural sociology" that drew explicitly on Catholic theology and derogated conventional social scientific claims to objectivity. From this perspective, he articulated a theological grounding for Catholic radicalism and "personalist action."[43]

The Worker movement had its critics among coreligionists who considered it too radical. Jesuit John LaFarge, writing in *America*, displayed the ambivalence that probably marked many sympathetic yet skeptical observers. Against its strident detractors, LaFarge defended the movement's right to its version of social action. He placed the workers firmly within the Catholic fold, stating, "Where they differ from the more current Catholic opinions, it is not on matters strictly of our Holy Faith, but on debatable topics." At the same time, LaFarge sounded a note of caution. Because it was a public movement, not merely a lone individual, the Catholic Worker had the responsibility not to contradict the public stands of American bishops, even on policy issues. LaFarge, fully cognizant of the distinction between social teaching and its application, nonetheless thought that the workers, as an organized public voice of Catholicism, owed deference to ecclesiastical authority when that application involved not "mere theory" but "directive action."[44]

As a whole, the Catholic Worker movement under Maurin and Day certainly set itself in opposition to the dominant economic trends of modernity. Eugene McCarraher is correct, then, in observing that, "Catholic Workers' implacable animus toward industrial technology proved injurious intellectually and politically." "Unwilling to face" key issues such as technology and efficient production," McCarraher argues, Catholic Workers "routinely retreated into a facile antimodernism."[45]

At the same time, other commentators have pointed out the ways in which Day's movement capitalized on currents within American culture. Mark Massa's unique but compelling interpretation sees Day and her workers as more "American" than Catholic Americanists because they resisted accommodation to the American mainstream. This policy of resistance placed the workers squarely within the venerable American tradition of Puritan antinomianism.[46]

Even if one does not accept Massa's interpretation, it must be admitted that the Worker movement comprehended certain ironies. James Fisher noted as much in his observation that, "[Day's] list of friends included the names of wealthy capitalists who often rescued the movement from disaster with generous contributions."[47] Day herself required material means to keep flesh and spirit together, and desired to bring aid to those she encountered; in doing so, she called on the assistance of those who had acquired their wealth through the mechanism of the American economic system. No matter how critical of the society within which they found themselves, Catholic Workers too were members of that society and had to come to terms with how to live as such. The question was not whether to engage modernity, capitalism, and America (they could not be avoided), but how to engage them.

New Deal Critics

Among Catholics who did comment on political developments, there were many who occupied positions ranging from ambivalent to hostile. Initially positive about Roosevelt, Frederick Kenkel had nonetheless detected as early as 1933 a drift toward "the bitter end of State Socialism."[48] Similar perceptions led to a growing chorus of Catholic critics as the thirties passed.

Frederick Kenkel

Kenkel's hesitancy concerning governmental solutions to social problems was evident even before the New Deal, as noted in chapter 3. In 1930, he explained that the Central Bureau was opposed to a bill under consideration by Congress, "primarily because it is unwilling the Federal government should engage in activities which, in their very nature, should be left to individuals, private organizations, municipalities, counties, and states."[49] Kenkel thus demonstrated succinctly his commitment to the principle of subsidiarity that would be formulated explicitly in the following year by Pius XI.

Kenkel's declamations against the dangers of state centralization took on added urgency in the context of the New Deal. While John Ryan continued publicly to count Kenkel as an ally and Kenkel did little to protest the association (see chapter 3), public amity concealed a deeper skepticism on Kenkel's part toward the validity of Ryan's project.

By 1935, in fact, Kenkel was indicating privately that he had serious qualms about Ryan's views and those qualms had been building for some time. "I have lost confidence in Msgr. Ryan," he wrote to Joseph Matt, citing a list of Ryan's problematic positions, including his "attitude on the Prohibition question" and his "attitude on the question of German Colonies." Kenkel criticized Ryan for being "strong for public works," in spite of "the great danger of corruption we invite when recommending and inaugurating a spending program." Paramount among Ryan's mistakes, Kenkel concluded, was his attack on the opponents of the child labor amendment (CLA), which was "ungentlemanly to an extent which would have merited public rebuke."[50]

The differences between Kenkel and Ryan expressed here point to the complicated motivations and rationales behind positions taken by Catholic social thinkers. The fact that Ryan's statements on German colonial policy irked Kenkel, for instance, had more to do with national sentiment than with any principle of Catholic social teaching.

Kenkel did not encourage public strife over these differences. "We have been very tolerant of him," he explained, "for the sake of the common cause, and because I did not think it wise to create further confusion in the mind of our people, for whom it is so difficult to understand what Christian Social Reform . . . really means and desires to accomplish." In Kenkel's estimation, he continued, Ryan had "always tended towards promoting the doctrines of the so-called armchair-socialists," and for this reason, Kenkel was "frequently, and in principle, not in agreement with him."[51]

Kenkel's criticism of Ryan's enthusiasm for Roosevelt's policies, then, indicates a clear difference between the two with respect to contemporary social reform efforts. Kenkel's major fear, growing through the 1930s, was state centralization resulting in socialism. If Ryan's positions lent support to developments in that direction, then he was little better than a socialist. For Ryan, while he shared Kenkel's dissatisfaction with American capitalism, he saw the government under Roosevelt more as an ally than as a threat in the quest for authentic social reform.

This difference would continue to play out for the remainder of the decade. Chapter 3 recounted the first installment of the child labor amendment debate; the amendment's reintroduction in the thirties ignited controversy again. Kenkel attacked the amendment and impugned the wisdom of its supporters (among whom was John Ryan). His views were preserved in a letter to Central Bureau members explaining the public support of the CLA offered by some Catholics:

> Astonishing as the move may seem, it is a sign merely of a divergence of opinion, the existence of which has been no secret for many years. There are among us those, whom I shall call opportunists, anxious to obtain as quickly and successfully as possible certain reforms without due regard for the dangers they court.
>
> An amendment to the Constitution which grants Congress the power to regulate the labor of every American up to his or her eighteenth birthday, implies a confidence in the views and integrity of coming generations of politicians I cannot contemplate except with trepidation. History has proven how dangerous it is to bestow so vast a power on either individuals or law-making bodies. In addition, the present trend toward a State vested with omnipotence should make us pause.[52]

In this way, Kenkel exemplified a typical Catholic suspicion toward lodging power in the state, a sentiment increasingly expressed in 1936 as the trend toward centralization in the Roosevelt administration became more evident. Particular reforms, Kenkel insisted, had to be assessed not only by their intended beneficial effects, but also by unintended effects whose damages might outweigh or even prevent the realization of the benefits.

Constitutional Critics: The CLA

A number of prominent Catholics joined in Kenkel's cautionary view of the child labor amendment. The lines of debate between Ryan and strict constitutionalists were elucidated in a 1928 exchange between Ryan and Moorhouse Millar, S.J., professor of philosophy at Fordham and an editor of the Jesuit journal *Thought*.[53]

That debate centered on the merits of a minimum-wage law that passed Congress but was subsequently declared unconstitutional by the Supreme Court. Millar defended the Court's ruling. The Jesuit agreed with Ryan on the necessity of the just wage, but he contended that, "the principles upon which these cases are decided are eminently sound and that their maintenance for the future of the country as a whole is of greater importance than the immediate solution of a particular economic problem." Millar believed that dangerous precedent was set by sweeping legislation that established a minimum wage across industries and occupations, without regard to companies' relative abilities to pay it. Ryan replied that he agreed with Millar's "technical and legal reasoning" but not with his "ethical and industrial principles." Ryan was willing to circumvent what he admitted were sound constitutional principles in order to attain the end of a living wage for American workers.[54]

In the 1934 debate, as the CLA was again being considered, Ryan again found himself fighting fellow Catholics. Ryan revealed his thoughts on the matter in a letter to Dorothy Day: "I hope that those Catholics who believe in social justice and yet who oppose the Children's Amendment will some day realize to what a great extent they have permitted themselves to be misled by the dishonest propaganda emanating from the National Association of Manufacturers and other agents of social injustice."[55]

Clarence E. Martin, a former president of the American Bar Association, in a critique of the amendment in *Commonweal*, admitted that in principle government could legislate on the issue of child labor, but thought such legislation should occur at the state level. The danger, he warned, was that Congress would interpret broadly the constitutional powers granted by an amendment. One possibility, in such an event, would be the federalization of the educational system and the prescribing, "through a federal bureau, [of] educational methods and standards." Adoption of the amendment, Martin cautioned, "is but a step in the destruction of our republican form of government and the substitution of a social democracy. Adopt it and other amendments, nationalizing and socializing our governmental structure, will follow."[56]

Not one to let the moment pass, Ryan responded the following month, making clear his own involvement in the CLA movement and assuring readers of the pure intentions of all his allies. These observations, of course, did nothing to address the objections raised by opponents such as Martin. Ryan went on to imply, once again, that there could only be two possible explanations for those who opposed the amendment: they must be (a) against social justice, or (b) deceived by the National Association of Manufacturers or certain other "superpatriotic" organizations.[57] Ryan simply denied that any of the fears voiced by Martin and others were substantive, though on the issue of the federalization of education he was less definitive, leaving open the possibility that the amendment could be construed in that way.

Martin got the last word in his June 8 rebuttal of Ryan's response. Taking umbrage at the suggestion that he was either socially insensitive or a tool of business interests, Martin repeated his claim: "my opposition lies in the fact that its adoption would undermine our present system of government—the best system of government yet devised. . . ."[58] Martin noted Ryan's willingness to trust Congress and the courts and take a risk as to whether the amendment would be construed to imply power over education. "What an argument!" he exclaimed, "Let us lay our heads on the block to determine whether the executioner's axe is sharp."[59]

Other Objections to the New Deal

Constitutional problems were not the only grounds on which objections to various pieces of the New Deal were raised. Catholic critics also enumerated reasons for concern ranging from the practical ineffectiveness of particular legislation to general warnings against the tendency of government to usurp too many functions of society.

Catholic businessmen were among those who objected most strenuously to the methods of the New Deal. While it is an oversimplification to think of New Deal politics as a simple alignment of government versus business interests, Roosevelt did cultivate the image of himself as defender of the common man against the corporate turpitude and greed that had plunged the nation into depression and kept it there. It is at least a plausible thesis that Roosevelt's anti-business polemic and, to some extent, policies, prolonged the economic distress.[60] Among Catholics, Georgetown University's Father Edmund Walsh, for one, worried that business cooperation—and therefore the long-term realization of social justice—would be dampened by the administration's exploitation of class division.[61]

In any case, business leaders often differed from Catholic clerics and academics in their assessment of the causes and solutions to the problem of economic downturns. In the early years of the depression, a writer sympathetic to business concerns admitted the need for reform in ameliorating the problem of unemployment, but argued that the European system of federal social insurance entailed a number of problems and that American business ought to invent its own solution to the problem.[62] Many Catholic commentators similarly took up a middle ground between those who saw business with no responsibilities other than profit-making and those who sought answers for social problems in governmental action.

Ernest Du Brul wrote in *Commonweal* of the "immorality" of the Agricultural Adjustment Act (AAA), the 1933 legislation intended to raise food prices by rewarding production decreases. Although Catholic reaction to the AAA was largely positive, Du Brul represented one of a small group of Catholic critics.[63] General manager of the National Machine Tool Builders Association in Cincinnati, Du Brul had been a vice president of the Catholic Conference on Industrial Problems and was, therefore, involved in promoting the dialogue among business leaders, academics, and clergy that the CCIP sponsored.

Du Brul objected to the AAA on two grounds. He argued, first, that taxes should be levied on those most able to pay and, second, that taxes should be collected only for general purposes of government that benefit all citizens and not for the enrichment of any particular group. The AAA, he argued, not only exploited wage earners in favor of farmers but did so indiscriminately, benefiting the wealthy farmer even more than the poor one.[64]

From a wider political perspective, Du Brul explained, the AAA should also be considered dangerous. "For the principles underlying the AAA are essentially antagonistic to our whole governmental system," he began. "This sort of legislation shifts the method of getting a living away from earning one's own bread by the sweat of one's brow, to a method of getting it by the sweat of other men's brows, through the exercise of political power."[65] Du Brul considered the AAA as a dangerous step toward a concept of government as a tool for the redistribution of wealth.

Although he did not indict the New Deal explicitly, the tendency of government expansion could readily be seen as the target of the Jesuit Samuel Wilson's article in *Thought* in 1937. Interpreting the crash of 1929 and the ensuing shift in popular attitudes toward government, Wilson claimed that "a prevailing materialistic concept of life was not dispelled. People were merely resentful that material benefits were denied to them."[66]

With government viewed as the guarantor of prosperity, the citizenry were open to abuses of power. In the mood prevailing after 1929, Wilson observed, "the underprivileged many will listen to any scheme that promises economic security." Economic security guaranteed by government, he asserted, "has never proved successful in the past and is unlikely to prove successful in the future." The circumstances of a serious depression, however, ensures that people will "acquiesce in any governmental changes which promise immediate material relief though such changes eventually may result in spiritual slavery."[67] Wilson offered no further specifics about the danger of which he warned, its connection to the New Deal, or prescriptions for alternative modes of reform. The thrust of his article was clear, however: A nation in the throes of economic distress must be careful lest proposed solutions entail destructive long-term side effects.

Later in 1937, Wilson's Jesuit confrere Paul Blakely issued a warning about the constitutional implications of New Deal reform. Blakely occupied a middle ground, admitting that the Supreme Court was justified in granting the federal government increasing powers over commerce, but warning that the danger in the future was likely to be too much legislation by Congress in that field.

The tendency to deal recklessly in the arena of economics was already evident among the political class, in Blakely's estimation. "In these days," he wrote, "politicians eagerly play with social experiments, heedless of the constitution, heedless of the unhappy result to the subject of their experimentation." Blakely enumerated the goals he shared with reformers of every stripe: "To crush rapacious capitalism, to give to everyman a free field and no favor, to insure to wage-earners adequate protection for the least of his rights. . . ." To reach these goals, however, he insisted that "we need legislation with more to recommend it than the good intentions of its framers."[68] Like Wilson, Blakely remained vague; he did not specify those pieces of current reform legislation that fit his description of being ineffective though born of good intentions. It can be inferred, however, that Blakely, like Wilson, sought to alert his readers to a dangerous trend in federal lawmaking that he had detected.

Less than a year later another priest, T. J. Brennan, offered another criticism of the New Deal, this time as part of a general critique of the state of the social question in the United States. There was no answer to the social question, Brennan insisted, and in his view much of the contemporary agitation for reform arose out of a dangerous belief that there was. "The social problem is the sum of all the problems of everybody," he observed, and attempting to solve them all by means of relief programs is mistaken.[69]

> The country is littered with agencies, bureaus, departments, and societies, all ladling out remedies, relief and monthly allowances, and all calling for still further appropriations to continue their activities, all of which appropriations must come from charity or taxation. The natural consequence is that taxation has grown beyond human endurance, and charity is growing cold because it sees such poor results from previous benefactions.[70]

Like Blakely, Brennan thought that many relief efforts were misguided, but Brennan widened the criticism to include not only governmental efforts but private charities as well. The most serious problem to solve at present, Brennan insisted, "is the number and variety and expense of the previous solutions and those who administer them."[71]

Brennan did not advocate indifference in the face of need. His target was a secular utopian spirit that had conquered government and infiltrated private organizations as well. He called, instead, for the renewal of spiritual and corporal works of mercy, by which suffering is alleviated but no delusions about the solution of mankind's problems are fostered.[72] In this way, Brennan trumpeted a traditional claim of Catholic social teaching: There is no solution to social problems apart from the Church.

Other Catholic commentators identified the source of the central economic problem, unemployment, in social forces. Father Edward Roberts Moore, a committee chairman at the National Conference of Catholic Charities, argued that the relative prosperity of the United States up to the 1930s was due primarily to its ever-expanding market. In other words, demographics drove economic growth. Declining birth rates and stagnating population growth in the 1920s, then, had been an important factor in the unemployment crisis of the early thirties. The implication of Moore's article—that expanding population was the key to economic growth—fit nicely with the moral teaching of Pius XI, who had reiterated the Church's opposition to birth control in the encyclical *Casti Connubii* (1930).[73]

Stephen DuBrul, an economist at General Motors Corporation, agreed that economic growth was the key, but he focused on productivity rather than population. His presentation at the First National Catholic Social Action Conference in 1938 set his position apart from that of many Catholics calling for government action on issues such as wages.

DuBrul did not defend laissez-faire economics, but he clearly thought that the contemporary American economic system had more to recommend it than many of his fellow Catholics conceded. A competitive system, DuBrul contended, far from being a distortion of human nature, was founded on "natural instincts and the unequal distribution by God of natural aptitudes."[74]

Instead of basic structural change, DuBrul recommended personal moral change. With Kenkel and others he shared a distrust of centralizing power in government, a trend he thought well underway. Conceding that minimum-wage laws could serve a useful purpose by "preventing economic adjustment from reducing wages to a demoralized social level," he also cautioned that "in establishing minimum wage laws we must be careful that our hearts do not get the better of our heads and actually result in reducing the real income of the workers we are trying to aid or in restricting the opportunities for employment. . . ."[75]

At the root of the problem of inadequate wages, DuBrul reminded his audience, was productivity. "The value of human labor," he observed, "has never been raised by pious aspirations or law, but only by efficient combinations of real capital in the sense of buildings and machinery, and new scientific knowledge, with a self-disciplined, well-coordinated organization fully appreciative of its problems and the limitations of their solution and directed by efficient management."[76] DuBrul meant to warn his academic and clerical interlocutors against promoting economic reform without having a real understanding of the workings of business.

A few Catholic businessmen were willing to call into question more fundamentally the economic system in which they operated. P. H. Callahan, president of the Louisville Varnish Company, was an atypical Catholic in many ways. Characterized by his biographer as a southern progressive, he counted H. L. Mencken and William Jennings Bryan among his friends, was a strident prohibitionist, and had opposed Al Smith's campaign for presidency. Callahan had collaborated earlier with Ryan in formulating a pioneering profit-sharing plan, which was often cited by Catholic commentators as a paragon of economic reform modeled on papal teaching. He backed John Ryan's endorsement of the New Deal and criticized the "Economic Tories" within the Church who ordered Ryan to desist.[77]

Oil executive Michael O'Shaughnessy broached a plan in the early 1930s for a cooperative rather than competitive industrial system. Industry would be regulated by trade associations made up of directors representative of corporate management, labor, and consumers. O'Shaughnessy's ideas borrowed heavily from the guild-like system praised by Pius XI in *Quadragesimo Anno*. At the same time, O'Shaughnessy noted with frustration that the New Deal itself was being undermined by the pursuit of self-interest by business and labor leaders alike, a problem that his own plan would have to confront.[78]

James Gillis

James Gillis, C.S.P. (1876–1957), was editor of *The Catholic World*, an influential monthly journal, from 1922 to 1948.[79] As Roosevelt pushed reform, Gillis held out hope that it would be the kind of radical reform the nation needed: "I hope he doesn't mean merely that the cards are to be shuffled again for the same old game. What we really need is a new pack, new rules and indeed a new game."[80] Far from being a defender of the status quo, Gillis was pleased that "the present capitalistic, industrialistic, materialistic organism is dying and all but dead."[81] Capitalism could be purified, he thought ("there is no essential defect inherent in the capitalistic system"), but he believed the same could be said of communism.[82]

One of the problems with much of the Catholic commentary on the social order during this period was the failure to define the terms by which the arguments were conducted. Gillis made an attempt, asserting that the enemy he had in mind was "orthodox Capitalism—that of Jay Gould, Jim Fiske [*sic*] ... Teapot Dome; the Capitalism that cornered gold, hoarded grain and built up huge monopolistic trusts; the Capitalism of 'God's Gold' and 'Mellon's Millions.'"[83] That kind of capitalism, he insisted, must be "completely metamorphosed as to become unrecognizable."[84] Gillis drew on a book by John Strachey, *The Coming Struggle for Power*, to show that Catholicism was not really compatible with capitalism; instead, Protestantism had given it rise and the individualism of the reformed ethic was more suitable to its thriving.[85] Wary that Catholicism be too closely aligned with a particular economic system, Gillis reminded readers that the Church "does not stand or fall with Capitalism. She was here a long time before Capitalism was created and she intends to be—and will be—here when Capitalism is gone."[86]

In Gillis's view, wealthy capitalists were primarily to blame for the depression in which the American economy wallowed. "At bottom all questions even economic questions are simple," he observed. "The Pope, for example, solved the problem of the depression, supposedly so intricate, with one word—greed."[87] Given this display of Gillis's views on the economy, it seemed that he was poised to celebrate the reforms recently enacted.

Through 1933 and 1934, Gillis wrote little on the legislation of the Hundred Days; perhaps he was trying to make up his mind about the character of Roosevelt's reform.[88] In a July 1935 editorial comment on the Supreme Court's nullification of the National Recovery Act (NRA), there appeared hints that Gillis was not enthusiastic about Roosevelt's approach. "The N.R.A. is gone," he began. "With it, for the moment, has gone the hope of social and economic reform." He forcefully argued that there must be reform, that a mere recovery, a normalization of business in imitation of pre-1929 times was insufficient: "It will be as though a sinner were to get absolution without contrition."[89]

Gillis argued that the president needed to move on, to try some other kind of reform—after all, he had promised experimentation: "If this plan doesn't work, we shall try something else." He expressed some dismay at Roosevelt's being so emotional and polemical about the loss of the NRA. He wrote acidly that Woodrow Wilson had demonstrated that it was not the case that "when the world needs a great man, God invariably sends one," implying that Roosevelt too might lack the qualities that a time of crisis demanded.[90]

Indeed, Gillis displayed no particular love for the NRA. It was, he argued, "so obviously and absolutely unconstitutional as to warrant unanimous repudiation by the Supreme Court." "I am one of those," he conceded, "who rejoiced at the vindication of the Constitution. To tell the truth, I have been alarmed at the recklessness with which the good old ship was being battered about."[91] While he continued to argue strenuously for economic reform, then, Gillis had begun to question the rectitude of Roosevelt's measures in that direction. The events of coming years, far from soothing Gillis's concerns, would raise heightened fears that the constitutional order on which the nation depended was being undermined.

Gillis's criticism of the president became explicit and charged with some emotion in February 1936. The occasion was Roosevelt's state of the union speech. The address, in Gillis's estimation, was laden with unnecessary rhetorical heat against perceived enemies both foreign and domestic. Especially galling was Roosevelt's "assumption that none of his critics can possibly be sincere." He continued:

> Every American who moves around among his fellow citizens could report to the President the existence of a fair number of advocates of social justice and economic reform who are beset with fears . . . that some of the administration's devices are dangerous. There are genuine patriots, not a few, who have a reasonable apprehension about the fate of the Constitution and of the fundamental principles of democracy because of the startling measures employed to bring back prosperity. These are honest if timid folk. It were better to recognize their honesty than to castigate their timidity. I know because, as it happens, I am one of them.[92]

He had not entirely abandoned Roosevelt, however. "We still believe that he is emotionally at least, on the side of the angels, on the side of social reform. As for the Bourbons who were thrown out, we hope they will never get in again."

Gillis simply wanted reassurance that the president was aware of the constitutional problems; he desired a "repudiation of the common allegation that he has veered too far to the left and that with reelection and more power he would rush even further into radicalism." But Roosevelt offered no such reassurance; instead, as Gillis described it, "It is nothing less than calamitous that our President saw fit to ignore us, and in effect to jeer at us."[93]

Gillis pointed to the venomous press attacks on the Supreme Court for its rulings, most lately its 6-3 decision against the AAA. He noted with concern the raising of the possibility that the Court might be circumvented by a Roosevelt-controlled legislature—by ignoring its decisions, perhaps, or by "packing" it. He ended by wondering, indeed doubting, whether, three years after Roosevelt's first inauguration and after much trial and error, the country was any better off than it had been in 1932.[94]

In April 1936, John Ryan responded to Gillis's criticism of Roosevelt, and Gillis responded to Ryan in turn. Gillis took exception to Ryan's insinuation that he might have been taken in by the propaganda of the American Liberty League, the National Association of Manufacturers (NAM), and other representatives of plutocracy. He went on to assert his independence and immunity to propaganda, including that of the Liberty League and the NAM. He professed again his fundamental loyalty to the spirit of Roosevelt's reforms, and enumerated again his qualms about their substance—this time specifying the concerns of still-high unemployment, an increasing federal deficit (despite campaign promises to reduce federal spending), and the creation of an immense federal bureaucracy that "can be so easily transformed into a political machine."[95]

It remained clear, however, that Gillis's difficulties with Roosevelt were not transforming him into a defender of the old order. In September, Gillis, commenting on Paul Hanly Furfey's *Fire on the Earth*, engaged in a polemic against those who hedged the teaching of the Church in order to curry favor with the wealthy and powerful. He proclaimed the preference of the Church for the poor and castigated the Church for losing the proletariat because it failed to proclaim as much. "Something is wrong," he wrote, "tragically wrong, with the Capitalistic system." He noted with pleasure the beginnings of the Catholic Worker movement and derided those who criticized it as communist or anticlerical.[96]

Two months later, Gillis leveled another criticism at Roosevelt. Much along the same lines as before, he professed his "wish to continue to believe in you," but was troubled by the "unprecedented concentration of power in the federal administration and more particularly in the White House," and the continued rumors of a court-packing scheme.[97] Gillis did not seem unalterably opposed to fundamental constitutional change, but he did want the president to be honest about it.

Again in December, following Roosevelt's landslide reelection, Gillis urged the president to consider the threat of communism and whether he played into the hands of those promoting it. He raised the specter that class conflict may have had an important part in the election. Gillis demonstrated cognizance of his ambivalence toward Roosevelt and by extension, one might assume, of Roosevelt's method of reform. Some will say, Gillis wrote, "'The man doesn't know his own mind about Roosevelt.' The honest answer," he replied in his column, "is that I don't."[98]

In May 1937, the president's court-packing plan was announced and Gillis went on the offensive. He first repeated earlier concerns that such a scheme would undermine checks and balances, abuse the Constitution, and establish Roosevelt as a dictator. "If the people and the President," he wrote, "are so eager for swift 'reform' that they are ready to justify any and all means to obtain it, if they think ... that in the circumstances in which the country now finds itself, a dictator is necessary, then so be it, but let us not, like the Romans trick ourselves by calling an Emperor 'Consul,' or an Autocrat President."[99]

Gillis's position on Roosevelt was summed up in an editorial later in 1937. He had voted for Roosevelt in 1936 and then he had rejoiced when the court-packing plan was scuttled; he hoped, however, that legislators would not overreact and reverse all the reforms of the New Deal.[100] Gillis articulated the ambivalence toward Roosevelt that characterized many socially conscious Catholics through the course of the 1930s. On one hand, he hoped that the president, freed from a slavish devotion to the capitalism of the past, would set in motion reforms that would bring about a social order more in line with Catholic teaching. On the other hand, he feared that Roosevelt's openness to aggrandizement of power by government and his cunning methods of reaching his goals were pushing the United States down a path that led not to a just and humane social order but to statism.

The passage of time has shown that Gillis and others, while their fears of socialism in America proved unfulfilled, were correct in discerning the nature of the course charted by Roosevelt. One of the major and lasting effects of the Great Depression was a shift in workers' outlook. Whereas previously they had been inclined to rely on local institutions and the welfare capitalism of employers for the solution of economic problems, they now turned more readily to the federal government.[101]

The Waning of Catholic Support

Catholic skepticism concerning the efficacy of state intervention increased after 1935. The number of prominent and vocal critics of Roosevelt in general seemed to increase around 1936.[102] Strikingly, the Democratic candidates of both 1924 and 1928 turned against Roosevelt. Al Smith echoed the antistatist sentiment of other Catholic critics: "All this is a long way from the traditional role of the Democratic Party, which has been since the days of Jefferson the party opposed to highly centralized Federal control."[103] One of the best-known Catholics of the time, Monsignor Fulton Sheen, while largely steering clear of political questions, was obliquely critical of Roosevelt and the New Deal.[104]

By 1936, Bishop James Ryan of Omaha, the former superior of John Ryan as rector of Catholic University from 1928 to 1934, was warning Catholics against viewing *Quadragesimo* as a clarion call for federal intervention. Bishop Ryan argued that the encyclical applied more directly to the individual states, not the federal government, as the primary vehicles of reform.[105] Indeed, as the reforms of the Roosevelt years became increasingly focused on the activity of the federal government, it was only natural that the traditional skepticism of American Catholics toward the state would reassert itself.

"At no time," Aaron Abell attests, "not even in the Depression Thirties—did Catholic social actionists think that government was the prime factor in the solution of economic and social problems."[106] Instead, most Catholic social thinkers saw federal intervention as a means of encouraging the ordering of society along the lines suggested by the papal encyclicals. The fact was indicated in the response to Ryan's efforts to get signatories to "Organized Social Justice," a statement calling for a renewed NRA under a constitutional amendment. Although the 131 signatories represented a broad swath of Catholic social thinkers, many refused to sign because of fear of the growing federal government. Many of those who did sign continued to hope that the New Deal would metamorphose into the vocational group system Pius XI advocated. As a modern guild system failed to materialize, however (the New Deal brain trust itself losing interest in industry cooperation), and power became ever more centralized in Washington, the Catholic critique of the New Deal gained steam.[107]

The turn in Catholic thinking was reflected even in the statements of the NCWC. "Present Crisis," a document released in 1933, had been the most caustic treatment of American capitalism to emanate from the NCWC. It excoriated "capitalists and industrialists" who, "driven by greed, monopolized the sources of wealth . . . to their own enrichment and to the impoverishment and enslavement of the masses."[108] The "Statement of Social Problems" of 1937, in contrast, while sounding some of the same themes as the 1933 document, also observed that "there are many honorable employers whose motives and purposes are dictated by justice and charity." The 1937 statement emphasized in different words the subsidiarity principle from Pius XI's *Quadragesimo Anno:* "The tendency of our time is to make more and more demands on government. Citizens and groups should not ask the government to do for them what they can do for themselves. Sound social policy requires government to encourage citizens to assume as much personal responsibility as possible."[109]

Ryan, however, stayed the course. In 1936, cajoled by his Democratic friends into countering Father Coughlin's criticisms of Roosevelt, Ryan went on the air with a speech that was taken almost universally to be an endorsement of Roosevelt's reelection campaign. The move provoked much reaction in the Catholic community, with many thinking Ryan had gone too far down the path of political activism.[110] The ensuing controversy between Ryan and Coughlin partisans led one Catholic periodical to opine: "If both the Reverend Gentlemen would retire for some time to the Carthusian Order where perpetual silence is observed, they would do a great favor to the Church and to the Country at large."[111]

The lengths to which Ryan was willing to go to achieve the ends that he viewed necessary to the country's well-being were demonstrated in his espousal and defense of Roosevelt's court-packing scheme. It was this action that led some Catholics to cross the line from disagreeing with Ryan's judgments to questioning his very ability to make independent judgments.[112] Ryan continued to befriend the Roosevelt administration throughout its tenure, ceremonially blessing the president with his invocation at Roosevelt's 1937 inauguration, and reminiscing, years later, that "practically all the reform measures enacted during the Roosevelt Administration have met with my hearty approval."[113]

It is fairly certain that Ryan and his allies did not have a formative influence on Roosevelt or his programs. As George Flynn concluded in his study of Catholics and Roosevelt: "Perhaps the most judicious conclusion that can be drawn from all this evidence is that while FDR and his advisers knew of the papal program, their knowledge was in the context of general American reform ideas. Some of these ideas were restatements of old Progressive movement principles. It seems clear that the New Deal would have developed even if the popes had not spoken."[114]

Although the well from which the most influential intellectual guides of the New Deal had drunk more deeply was American liberalism, not Catholic social teaching, the question of the degree to which the two were compatible remained an issue of contention. John Ryan, sympathetic to much of the content of American liberalism, found the New Deal appealing. Frederick Kenkel and Virgil Michel, leery of both liberalism and capitalism, were indifferent to or critical of Roosevelt's reforms. There was a third strand in Catholic thinking, inchoate in the thirties, but represented among the businessmen who were more favorable toward capitalism than Kenkel or Michel. With the conservative shift beginning in the 1940s, this strand would assume greater importance and find new spokesmen.

Notes

1. Richard Hofstadter, *The Age of Reform: From Bryan to F. D. R.* (New York: Alfred A. Knopf, 1989 [1955]), 300ff.

2. Crunden, Robert M. *Ministers of Reform: The Progressives' Achievement in American Civilization, 1889–1920* (New York: Basic Books, 1982), xi.

3. Alan Dawley, *Struggles for Justice: Social Responsibility and the Liberal State* (Cambridge, Mass.: Belknap, 1991), 343–70. Dawley notes that Roosevelt did promote more radical reform during the "Second New Deal" of 1935 (378ff.) .

4. Alan Brinkley, *The End of Reform: New Deal Liberalism in Recession and War* (New York: Vintage, 1995), 5. See also Terry A. Cooney, *Balancing Acts: American Thought and Culture in the 1930s* (New York: Twayne, 1995), 45–46, 57–58.

5. Brinkley, *End of Reform*, 17.

6. David J. O'Brien, *American Catholics and Social Reform: The New Deal Years* (New York: Oxford, 1968), 51; George Q. Flynn, *American Catholics and the Roosevelt Presidency, 1932–1936* (Lexington: University of Kentucky, 1968): "It was under Franklin Roosevelt and the New Deal that American Catholics were given recognition as a major force in society and were raised to 'a new level of association . . . indicating a change in the "official" American attitude toward the Church, and equally important, in the Church's disposition toward the government'" (xi). Flynn is quoting from another author who makes the same claim, Francis J. Lally, *The Catholic Church in a Changing America* (Boston: Little, Brown, 1962), 48.

7. On Protestant churches' "move to the left," see Robert Moats Miller, *American Protestantism and Social Issues, 1919–1939* (Chapel Hill: University of North Carolina Press, 1958), chaps. 5, 6, and 7. As Miller shows in chapter 8, however, the appearance of radicalism may have hidden conservatism among the rank and file, as well as a significant number of clergy. This, again, parallels the story of this chapter concerning Catholics, among whom criticism of Roosevelt grew over the course of the 1930s.

8. James Fisher argues along these lines, suggesting that Catholics were slow to embrace the competitive capitalist culture of the United States and, therefore, slow to realize the economic gain it promised; for instance: "The bitterness of many Catholics in the 1930s reflected anxieties over real threats to their social status as well as their ambivalent attitude toward economic opportunity. Stephan Thernstrom's contention that the Irish in Boston demonstrated a higher rate of 'slippage'—or downward mobility—than other groups bolsters the argument that powerful forces within Catholicism cast a shadow over economic aspirations." James Terence Fisher, *The Catholic Counterculture in America, 1933–1962* (Chapel Hill: University of North Carolina Press, 1989), 87, referring to Stephan Thernstrom, *The Other Bostonians: Poverty and Progress in the American Metropolis, 1880–1970* (Cambridge, Mass.: Harvard University Press, 1973), 152–60.

9. On the relation of Hutchins and Adler to Catholics, see Cooney, *Balancing Acts*, 191–94; and Philip Gleason, *Contending with Modernity: Catholic Higher Education in the Twentieth Century* (New York: Oxford University Press, 1995), 163–64, 246–47.

10. On Francis Haas, see Thomas E. Blantz, C.S.C., *A Priest in Public Service: Francis J. Haas and the New Deal* (Notre Dame, Ind.: University of Notre Dame Press, 1982). On Catholic support for the New Deal, see Monroe Billington and Cal Clark, "Catholic Clergymen, Franklin D. Roosevelt, and the New Deal," *Catholic Historical Review* 79 (January 1993): 65–82; O'Brien, *American Catholics*, 51–56; and Flynn, *American Catholics*, chap. 3.

11. Kerby, "The Old Deal and the New," *Catholic Mind*, July 22, 1934, 276.

12. Ryan, *Social Doctrine in Action: A Personal History* (New York: Harper, 1941), 242

13. Secretary of Agriculture Henry Wallace, quoted in Brinkley, *End of Reform*, 30. The struggle to identify and offer a solution to the recession, Brinkley observes, was a "struggle to define the soul of the New Deal." On Ryan's acceptance of Hobson's theory, see Patrick W. Gearty, *The Economic Thought of Monsignor John A. Ryan* (Washington, D.C.: Catholic University Press, 1953), 24, 69n44.

14. Brinkley, *End of Reform*, 74–85, 104. Brinkley notes the important role of Marriner Eccles, chairman of the Federal Reserve Board, in this development.

15. On economics during the Great Depression, see Joseph Dorfman, *The Economic Mind in American Civilization*, 5 vols. (New York: Viking Press, 1959 [1949]), vol. 5, pt. II, esp. chap. 22. See also Márcia L. Balisciano, "Hope for America: American Notions of

Economic Planning between Pluralism and Neoclassicism, 1930–1950," 153–78, in *From Interwar Pluralism to Postwar Neoclassicism*, eds. Mary S. Morgan and Malcolm Rutherford (Durham, N.C.: Duke University Press, 1998).

16. Dorfman, *Economic Mind*, vol. 5, chap. 22, 775–76. In support of his proposal, Ely adverted to William James's essay on "The Moral Equivalent of War."

17. Testimony of Father John A. Ryan, Oct. 27, 1931, in *Establishment of a National Economic Council: Hearings Before a Subcommittee of the Senate Committee on Manufactures*, 72nd Cong., 1st sess., 265. Quoted in Dorfman, *Economic Mind*, vol. 5, 659.

18. Ryan, *A Better Economic Order* (New York: Harper and Brothers, 1935), chap, 2. See chapter 2 above for reference to the influence of Hobson on Richard Ely. Economists have raised considerable doubts about the likelihood of underconsumption being the cause of the Depression. See, for instance, Richard Vedder and Lowell Gallaway, *Out of Work: Unemployment and Government in Twentieth-Century America* (New York: Holmes and Meier, 1993); and Murray N. Rothbard, *America's Great Depression* (Los Angeles: Nash, 1972 [1963]). Both argue that artificially inflated wages, promoted by both Hoover and Roosevelt, prevented a recovery in employment that would have quickly ended the recession.

Vedder and Gallaway disagree with Peter Temin, who holds a Keynesian interpretation of the Depression, viewing the prolonging of the slump as a result of a decline in consumption that followed the onset of the Depression. As to the cause of the onset itself, however, Temin agrees with Vedder and Gallaway that underconsumption could not be the cause, since consumption as a percentage of GDP was relatively stable, not falling, over the course of the 1920s. Peter Temin, *Did Monetary Policy Cause the Great Depression?* (New York: W. W. Norton, 1976).

19. Ryan, *Economic Order*, 79–81. See also Ryan, "The New Deal and Social Justice," *Commonweal*, April 13, 1934, 657–59.

20. Ryan, *Economic Order*, 84–85. On Catholic critics of the New Deal, see below. For a view of the differences between Ryan and others on this point, though with reference to an earlier debate on minimum wage legislation, see Moorhouse F. X. Millar, S.J., "Declining Liberty and Other Papers," with Ryan's reply and Millar's rejoinder, *Catholic World* 127 (April 1928): 70–75. Millar and Ryan differed again in 1934 on the child labor amendment: See letter to the editor from John A. Ryan, *Commonweal*, May 25, 1934, 104–5.

21. Ryan, *Economic Order*, 86–87, 181. On the widespread acceptance of NRA among Catholics, see Flynn, *American Catholics*, chap. 5. Flynn does note a few of the scattered opponents, including Frederick Kenkel (95–96). Many Catholics, moreover, shared Ryan's view of the New Deal's defects vis-à-vis Pius XI's program. See O'Brien, *American Catholics*, 56–57. Father Raymond McGowan, Ryan's assistant at the SAD, warned against overly enthusiastic reception of the NRA by Catholics not only because it did not mirror the papal program but also because it could fail. Such a failure, paired with its identification with Catholicism, would make it even "harder to convince persons of the truth of Catholic social teaching with the example of a presumably 'Catholic' NRA before them." McGowan to Kenkel, April 23, 1934, CCCV, 4/49.

22. Ryan, *Economic Order*, 187–88. Throughout his writings, Ryan displayed respect for the medieval guild system and for the updated cooperative version offered by Pius XI in *Quadregismo Anno*. At the same time, he was an enthusiastic supporter of Roosevelt and the New Deal. These facts puzzled commentators at the time and remain something

of a puzzle. An insight into the problem is afforded by a brief exchange recorded from a social action conference in 1939. The secretary summarized Ryan's remarks as saying "that our present stage of social and economic development made the establishment of the Christian guild and the corporate society a matter of idealism for the time being. However, he intimated that the perfection of society which must follow the more pressing need of immediate economic adjustment, calls for the corporate society and the Christian guild." "American Economic Life Forum (Secretary's Report)," *Proceedings, Second Annual National Catholic Social Action Conference* (1939), 35–36. By employing this distinction between the ideal and the realistic or practical, Ryan justified support for admittedly imperfect economic reform. This explanation for Ryan's seeming ambivalence with respect to the corporate system is even more compelling when one considers that he used the same distinction in a similar way when writing on the issue of church and state. See John A. Ryan and Moorhouse F. X. Millar, *The State and the Church* (New York: Macmillan, 1922).

23. O'Brien, *American Catholics*, 212. Lawrence DeSaulniers, who has documented the Catholic press's reaction to the New Deal, similarly notes the obverse: Despite significant diversity on specific policy questions, most Catholics were united in their belief that the papal encyclicals held the key to the solution of economic problems. Lawrence B. DeSaulniers, *The Response in American Catholic Periodicals to the Crises of the Great Depression, 1930–1935* (Lanham, Md.: University Press of America, 1984), 117.

24. On connections between Kenkel and Michel (and between the CCV and the liturgical reform movement), see Philip Gleason, *The Conservative Reformers: German-American Catholics and the Social Order* (Notre Dame: University of Notre Dame Press, 1968), 190–91; and Jay P. Corrin, *Catholic Intellectuals and the Challenge of Democracy* (Notre Dame, Ind.: University of Notre Dame Press, 2002), 264–65.

25. The liturgical reform movement, initiated in certain French and German monasteries, had as its goal a fuller understanding of and participation in Catholic liturgy, especially among the laity. On the liturgical movement in general, see The Sacerdotal Communities of Saint-Severin of Paris and Saint-Joseph of Nice, *The Liturgical Movement*, trans. Lancelot Sheppard (New York: Hawthorn, 1964 [1960]). For a brief synopsis of the movement in the United States, see William J. Leonard, S.J., "The Liturgical Movement in the United States," chap. 24 in vol. 2 of *The Liturgy of Vatican II: A Symposium in Two Volumes*, ed. William Baraúna; ed., English edition, Jovian Lang, O.F.M. (Chicago: Franciscan Herald, 1966). On the connections between the liturgical movement and social thought and action during this period, see chapter 4 of Keith F. Pecklers, S.J., *The Unread Vision: The Liturgical Movement in the United States of America, 1926–1945* (Collegeville, Minn.: Liturgical Press, 1998).

26. For Michel's biography, I draw on Rev. Paul Marx, O.S.B., *The Life and Work of Virgil Michel* (Washington, D.C.: Catholic University of America Press, 1957). For an overview of the context of Catholic social movements in the 1930s, see chapter 3 in Marvin L. Krier Mich, *Catholic Social Teaching and Movements* (Mystic, Conn.: Twenty-Third Publications, 1998). Another treatment of Michel's social thought is Seamus Paul Finn, "Virgil Michel's Contribution to Linking the Liturgical and Social Apostolate in the American Catholic Church: A Fifty Year Perspective" (Th.D. diss., Boston University, 1991).

27. Despite Michel's prominence within the liturgical reform movement, among social ethicists "his impact has been almost nil." Michael Baxter, C.S.C., "Reintroducing Virgil Michel: Towards a Counter-Tradition of Catholic Social Ethics in the United

States," *Communio* 24 (Fall 1997): 515. For another attempt to recover Michel's social thinking, see Kenneth R. Himes, "Eucharist and Justice: Assessing the Legacy of Virgil Michel," *Worship* 62 (May 1988): 201–36.

28. Michel, "Catholic Leadership and the College," *OF*, November 30, 1935, 22–27.

29. Michel, "Natural and Supernatural Society," *OF*, April 18, 1936, 246.

30. Michel, untitled editorial, *OF*, December 27, 1936, 78–80. For more on Michel's support of Day and the Catholic Worker movement, see Pecklers, *Unread Vision*, 107–9.

31. Michel, "The Bourgeois Spirit and the Christian Renewal," *OF* April 14, 1940, 257, 258.

32. Michel, "Political Catholicism," *OF*, December 25, 1938, 79–81. On Michel and cooperativism, see Corrin, *Catholic Intellectuals*, 264–67.

33. Quoted in R. W. Franklin and Robert L. Spaeth, *Virgil Michel: American Catholic* (Collegeville, Minn.: Liturgical Press, 1988), 87.

34. Franklin and Spaeth, *Virgil Michel*, 13; Michel, "Individualism and Its Social Effects," reprinted from *Social Concepts and Problems*, Book One of *The Social Problem* (Collegeville: St. John's Abbey, 1936), in *The Social Question: Essays on Capitalism and Christianity by Father Virgil Michel, O.S.B.*, ed. Robert L. Spaeth (Collegeville, Minn.: St. John's University, 1987), 14; Michel, "The Nature of Capitalism," reprinted from *Economics and Finance*, Book Two of *The Social Problem* (Collegeville: St. John's Abbey, 1936), in *The Social Question*, 23.

35. Ryan, "New Deal and Social Justice," *Commonweal*, April 13, 1934, 657–59.

36. Michel, "Defining Social Justice," *Commonweal*, February 14, 1936, 425–26. The definition of the term *social justice* has been a subject of much debate, both within and outside of Catholic circles. Among Catholics, the main problem has been trying to locate social justice within the schema of justice developed by Thomas Aquinas from an Aristotelian foundation. Frederick Kenkel's observation reflected the problem. He thought that the term invited misunderstanding: "Men speak of 'social justice' when they should say 'legal justice' or, in another case, 'commutative justice.'" Kenkel to J. J. Tompkins, August 20, 1942, CCCV, 5/15. See also Leo W. Shields, "The History and Meaning of the Term Social Justice" (Ph.D. diss., University of Notre Dame, 1941).

37. Pecklers, *Unread Vision*, 89.

38. Ryan to Catharine O'Keefe, March 9, 1937. Quoted in Broderick, *Right Reverend*, 116–17.

39. Fisher, *Catholic Counterculture*, 34. See also 43–47. On the connection between Michel and the Catholic Worker, see Corrin, *Catholic Intellectuals*, 263. For more on the Catholic Worker movement, including Maurin and a later figure, Ammon Hennecy, see *A Revolution of the Heart: Essays on the Catholic Worker*, ed. Patrick G. Coy (Philadelphia: Temple University Press, 1988); see also Nancy L. Roberts, *Dorothy Day and the Catholic Worker* (Albany: State University of New York Press, 1984); Fisher, *Catholic Counterculture*, chaps. 1–3; Marc H. Ellis, *Peter Maurin: Prophet in the Twentieth Century* (New York: Paulist, 1981); William Miller, *A Harsh and Dreadful Love: Dorothy Day and the Catholic Worker Movement* (New York: Liveright, 1973).

40. Fisher, *Catholic Counterculture*, 38, 52. Quote from Maurin, *Catholic Worker* 1 (April 1934): 3.

41. Mel Piehl, *Breaking Bread: The Catholic Worker and the Origin of Catholic Radicalism in America* (Philadelphia: Temple University Press, 1982), 116.

42. See Piehl, *Breaking Bread*, 120. See 136–38 for the differences between the Catholic Worker and social gospel movements in the 1930s.

43. Piehl, *Breaking Bread*, 126–27; Charles E. Curran, *American Catholic Social Ethics: Twentieth-Century Approaches* (Notre Dame, Ind.: University of Notre Dame Press, 1982), chap. 4.

44. John LaFarge, S.J., "Some Reflections on the Catholic Worker," *America*, 26 June, 1937, 275; "Catholic Workers," *America*, 24 July, 1937, 371.

45. Eugene McCarraher. *Christian Critics: Religion and the Impasse in Modern American Social Thought* (Ithaca, N.Y.: Cornell University Press, 2000), 86, 87.

46. Mark Massa, *Catholics and American Culture: Fulton Sheen, Dorothy Day, and the Notre Dame Football Team* (New York: Crossroad, 1999), 109, 121–27.

47. Fisher, *Catholic Counterculture*, 48. Fisher also observed the difficulties inherent in Day's attempt to raise a daughter in the context of the Catholic Worker house in which they dwelt (63).

48. Gleason, *Conservative Reformers*, 207.

49. Kenkel to Members of the Major Executive Committee of the Catholic Central Verein of America, April 28, 1930, CCCV, 1/28: "Central Bureau Correspondence." See also DeSaulniers, *American Catholic Periodicals*, 102–3, for evidence of the *Central Blatt*'s increasing concern with centralization of government power, from 1930 on. DeSaulniers notes similar expressions of concern from other quarters of the Catholic community, including the National Council of Catholic Women (104).

50. Kenkel to Joseph Matt, August 12, 1935, CCCV 3/07: "Joseph Matt." Matt was the editor of *The Wanderer*, a Catholic newspaper based in St. Paul (historically German-language, the paper went to English in 1930).

51. Kenkel to Matt, August 12, 1935.

52. Kenkel to Members of the Major Executive Committee of the CCV, March 5, 1936, CCCV, 1/28: "Central Bureau Correspondence."

53. Like most Catholics opposed to the CLA, Millar did not in any way found his opposition on a defense of American capitalism. Elsewhere, Millar argued that social and political problems were primarily the result of spiritual deficiency. Both "Liberal Capitalism" and "Marxist Socialism," in Millar's view, were "vitiated by a bias towards materialism." Millar, "What Makes Man Go?" *Thought* 12 (March 1937): 15.

54. Moorhouse F. X. Millar, "Declining Liberty and Other Papers," with Ryan's reply and Millar's rejoinder, *CW* 127 (April 1928): 70–75.

55. Ryan to Dorothy Day, January 29, 1934, JRP, box 8, folder "CLA [Child Labor Amendment] 1933–1934."

56. Clarence E. Martin, "Shall Americansim [*sic*] Remain?" *Commonweal*, April 13, 1934, 650, 651.

57. Ryan, Letter to Editor, *Commonweal*, May 25, 1934, 104–5.

58. Martin, Letter to Editor, *Commonweal*, June 8, 1934, 160.

59. Ibid.

60. Gary Dean Best, *Pride, Prejudice, and Politics: Roosevelt Versus Recovery, 1933–1938* (New York: Praeger, 1991). Oliver McKee Jr., reported sympathetically in 1938 on the views of small businessmen who opposed many of Roosevelt's reforms. "Little Business Men Consolidate," *Commonweal*, June 17, 1938, 205–6.

61. O'Brien, *American Catholics*, 57.

62. G. Hirschfeld, "The Unemployment Puzzle," *Commonweal*, November 19, 1930, 67–69.

63. Flynn, *American Catholics*, 70–71. Father Coughlin was also critical of the AAA.

64. Ernest Du Brul, "The Immorality of the AAA," *Commonweal*, January 24, 1936, 341.

65. Ibid., 342.

66. Samuel K. Wilson, S.J., "State Materialism in the United States," *Thought* 12 (March 1937): 40.

67. Ibid.

68. Paul L. Blakely, S.J., "The Constitution and Industrial Reform," *Thought* 12 (December 1937): 566.

69. Rev. T. J. Brennan, "Will Things Ever Be Right?" *AER* 99 (October 1938): 353.

70. Ibid., 354.

71. Ibid.

72. Ibid., 355.

73. Edward Robert Moore, "The Contraception of Prosperity," *Commonweal*, April 15, 1931, 654–56. Lawrence de Saulniers sees Moore's argument as implicit acceptance of the possibility of an ever-expanding economy, a position differentiating him from most other Catholic commentators; De Saulniers, *Response*, 99n92.

74. Stephen DuBrul, "Some Comments on the Automobile Industry," in *Proceedings of the First National Catholic Social Action Conference* (1938), 137.

75. Ibid., 141.

76. Ibid.

77. Callahan to Rev. Maurice Sheehy, undated, CLN; William E. Ellis, *Patrick Henry Callahan (1866–1940): Progressive Catholic Layman in the American South* (Lewiston, N.Y.: Edwin Mellen Press, 1989), ii, 50–57. On the Callahan-Ryan Plan of Partnership, see 12–14 and 67–72; on Callahan and the New Deal, see chap. 5.

78. Aaron I. Abell, *American Catholicism and Social Action: A Search for Social Justice, 1865–1950* (Garden City, N.Y.: Hanover, 1960), 250. O'Shaughnessy's plan is summarized on 242–45.

79. For a full biography of Gillis, see Richard Gribble, C.S.C., *Guardian of America: The Life of James Martin Gillis, C.S.P.* (New York: Paulist Press, 1998).

80. Gillis, "Editorial Comment," *CW* 137 (August 1933): 615.

81. Ibid., 614.

82. Ibid.

83. Gillis, "Editorial Comment," *CW* 137 (October 1933): 2.

84. Ibid., 3.

85. This argument, of course, has a long pedigree. Recent decades have seen a concerted effort to revise the view that Protestantism is singularly suitable to market economics. See, for instance, Michael Novak, *The Catholic Ethic and the Spirit of Capitalism* (New York: Free Press, 1993). For a recent and novel revision of the view, see Liah Greenfeld, *The Spirit of Capitalism: Nationalism and Economic Growth* (Cambridge, Mass.: Harvard University Press, 2001).

86. Gillis, "Editorial Comment," *CW* 137 (October 1933): 6.

87. Gillis, "Editorial Comment," *CW* 138 (October 1933): 261.

88. For a thorough account of Gillis's commentary on the New Deal, see Richard Gribble, C.S.C., *Guardian of America: The Life of James Martin Gillis, C.S.P.* (New York: Paulist Press, 1998), 127–35.

89. Gillis, "Editorial Comment," *CW* 141 (July 1935): 385.

90. Ibid., 386, 388.

91. Ibid., 386–87. Gribble points out that Gillis had earlier defended the NRA, even though he intimated that its legality was questionable. Gribble, *Guardian*, 128.

92. Gillis, "Editorial Comment," *CW* 142 (February 1936): 515.

93. Ibid., 519, 520.

94. Ibid., 520–23.

95. John A. Ryan, "An Open Letter to the Editor," *CW* 143 (April 1936): 22–27; Gillis, "Editorial Comment," *CW* 143 (April 1936): 9.

96. Gillis, "Editorial Comment," 143 (September 1936): 651–52.

97. Gillis, "Editorial Comment," *CW* 144 (November 1936): 133, 131.

98. Gillis, "Editorial Comment," *CW* 144 (December 1936): 265.

99. Gillis, "Editorial Comment," *CW* 145 (May 1937): 136.

100. Gillis, "Editorial Comment," *CW* 145 (September 1937): 646–47.

101. Lizabeth Cohen, *Making a New Deal: Industrial Workers in Chicago, 1919–1939* (New York: Cambridge University Press, 1990).

102. Best, *Pride, Prejudice, and Politics*, 131–37. On the initial concern in the Roosevelt camp over such high-profile criticism, see Flynn, *American Catholics*, 195–97. Despite these defections among both Catholics and non-Catholics, Roosevelt won in a landslide with the strong support of both groups.

103. "Business Control," *New Outlook* 162 (July 1933): 9–10. Quoted in Robert A. Slayton, *Empire Statesman: The Rise and Redemption of Al Smith* (New York: Free Press, 2001), 379.

104. Thomas C. Reeves, *America's Bishop: The Life and Times of Fulton J. Sheen* (San Francisco: Encounter Books, 2001), 90–93.

105. James H. Ryan, "What is the State?" *Commonweal*, May 29, 1936, 117–18.

106. Aaron I. Abell, Introduction to *American Catholic Thought on Social Questions*, ed. Abell (Indianapolis: Bobbs-Merrill, 1968), xxxi.

107. Flynn, *American Catholics*, 101–2; Abell, *American Catholicism*, 251; Brinkley, *End of Reform*, 39–40. For a case study of Catholics during the New Deal that concretizes these generalizations, see Kenneth J. Heineman, *A Catholic New Deal: Religion and Reform in Depression Pittsburgh* (University Park: Pennsylvania, Pa., 1999). See, for instance, the views of labor priest Carl Hensler, 159–60.

108. "Present Crisis," issued with the Authorization of the American Hierarchy, in *Pastoral Letters of the United States Catholic Bishops*, vol. 1, 1792–1940, ed. Hugh J. Nolan (Washington, D.C.: United States Catholic Conference, 1984), 386. Even the 1933 statement warned against the "tendency to place too much reliance on government to accomplish our economic salvation" (395).

109. "Statement on Social Problems," issued by the Administrative Board of the National Catholic Welfare Conference, November 28, 1937, in *Pastoral Letters*, 424, 425.

110. Broderick, *Right Reverend*, 225.

111. *Catholic Review*, October 16, 1936. Quoted in Broderick, *Right Reverend*, 228.

112. See Broderick's account, including Baltimore *Catholic Review*'s reaction, in Broderick, *Right Reverend*, 230–31. On Catholic reaction to the court plan, see O'Brien, *American Catholics*, 72–74. On the court plan, see Marian C. McKenna, *Franklin Roosevelt and the Great Constitutional War: The Court-Packing Crisis of 1937* (New York: Fordham University Press, 2002).

113. Ryan, *Social Doctrine*, 248; on Ryan's inaugural invocation, see "The Defense of Democracy," [unsigned editorial], *Commonweal*, January 29, 1937, 369–70.

114. Flynn, *American Catholics*, 49. O'Brien's judgment with respect specifically to John Ryan concurs with Flynn's more general judgment. O'Brien, *American Catholics*, 148.

5

War, Anticommunism, and the Rise of Conservatism

The End of Reform

The coming of war and the end of the Great Depression in the late 1930s signaled changes in the tenor of American intellectual life. Reinhold Niebuhr called the previously "acrimonious" relations between Catholics and Protestants "scandalous" and his writings exemplified a new spirit of amity between the two groups. Catholics detected among their non-Catholic countrymen a notable revival of interest in religion along with a reappraisal and rehabilitation of some of the ideas referred to above as "American innocence." The defense of democracy against totalitarianism prompted attacks on relativism and increasing openness to a natural law position that admitted the possibility and the promise of objective standards of reason and morality.[1]

There were also significant shifts underway among American attitudes toward social reform. Opinion polls showed rising opposition to the New Deal agenda as the 1940s began, and congressional elections substantiated the polls. While Roosevelt had enough personal appeal left to ensure reelection in both 1940 and 1944, his allies in Congress were being eliminated. The Republican gains began in 1938, continued in 1940, and achieved critical mass in 1942. By the end of that year, the Democratic advantage in the House, which had been 242 in 1936, was reduced to 10. Enough of them were conservative southern Democrats, moreover, that Roosevelt was bound to be frustrated in any continuing efforts at enacting social programs. By 1944, the Civilian Conservation Corps and the Works Progress Administration were only the two most prominent of the New Deal programs to have been abolished.[2]

John Ryan remained enthusiastic about Roosevelt's project to the end, but his dissatisfaction with the level of Catholic support for it was clear. His discontent with the lack of consensus was manifest in a 1941 article celebrating the anniversary of the social encyclicals. Ryan was pleased at the reception of the papal teaching in the United States, believing that the "doctrine" contained therein had been disseminated effectively. He was less pleased with the "application" of that doctrine, as evidenced by such problems as low wages paid by Catholic employers and a negative attitude toward labor unions on the part of the same. For Ryan, theory and practice had not yet merged.[3]

Ryan continued to advocate the reforms of the Roosevelt era into the 1940s, although his position at the National Catholic Welfare Conference (NCWC) mandated that he avoid statements of endorsement for political candidates in the elections of 1940 and 1944.[4] In 1945, nonetheless, he was able to deliver the blessing again for the inauguration of his president's fourth term. Ryan passed away in September of that year.

The liberalism with which Ryan had aligned himself was itself changing, and it may be that he would have found the new form a less amenable ally. Any effort to create cooperative associations, for instance, was decisively left behind. By 1945, few "New Dealers" championed any longer the more radical reforms at the heart of the New Deal. Advocacy of central planning by the state, fundamental restructuring of capitalism, and the formation of cooperative associational arrangements was mostly abandoned.[5]

The NCWC still reflected Ryan's reform concerns, though its statement on social order at the beginning of the decade reflected a moderated tone devoid of the polemics of the 1930s. It still condemned laissez-faire in economics, seeing danger in the "concentration of ownership and control of wealth" and "the anonymous character which results from some of the existing business and corporation law, whereby responsibility toward society is greatly impaired if not completely ignored."[6]

The statement reiterated the traditional call for a "guild or corporative system," but it made explicit the demand that the state not be the driving force in such a system. The state, it directed, should not be "mere policeman or umpire. It has the responsibility of providing for the common good. On the other hand it may not and should not become totalitarian in attempting to fulfill all social functions in the way of economic planning and direction. It should leave to the smaller vocational groups the settlement of business of lesser importance."[7]

War and the Catholic Worker

The coming of war also brought to the surface fault lines within the Catholic Worker movement. The relationship between the Catholic Worker and mainstream liberalism had always been a tenuous one. With the outbreak of war in 1939, the lines of division between "radical" workers and "liberal" workers became more apparent. Two important leaders and branches of the Worker movement—John Cogley (Chicago Worker) and Dorothy Day (New York Worker)—split in 1939 over differences in opinion on the war.[8] Day's strict adherence to pacifism would be a sticking point for many Catholic Workers, including H. A Reinhold, an exile from Nazi Germany, head of the Seattle Worker house, and Virgil Michel's successor as leading figure in the liturgical movement.[9]

Mel Piehl has explicated well the differences between the two types of workers and the problems endemic to both approaches to relating religion to the American polity. John Cort, in Piehl's typology, exemplified the liberal Catholic Worker. As he sought increasing influence within the political sphere and became more deeply involved in the Association of Catholic Trade Unions (ACTU), Cort came to accept mass production and industrialization as sources of wealth growth. Cort was able, by abandoning the radical countercultural stance of the Catholic Worker, to exert tremendous influence in political circles, coming to have a major role as advisor to John F. Kennedy.[10] His rapprochement with liberalism, however, opened Cort and his fellow former radicals to the charges of those who saw the move as an illicit compromise: "Through this 'Christian industrialism,' Catholic corporatists . . . commended their spirits into the hands of New Deal liberalism, to rise again as denatured ideologues for the Democratic coalition."[11]

The story of the Catholic Worker's relationship with American liberalism shows that the Worker movement itself was not exempt from grappling with the same issues of engaging the world that confronted all American Catholics. Many who saw value in the project of the Catholic Worker project nonetheless came to see that fidelity to Day's social and religious ideas might be as well expressed by participation in labor organization or political activism. Capitalism, too, if that was the right term for the economic system regnant in the United States, could be berated, but not really avoided. John Cort, without abandoning Day's goal of helping the disadvantaged, could embrace the industrial economy as the means by which poverty would be alleviated.

A "Strong Moral Foundation" for Free Enterprise

Apart from the war and its impact on the Catholic left, the economic and political conservatism of the 1940s found representatives among Catholic thinkers as well. Father Edward Keller, C.S.C. (1903–1989), proposed ideas contrary to the way many Catholic social thinkers had previously conceived of the relation between Catholic teaching and economics. In many ways, Keller's economic ideas, and the political allegiances flowing from them, can be seen as diametrically opposed to those of Catholic social thinkers in the tradition of John Ryan. Historians of American Catholicism have not paid much attention to Keller, but his work represents a significant and unique contribution to Catholic economic thought.

Born in Cincinnati, Keller joined the Congregation of Holy Cross and studied economics at the University of Minnesota. As was often the case in the early twentieth century, the needs of Catholic schools and colleges for teachers outstripped the resources of the religious orders that ran them, and Keller was sent to teach at Notre Dame before finishing his dissertation. He remained there as a professor of economics for the duration of his career.

Like many of his coreligionists, Keller derived lessons from the experience of the Great Depression. Unlike many other Catholics, however, his interpretation of that event did not result in admiration for Franklin Roosevelt. Keller had known personally ex-President Hoover during the 1930s and 1940s and he believed that the picture of Hoover drawn by Roosevelt and the mainstream press was a caricature. Hoover had been deeply concerned about Americans suffering impoverishment, he observed, and had, in fact, implemented measures to relieve the depression, such as the Reconstruction Finance Corporation and spending on public works.[12]

Keller's view of the relation of Hoover's and Roosevelt's respective policies regarding the depression was contrary to Ryan's. "It is my conviction," he reflected late in life, "that Mr. Hoover's economic policies would have brought the country prosperity because the Depression 'bottomed out' in 1932 and the economy was on the upswing in 1933, and prosperity would have been attained by 1934 if the economy had not be[en] structured into depression by the Roosevelt New Deal."[13]

Besides his interpretation of the depression, Keller's views were also dependent on his assessment of the current state of the American economy in the late 1940s. The focus of his economic research was income distribution, a topic of some importance to the tradition of Catholic teaching on the economy. Keller outlined his evaluation of income distribution in two books published in 1947 and 1948.

In the first book, Keller linked his view of Roosevelt and the depression with the topic of distribution. Prior to the question of distribution, he noted, was the question of wealth production. The relatively high standard of living obtaining among Americans in general was a result of "labor-saving Tools," acquired by "individuals who do not spend all of their income for consumer goods and services but save part of their income and invest it in Tools."[14] The debacle of the thirties—the first decade during which the American economy "went backward instead of forward"—was due to the new tax policy of 1933, which appropriated a large part of the savings of those in the higher income brackets. As a result, Keller concluded, "Private investment in business practically ceased."[15] Keller thus reminded his readers that excess income was not itself a problem, but was in fact—when invested properly—the source of fecundity in the national economy.

His 1948 book, written with coauthors Fred Clark and Richard Rimanoczy, reinforced the analysis of his previous work. The authors presented extensive statistics concerning the reception of income and the possession of wealth in the

United States. Using these figures they argued that income distribution was essentially fair and that popular impressions to the contrary were based on faulty interpretations of the data. For instance, the income of the "rich," they pointed out, must be considered after, not before taxation, a consideration that decreased substantially the percentage of the national income received by that group.[16] Reiterating the point of the earlier book, Keller and his collaborators wrote that the rich were an important source of "new enterprise, new jobs and better tools of production," and wondered "whether the high surtax on large incomes is not destroying an important element of progress in the nation's life."[17]

In 1947, Keller published a series of articles in *Ave Maria* magazine that outlined his interpretation of Catholic social teaching and its relation to the American economy. In the opening paragraph of the first article, he stated two theses that set him at odds with the claims of many of his American Catholic colleagues. "The encyclicals do not condemn our economic system of free enterprise," he wrote, "but instead give a strong moral foundation for such a system." Secondly, "the main economic problem in the United States is not extreme concentration of wealth and income but rather a lack of balance among different worker groups and different geographical segments of the economy."[18]

Keller admitted that Pius XI, in *Quadragesimo Anno*, condemned "unlimited competition," or laissez-faire capitalism. Keller asserted in response that such unlimited competition "was never the dominant ruling principle of our economic system even though at present the attitude of some groups."[19] Pius did not condemn great wealth, Keller further observed; the pontiff instead emphasized the responsibilities of those with wealth to use it to the benefit of others. In the United States, Keller pointed out, superfluous income had been largely invested in capital, fulfilling admirably *Quadragesimo*'s exhortation to use wealth to increase employment opportunities.[20]

Keller's second article demonstrated his acceptance of the conventional language of Catholic social thought as a via media between "the extremes of nineteenth-century individualism and socialism."[21] This position was reflected in the Church's position on property, he explained, which preserved property as an individual right, yet insisted on the social responsibilities of ownership. It was also reflected in its position on government intervention in the economy, which saw a positive role for government beyond merely that of policeman, yet placed limits on it and warned of the dangers of excessive government interference.[22]

Keller quoted Leo XIII on the desirability of the distribution of property ownership among workers. "The ideal," Keller observed, "comes closer to realization in the United States than in any other country in the world." He cited the widespread ownership of homes, automobiles, and other goods as indications of fulfillment of Leo's teaching. Similarly, productive wealth is widely distributed, Keller claimed, pointing to the half-million American corporations and the thousands of stockholders in the larger corporations.[23]

Keller posited the main reasons for this wide distribution to be two: the youth of the American nation (thereby lacking a landed elite), and the astounding

productivity of the American worker (aided by unprecedented capital investment). Citing numbers to show productivity increases over the past half-century,
Keller asserted: "Most of this increased productivity was passed on to the workers, in the form of higher wages and lower prices." The concern shown by the
popes for pauperism and for extreme concentrations of wealth did not apply to
the United States, Keller insisted. The American worker was relatively well-off,
he reiterated, and asserting otherwise would be "terribly dangerous," feeding
"fuel to the spreading fire of world communism."[24]

All of this was not to say that there was no room for improvement in the
American economy. "There are serious weaknesses in the national economy,"
Keller wrote; this fact necessitated locating and addressing those weaknesses and
not being distracted by false problems such as the gap between rich and poor.
The major source of distortion in distribution in the American context, according
to Keller, was the differences between worker groups—namely between "agricultural workers and the non-agricultural workers, and between the highly organized, highly paid workers and the unorganized, lower-paid workers."[25]

Citing income figures, Keller substantiated his claim that maldistribution
was more severe between worker groups than between workers and the wealthy.
He also observed that southern states were the locus of the most serious poverty:
"The South is," he wrote indelicately, "the cancer-sore of our national economy."[26] The answer to the South's predicament, he explained, could only come
through industrialization and agricultural diversification.

Keller's controversial articles did not go without notice. Carl Hensler, a
priest and professor of sociology at Seton Hill College in Greensburg, Pennsylvania, contested Keller's claims in the *Catholic Educator*. Hensler quoted Pius
XII on the evil of "economic dictatorship" and claimed that, if Keller did not
think such harmful concentration of wealth and power were "the dominant characteristic of American economic life," then he was "not very well acquainted
with the facts." Hensler also disputed Keller's portrayal of the ownership of productive capital, highlighting the "separation of ownership and control" that characterized most large firms with widespread stock ownership. The "men who rule
over the American economy," Hensler charged, were "socially irresponsible."
Claims that consumers, stockholders, and government served to keep in check
the immoral tendencies of business leaders, he insisted, were true in theory, but
not in practice.[27]

Keller's series of articles has been treated extensively because it demonstrates so well (as did John Ryan's work) the relationship between Catholic social
teaching and its application to the American situation made by Catholic commentators on social questions. Keller's contentions, insofar as they differed from
those of other Catholic thinkers, were based not on misinterpretations or misrep-
resentations of the encyclical tradition. They were not based on the encyclicals at
all. Keller knew and articulated the fact that the popes condemned harmful disparities of wealth. His economic studies (and perhaps to some degree his political allegiances), however, led him to conclude that, insofar as such disparities

existed in the United States, they were located between worker groups rather than between workers and capitalists. The policy recommendations deduced from such a conclusion—both the extent and character of government intervention called for—would differ dramatically from those derived from a New Deal interpretation such as that offered by John Ryan.

Conservatism and Anticommunism

Keller's views on economics made him a more willing ally of political conservatism than most of his fellow Catholics. Another feature of Keller's view, moreover—an issue that was assuming center stage just as Ryan was leaving the scene—would bring American Catholics in general into friendlier relations with non-Catholic conservatives. This feature was Keller's anticommunism.

The rise of totalitarianism in the 1930s had led many American intellectuals to distance themselves from ideas associated with fascist and communist regimes and to defend more forthrightly political democracy. Most refused to accept the Catholic critique of totalitarianism, however, implying as it did acceptance of the reality of natural law and a rejection of social scientific naturalism. In fact, they continued to view the Catholic Church as an abettor rather than a foe of the totalitarian mindset. Philosophers such as John Dewey and Sidney Hook fashioned a "relativist theory of democracy" that denied the concept of ethical absolutes entailed by natural law.[28]

Developments in Europe led other intellectuals to embrace aspects of the Catholic critique. Legal realism, under assault by Catholic legal theorists, came under fire from erstwhile advocates such as Robert Maynard Hutchins, as well. Reappraisal of ideas touted by Catholic scholars placed figures such as Walter Lippman and Reinhold Niebuhr "among those who followed from the late twenties to the late thirties paths that seemed at the time roughly parallel to the one Hutchins had trod."[29]

Hutchins, Lippman, and Niebuhr were not, however, at the center of the conservative movement gaining steam in the late 1940s. With the fascist threat frustrated, fear of communism drove the rise of the new conservatism. As John Diggins has documented, many important figures in the incipient conservative movement were former communists, disillusioned during the 1930s by the totalitarian tendencies they perceived as endemic to communism as a political system.[30] As Diggins's work also shows, this group of conservative intellectuals was a diverse lot, impelled by various motives and taking up divergent positions on a range of issues. Their only points of commonality were their former involvement with communism and their developing antipathy to it. While anticommunism could serve as a bridge connecting Catholic thinkers and non-Catholic conservatives, that bridge would be more or less stable depending on the nature of an individual's "conservatism."

Novelist and literary critic John Dos Passos (1896–1970) was one communist-turned-conservative. Dos Passos's conversion occurred during the 1930s and was spurred by his experience of the Spanish Civil War. Rare among non-Catholic Americans, Dos Passos joined many American Catholics in their support of the Nationalist side during that conflict. Dos Passos's conservatism, however, was of an aesthetic antitechnological, anti-industrial sort. Few American Catholic social thinkers shared that viewpoint. While many were enamored by the Middle Ages, most recognized the benefits of material progress and were uninterested in cultivating a sense of detachment from and disdain for American culture in the way that Dos Passos did. While, during World War II, Dos Passos exhibited some of the patriotism that Catholics generally shared, his criticism of big business, big government, and big labor in the 1950s set him on a course orthogonal to that of most Catholic thinkers.[31] The buoyant attitude of 1950s Catholicism would find little value in Dos Passos's truculent pessimism.

Max Eastman (1883–1969), a prominent figure in the founding of the conservative flagship publication *National Review*, was even less a potential Catholic ally. Eastman turned from both communism and the American Left, which he perceived to be driven by similar utopian visions, in the 1930s. Eastman never turned from his hostility to religion, however, a fact that led ultimately to his breaking with the periodical that he had helped to launch.[32] Catholics may have appreciated Eastman's anti-utopianism, but his indifference to traditional morality and negative view of Christianity's role in the social order would have made any alliance problematic.

Catholics could—and did—find more common ground with a third figure in the conservative pantheon, Jewish sociologist Will Herberg (1901–1977). Herberg's own odyssey out of communism was prompted by his observation of its decline into totalitarianism in the Soviet Union. Driven less by aesthetic sensibilities, like Dos Passos, or political and economic considerations, like Eastman, Herberg was keenly aware of the spiritual aspect of American opposition to communism. Herberg did not turn to the Enlightenment or eighteenth-century rationalism as antidotes to modern ills, as did other conservative thinkers. For him, rationalism, with its exaltation of science, reason, and progress, contained the seeds of twentieth-century totalitarianism.[33]

The only effective counterbalance to communism, then, was recognition of the limitations of human reason and perfectibility, a recognition that came through understanding man's relationship to God. Religion was, therefore, needed even to explain fully the evils of totalitarianism. Marxism, he averred, was itself a religion, one based on economics. It proclaimed that "man's essence was economic, the root of his frustration and miseries was economic, and his salvation would be economic as well."[34]

To counter the Marxist system, Herberg, drawing on his reading of Reinhold Niebuhr, recovered the concept of sin and its effects on social and political organization. The human person's dual capacity for selflessness and sin, he explained, made possible and necessary the democratic system—in which men could act for the common good, yet were checked by divisions of power and democratic rule from becoming autocrats. Herberg viewed his reassertion of Orthodox Judaism not as a repudiation of his longing for economic justice, but as a fulfillment of it. "I found in religion what I sought," he reflected, "and that was not an escape from social responsibility, but a more secure spiritual groundwork for a mature and effective social radicalism." A solid grounding for democracy, he believed, could ultimately be found only in the theological concept of the "Fatherhood of God."[35]

Herberg thus appeared as an ally of religion in the mid-century strife between religious and secular thinkers. Herberg lauded Catholic and Protestant scholars such as Jacques Maritain, Emil Brunner, and Karl Barth in the face of dismissal by major American intellectuals such as John Dewey and Sidney Hook. Catholics, for their part, did not ignore Herberg. The Jesuit journal *Thought* published several articles and his magnum opus, *Protestant, Catholic, Jew*, was received with accolades by the Catholic community.[36]

Conservatism Complicated: The Persistence of Corporatism

While anticommunist and politically conservative Catholics viewed hopefully the rightward shift of figures formerly prominent on the Left, the ranks of "conservative" Catholics were by no means drawn up in a unified formation. There remained division between those who, like Edward Keller, defended the American economic system and those who, like the leaders of the Catholic Central Verein, urged fundamental reform according to corporatist theory.

The complexity of drawing lines of distinction between the various groups of American Catholic social thinkers is captured in a 1943 letter from Georgetown University professor Franz Mueller to Frederick Kenkel. On the one hand, Mueller distanced himself and his corporatist allies from John Ryan. "It looks as if Msgr. Ryan approves of about everything Roosevelt and the New Deal do or propose," he observed. Ryan's willingness to accept state intervention was unacceptable to Mueller: "I wouldn't be surprised if he would endorse 100 percent a 'cradle-to-grave' scheme in [the] U.S.A."[37]

Mueller (1900–1994), like Kenkel, was a disciple of the German Catholic economist Heinrich Pesch.[38] In the same letter, Mueller noted with dismay the reception of his pamphlet on Pesch by Will Lissner, the Catholic editor of the *American Journal of Economics and Sociology*. Lissner was critical of Pesch's corporatism because, in his view, it lent itself to cooptation by fascism, which in fact happened in Germany. Lissner's journal, Mueller pointed out, was an organ for the spread of the principles of Henry George, and counted among its editors Franz Oppenheimer, a "well-known land socialist," and John Dewey.[39]

The jumbled allegiances of American Catholic intellectuals became evident as Mueller delved deeper into the list of the board of editors. For also on the board was Mortimer Adler, a well-respected figure among Catholics. What Adler was doing on the board, Mueller wrote in bafflement, "is beyond me." Most puzzling to Mueller was the presence of Monsignor Luigi Ligutti, director of the National Catholic Rural Life Conference. "I wrote the Msgr.," Mueller informed Kenkel, "drawing attention to this strange company of his."[40]

In the end, Mueller determined that Lissner should be lumped with "that group of American Catholics, who ... cast suspicion upon everything that has corporate (non-parliamentary?) features." This sort of Catholic tended, Mueller added, to be "for the Reds in Spain" and to consider Peschian corporatism as "at least dangerously close to Italian Fascism."[41]

In fact, some Catholics (more in Europe than in the United States) did exhibit some affinity for fascism, and such Catholics often came from the ranks of distributist and corporatist circles.[42] The appearance of a connection caused Frederick Kenkel, for one, to reconsider his advocacy of corporatism.[43] He perceived the presence of fascist fellow travelers among his countrymen and distanced himself from their position. "While we pretend to be horrified by the totalitarianism of the State," he wrote of his fellow Catholic Americans, "there are those among us who pin their faith for the future of the Church in this country on totalitarian policy, repugnant to true Christian freedom."[44] If there were any tension between Kenkel's corporatist and antistatist inclinations with respect to the issue of fascism, there was no question as to which would prevail.

Virgil Michel had shared Kenkel's fundamental critique of the American economic order, and Michel's successors maintained that position. H. A. Reinhold, priest and editor of *Orate Fratres* following Virgil Michel's death in 1938, was a German exile, forced to flee because of his criticism of Nazism. Stridently critical of both communism and Nazism, Reinhold nonetheless remained critical of American capitalism. He deplored the bourgeois spirit that created the "hideous suburbs," where "church buildings look out of place." The "monopolistic capitalism" that he perceived as regnant in the United States was no different from Nazism and communism, he averred, insofar as it "adheres to the same depersonalizing economism."[45]

Reinhold had kind things to say about American democracy and had no sympathy for the call of some European Catholics to return to older political systems: "Don't let us fix our Christianity to period and other nostalgic *ressentiments*." "The ugly things here," he explained, "don't stem from democracy, but from a misconceived idea of economic freedom, resulting industrialism, efforts of worthless individualists to establish themselves as aristocrats, and our own failing as Christians to show them up through a good example."[46]

A lifelong antitotalitarian, Reinhold was not concerned with proving his credentials by a full-throated defense of the United States. The Catholic Church's opposition to communism, he stated, had a foundation entirely different from the mass of American "bourgeois crusaders." Catholicism was diametrically opposed to communism, not because of the latter's economic doctrines, but because of its "complete secularism." Catholics, aligned with the defenders of capitalism in their anticommunism, must be careful, he insisted, to avoid embracing capitalism in the process.[47] Reinhold was one Catholic social thinker whom the rise of total-itarianism did not force into a reconsideration of American capitalism. Instead, his critique continued in a different American tradition, deprecating the moral and aesthetic effects of a mass consumer society.[48]

Academic Economics: The Catholic Economics Association

The divisions that pitted orthodox versus heterodox among American econo-mists cleaved Catholic economists as well. Eva Ross, one of the first American Catholic laywomen to hold an academic post, was more orthodox than most of her colleagues. In her 1939 text, Ross defined economics conventionally as "the scientific study of man's activity in providing for such human needs as hunger, shelter, clothing, and education. . . . [It is] the science of wealth and of the wealth-getting activities of mankind." The bibliography of her book was filled with stan-dard economic texts; only a few citations—to authors such as Oswald von Nell-Breuning and Waldemar Gurian—stood out as indicating Ross's Catholicism.[49]

Indebted to the orthodox economics of the day, Ross nonetheless departed from the mainstream in various ways. She appreciated the many benefits brought by capitalism but also conceded that the "unplanned market mechanism has indeed led to great extremes of poverty and wealth and to ever increasing inse-curity." She presented mostly a standard account of traditional subjects such as utility, marginal utility, wants, economic goods, exchange, value, and prices, but she added caveats that were not usual in orthodox economics. The division of labor, for instance, had not been an unalloyed good for mankind, she observed. It meant that the "joy of the craftsman" was denied to the modern assembly-line worker. At the same time, Ross avoided the celebration of earlier economic arrangements that were characteristic of some of her coreligionists. "A great pro-portion of workers in precapitalist days," she pointed out, "were but servants and drudges and were not engaged in work which required great skill or provided variety."[50]

Ross similarly took middle-of-the-road positions on issues of prices and wages. She argued against fixed prices but stated that a just price implies that "all factors in production are adequately remunerated." She warned against the economic impact of government regulation such as profit taxes, worrying that such moves destroyed the incentive structure that drove the capitalist economy. But, on the issue of minimum-wage laws, Ross believed that government inter-vention was justified. "While it is undoubtedly best that people should take care of their own interests by private endeavor," she wrote in echo of *Quadragesimo Anno*'s principle of subsidiarity, "where this is not done or seems impossible, then it is the State's duty to intervene." The minimum wage was one such area, she thought, stipulating that such legislation could allow for smaller wages for the aged, handicapped, and others "whose output might be less than a reasonable normal production."[51]

On the issue of economic systems, Ross again attempted to strike a balance. She understood capitalism to be "largely the outcome" of a "philosophy of liberalism" that led to an "individualistic lack of social responsibility." She, therefore, had sympathy for reform plans such as distributism and corporatism. But these ideas were not devoid of problems, either. Distributism, she observed, seemed to involve a retreat from modern technology that was unnecessary and even harmful. Corporatism represented the best system, ideally, but its problem was implementation. Ross questioned how the industry groups could be organized without the rise of an authoritarian state and a planned economy (against which Ross upheld the "liberty" of economic life "privately organized and maintained"). Corporatism would be beneficial, then, if the "government can induce" citizens to organize into groups while simultaneously avoiding slipping into authoritarianism.[52]

Ross understood that her deference to economic science put her at odds with some Catholic social thinkers. Of her book, she wrote to Frederick Kenkel, "It is much more orthodox than Father Virgil Michel would have it, but then I fear the danger of too much radicalism from those who do not know too much economics."[53] Although Ross characterized the difference as proceeding from ignorance of economics, diverse positions on economic questions were found within the ranks of the economics profession itself.

The division is reflected clearly in the deliberations of the Catholic Economics Association (CEA), founded in 1941. From the beginning of that organization there were two distinct perspectives apparent. The first, represented by Thomas F. Divine, S.J., of Marquette University, essentially accepted the premises of conventional economics. The other, whose champion was Divine's Jesuit confrere Bernard W. Dempsey of St. Louis University, was situated within the social economics tradition, more fundamentally critical of orthodox economics.[54]

The most obvious influence on Divine's economic thinking was British economist Lionel Robbins. Divine shared Robbins's definition of economics as "the science which deals with human conduct in its administration of scarce means for the attainment of alternative ends or purposes." Divine also shared the broadly orthodox understanding of economics as a science in the mold of the natural sciences. As such, it encompassed both pure theory and applied economics, which uses the tools of economics to solve practical problems.[55]

The junction at which economic science met ethics, in Divine's schema, was in economic policy, which involved prescribing action and passing value judgments on economic ends, behavior, and institutions. While there could, therefore, be a meeting of economics and other fields such as social philosophy, economics itself remained a strictly positive (non-normative) discipline. The CEA, therefore, according to Divine's vision, would be a place where the goals derived from Christian social teaching could meet the science needed to bring them about.[56]

Although economists such as Keller and Divine sought to use orthodox economics in a way compatible with the Church's social teaching, the attitudes of major figures in the neoclassical school toward religion ranged from indifference to hostility. Frank Knight (1895–1972), whose *Risk, Uncertainty, and Profit* (1921), had become a classic text and who also wrote on the relationship between ethics and economics, considered Christianity and "liberalism" (by which he meant the ideas of economic, political, and religious freedom) to be incompatible.[57]

Throughout the positive developments of the Enlightenment, Knight believed, the Christian churches "remained fundamentally reactionary. Religion opposed tooth and nail every phase of what we now view as progress, particularly the intellectual advance." Accepting Enlightenment distinctions as gospel truth, Knight declared his devotion to "modern standards of credibility" and "facts and reasoning," and deplored any deference to "supernatural authority." He viewed religion not as providing any real human knowledge but as merely sanctioning views already held. Determining the "origin and content" of those views, he averred, "is a task for social psychology and culture history."[58]

It is no wonder that Knight had little use for religion when one considers his impression of it. "Most of what we think of as belonging to the higher life of the mind and spirit is ignored or repudiated in the New Testament and in historical Christian teaching," he observed. "The esthetic and intellectual life, science in all its branches and philosophic thought, find no place or are negatively regarded along with business and politics." Knight considered it enough to cite the names of Galileo and Darwin to prove Christian antipathy to science, and to mention "medieval scholasticism" as a proof against the philosophical mettle of religious folk. "The religious ideal of the intellectual life," he explained, "is the conditioning of children in infancy to the unquestioning acceptance of dogma, myth, and authority, and the sinfulness of all criticism and questioning."[59]

While much of Knight's characterization approaches caricature, there are points at which his criticism of Christianity parallels self-criticism within the Christian fold. Knight's perception of the churches' derogation of business and politics, in practice if not in theory, had grounding in reality, as the earlier discussion of the CCIP shows. Knight was also concerned to refute what he perceived as the widespread Christian view (which he called "moralism") that moral goodness or good intentions alone could solve social and economic problems. Repeated Catholic assertions that their social teaching held the key to the solution of the social question could be interpreted in such a way. Catholic scholars as diverse as John Ryan, Thomas Divine, and John Cronin (below and chapter 6), criticized fellow Catholics who seemed willfully ignorant of the role that economic knowledge should play in addressing social problems.[60]

While Catholics such as Divine largely agreed with orthodox economists such as Knight on the nature and content of economics, others in the CEA were highly critical of the mainstream position. At the first CEA meeting, John Ryan expressed his hope that the CEA could reinvigorate Richard Ely's ethical approach to economics, which, "unfortunately, has not been able to convert or strongly influence the great body of economists in the United States." Positive and normative elements in economics, he thought, should not "indiscriminately mingle," but the discipline did involve both elements.[61]

Bernard Dempsey, a student of Joseph Schumpeter at Harvard and an admirer of Pesch, sought to align the teaching of the popes with the opposition to orthodox economics. The economics of *Quadragesimo*, he argued, is "obviously an institutional economics, very much in the same sense as John R. Commons uses the term." Dempsey viewed mainstream American economics as one branch in the malevolent tree that had its roots in the soil of French Liberalism. In this way, Dempsey linked Ricardian economics, the branch that had been grasped by most American economists, with Marxian economics, the other main fruit of anti-Christian liberalism.[62]

If Divine and Dempsey represented opposite wings of the CEA, there was also a middle ground occupied by scholars such as John Cronin, S.S. Cronin was a professor of economics at St. Mary's Seminary in Baltimore and president of the CEA in 1946. His *Economic Analysis and Problems* was an impressive introductory text intended for a broad audience and published by a mainstream publisher.

Like Eva Ross, Cronin demonstrated conversance with the important figures and arguments of contemporary economics. Like Ross, too, he defined economics conventionally as the "science, which treats of the laws of wealth production, exchange, distribution, and consumption." More than some other Catholic economists, Cronin displayed knowledge of a broad range of economic thinkers from a variety of perspectives. Hayek, Mises, Schumpeter, Ely, Veblen, Sombart, Hobson, Commons, Spahr, and Knight represent a sampling of the authors on whom Cronin drew in the course of the book.[63]

His wide reading led Cronin to begin his treatment of economics by noting that although some areas of consensus existed among economists, there also persisted "deep cleavages" on a number of particular questions. This diversity notwithstanding, Cronin insisted that those concerned with social and political reform—including religious reformers—must be knowledgeable in the field of economics. A reform program, he warned, should not be adopted "merely because it is highly desirable. It must also be shown that it is feasible." It was the tendency of some churchmen, ignorant of social science, to make "loose statements on concrete matters," that Cronin thought gave rise to the kind of criticism of religion raised by Frank Knight.[64]

If religious reformers and economists were at an impasse, in Cronin's estimation there was blame enough to distribute. Christians were correct to assert the subordination of economic life to morality, he thought, but he discerned the need to return to a more temperate attitude toward economic reform: "While in the past, economists have claimed more power than was sound, there is a danger lest liberal reformers unwisely disregard economic law and accumulated experience."[65]

Addressing the CEA on the implementation of Church social teaching in the United States, Cronin again struck a note of balance and moderation. There certainly ought to be space for the Catholic economist within the profession, he avowed. "The economist who accepts Catholic social principles in one sense does bring outside considerations into his study of economic problems," he began. "But so does every other economist who is not content to deal with pure abstractions." Bringing considerations other than pure theory (including not only ethical arguments, but also psychological and historical) did not compromise the scientific value of economics, Cronin claimed; it enhanced it. Economics "has estimated too narrowly its field," he stated. To be relevant to the actual economy, it must take into account the complexity of economic actors who do not conform neatly to theory: "If we desire that our science reach precise mathematical conclusions, based upon highly limited assumptions, then we must admit that it applies to real life only when such assumptions are fulfilled."[66]

Cronin used the example of wage theory to exemplify the mediating role that economic theory played in the application of social teaching to the American situation. There were two main theories of wages currently popular, Cronin explained: wages as a source of purchasing power and wages as an outcome of productivity. Catholic adherents of each school were attempting to "apply and interpret the social encyclicals" according to their respective philosophies. The encyclicals themselves, Cronin insisted, do not settle the matter of application. "It is unfair," he declared, "to put out in the name of the Catholic Church the ideas which are in fact those of the Keynes-Hansen schools in the United States. It is equally unfair to baptize Pigou or Hayek and make them exponents of the encyclicals."[67]

The CEA encompassed a vibrant interaction of differing approaches through the 1940s. Its journal contained a defense of profit by Divine, an endorsement of Philip Murray's Industry Council Plan, and an examination of the thought of Heinrich Pesch. The relation of ethics to economics remained an important topic.[68]

It is evident that the same debates occurring among economists in the broader profession were also taking place among Catholics affiliated with the CEA. Divine and his allies drew on the writings of Marshall and Robbins, while Dempsey and others were indebted, through Pesch, to the German historical school. There is no evidence, meanwhile, to suggest that any of the interlocutors in these CEA debates held theologically heterodox views. The history of professional Catholic economists fits comfortably within the larger story of Catholic views on economics.

Notes

1. James Leo Garrett Jr., *Reinhold Niebuhr on Roman Catholicism* (Louisville, Ky.: Seminary Baptist Book Store), 39–40; William M. Halsey, *The Survival of American Innocence: Catholicism in an Era of Disillusionment, 1920–1940* (Notre Dame, Ind.: University of Notre Dame Press, 1980), 164–66; Edward A., Purcell Jr., *The Crisis of Democratic Theory: Scientific Naturalism and the Problem of Value* (Lexington: University Press of Kentucky, 1973), chap. 13. One marker of the religious revival of the 1940s was the organization of the National Association of Evangelicals; see Joel Carpenter, "The Fundamentalist Leaven and the Rise of an Evangelical United Front," in *The Evangelical Tradition in America*, ed. Leonard Sweet (Macon, Ga.: Mercer University Press, 1984), 257–88. During the two decades following World War II, church membership rose to 65 percent of the population, the highest point in American history, and, among Catholics, church attendance was 60 percent. Edwin Scott Gaustad, *A Religious History of America*, new rev. ed. (San Francisco: Harper and Row, 1990 [1966]). For a nuanced interpretation of the postwar religious revival, recognizing the churches' accomplishments but also detecting too much cultural accommodation, see Mark A. Noll, *A History of Christianity in the United States and Canada* (Grand Rapids, Mich.: William B. Eerdmans, 1992), 436–41.

2. Brinkley, *End of Reform*, 140–43.

3. Ryan, "On the Anniversary of the Encyclicals," *American Catholic Sociological Review* 2 (June 1941): 86.

4. Francis L. Broderick, *Right Reverend New Dealer: John A. Ryan* (New York: Macmillan, 1963), 257.

5. Alan Brinkley, *The End of Reform: New Deal Liberalism in Recession and War* (New York: Vintage, 1995), 265.

6. "Statement on Church and Social Order," issued by the Administrative Board and Assistant Bishops of the National Catholic Welfare Conference, February 7, 1940, 436–53, in *Pastoral Letters of the United States Catholic Bishops*, vol. 1, 1792–1940, ed. Hugh J. Nolan, ed. (Washington, D.C.: United States Catholic Conference, 1984).

7. Ibid., 450.

8. On Catholic Workers and liberalism, see Mel Piehl, *Breaking Bread: The Catholic Worker and the Origin of Catholic Radicalism in America* (Philadelphia: Temple University Press, 1982), chap. 5. On pacifism, see 150–9. See Robert Moats Miller, *American Protestantism and Social Issues, 1919–1939* (Chapel Hill: University of North Carolina Press, 1958), chapter 22, on the division among Protestants over the same issue. It should be noted that the issue of pacifism was probably more divisive among Protestants than among Catholics. In this period, outside of the Catholic Worker, Catholic pacifism was almost nonexistent.

In addition to the Catholic Worker's difficulties mentioned here, elements of the movement were at times under suspicion of theological error relating to their radical rejection of the world (viewed by some theologian opponents as an annihilation of nature in favor of grace). Two priests closely associated with Day and the movement were disciplined by ecclesiastical authorities in the early 1940s. James Terence Fisher, *The Catholic Counterculture in America, 1933–1962* (Chapel Hill: University of North Carolina Press, 1989), 58–59.

9. Piehl, *Breaking Bread*, 197.

10. Ibid., 160–5. See also John C. Cort, *Dreadful Conversions: The Making of a Catholic Socialist* (New York: Fordham University Press, 2003).

11. McCarraher, *Christian Critics*, 94–95.

12. "Oral History Interview with Edward A. Keller, C.S.C.," by Raymond Henle, November 4, 1969 (Hoover Library, 1971), 2–4, 17–19, CKEL 1/10.

13. Ibid., 19. Keller has not been the only scholar to argue that Roosevelt's policies prolonged rather than ameliorated the depression. See, for instance, Gary Dean Best, *Pride, Prejudice, and Politics: Roosevelt Versus Recovery, 1933–1938* (New York: Praeger, 1991). While Best's thesis that Roosevelt's antagonism toward business prevented economic recovery remains controversial, it is generally accepted that many New Dealers shared a belief that big business represented the main obstacle to recovery. See Brinkley, *End of Reform*, 48.

14. Edward A. Keller, C.S.C., *The National Income and Its Distribution* (Notre Dame, Ind.: Bureau of Economic Research, 1947), 21.

15. Keller, *National Income*, 22.

16. Edward A. Keller, C.S.C., Fred G. Clark, and Richard Stanton Rimanczy, *Who Gets How Much for Doing What in America: A Primer on the Distribution of Income and Property in the United States* (New York: American Economic Foundation, 1948), 19ff. Keller followed this study with two more, similar ones: Keller and Frank A. Brady Jr., *An Inventory of Wealth in the United States* (New York: American Economic Foundation, 1951); and Keller and Brady, *National Income in the United States* (New York: American Economic Foundation, 1954)

17. Keller, *Who Gets How Much*, 23.

18. Edward A. Keller, C.S.C., "The Church and Our Economic System [I]," *Ave Maria*, March 1, 1947, 263.

19. Ibid., 264.

20. Ibid.

21. Keller, "The Church and Our Economic System [II]," *Ave Maria*, March 8, 1947, 304.

22. Ibid., 304–5.

23. Ibid., 306–7.

24. Ibid., 307–8; Keller, "The Church and Our Economic System [III]," *Ave Maria*, March 15, 1947, 339.

25. Ibid.

26. Ibid., 340.

27. Rev. Carl P. Hensler, "Does Church Approve the American Economic System?" *Catholic Educator* 18 (January 1948): 239–43.

28. Edward A. Purcell Jr. *The Crisis of Democratic Theory: Scientific Naturalism and the Problem of Value* (Lexington: University Press of Kentucky, 1973), chap. 11, 203. On prominent American intellectuals' views of Catholicism through this period, including their view of the Church as antidemocratic, see John T. McGreevy, "Thinking on One's Own: Catholicism in the American Intellectual Imagination, 1928–1960," *Journal of American History* 84 (June 1997): 97–131. There were, at the same time, many American intellectuals who were attracted to Communism during the 1930s; Terry A. Cooney, *Balancing Acts: American Thought and Culture in the 1930s* (New York: Twayne, 1995), 132–36.

29. Purcell, *Crisis*, 141ff., 152, 164–74.

30. John P. Diggins, *Up from Communism: Conservative Odysseys in American Intellectual History* (New York: Harper and Row, 1975).

31. Ibid., 88–93, 114–15, chap. 6.

32. Ibid., chap. 5, 346–47.

33. Ibid., 154–59, 271. On Herberg and Catholicism, see Patrick Allitt, *Catholic Intellectuals and Conservative Politics in America, 1950–1985* (Ithaca, N.Y.: Cornell University Press, 1993), 102–5.

34. Will Herberg, "From Marxism to Judaism: Jewish Belief As a Dynamic of Social Action," *Commentary* 3 (January 1947): 25.

35. Herberg, "From Marxism," 27, 29; Diggins, *Up from Communism*, 276–77.

36. Diggins, *Up from Communism*, 285; Will Herberg, "From Marxism," 32. See also McGreevy, "Thinking," 117–31. McGreevy argues that, amid the undulations of American intellectual attitudes toward Catholics, the dominant 1940s view of Catholicism considered it to be a threat to democracy. For Herberg's articles in *Thought*, see chap. 6 below.

37. Franz Mueller to Frederick Kenkel, March 20, 1943, 5., CKNA 5/16.

38. See John J. Kelley, S.M., *Freedom in the Church: A Documented History of the Principle of Subsidiary Function* (Dayton, Ohio: Peter Li, 2000), 26, for Mueller's biography.

39. Mueller to Kenkel, March 20, 1943, 5–7.

40. Mueller to Kenkel, March 20, 1943, 7. Ligutti (1895–1984) would have some influence in the drafting of John XXIII's and Paul VI's social encyclicals. See Raymond W. Miller, *Monsignor Ligutti: The Pope's Country Agent* (Lanham, Md.: University Press of America, 1981).

41. Mueller to Kenkel, March 20, 1943, 7.

42. See, for instance, Jay P. Corrin, *Catholic Intellectuals and the Challenge of Democracy* (Notre Dame, Ind.: University of Notre Dame Press, 2002), chap. 8; and Patrick Allitt, *Catholic Converts: British and American Intellectuals Turn to Rome* (Ithaca, N.Y.: Cornell University Press, 1997), chap. 10.

43. Philip Gleason, *The Conservative Reformers: German-American Catholics and the Social Order* (Notre Dame: University of Notre Dame Press, 1968), 207.

44. Kenkel to Rev. Francis Borgia Steck, OFM, CCCV 3/43.

45. H. A. Reinhold, "Catholic Puritanism," *OF*, June 11, 1939, 367–69; Reinhold, "That Interesting Fiction: The American Standard of Living," *OF*, July 21, 1940, 409–12; Reinhold, "They Fought a War Over It!" *OF*, April 19, 1942, 271–74. For Reinhold's biography and antifascism, see Jay P. Corrin, "H. A. Reinhold: Liturgical Pioneer and Anti-Fascist," *CHR* 82 (July 1996): 436–58; see also Corrin, *Catholic Intellectuals*, chap. 10.

46. Reinhold, "The Menace of the Herd," *OF*, October 3, 1943, 505–10.

47. Reinhold, "Decent Godless People," *OF*, November 4, 1945, 555–58.

48. See Daniel Horowitz, *The Morality of Spending: Attitudes Toward the Consumer Society in America, 1875–1940* (Baltimore: Johns Hopkins University, 1985). Horowitz outlines two traditions of consumer criticism, the first critical of the profligacy and intemperance of workers and immigrants, the second of bourgeois standards and mass consumption. Reinhold's perspective mirrors the second, which Horowitz identifies arising after World War I.

49. E. J. Ross, *What is Economics? A Brief Survey of Our Economic Life* (Milwaukee: Bruce Publishing Company, 1939), 2, 245–46.

50. Ibid., 4, 22–24.

51. Ibid., 34–35, 87, 109–11.

52. Ibid., 215, 236–42.

53. Ross to Kenkel, May 4, 1938, CCCV, 3/27. On Ross, see Allitt, *Catholic Converts*, 154–55.

54. William R. Waters, "Evolution of Social Economics in America," in *Social Economics: Retrospect and Prospect*, ed. Mark Lutz (Boston: Kluwer Academic, 1990), 91–94. Another important orthodox economist on the early rolls of the CEA was Raymond J. Saulnier. Saulnier was a professor of economics at Columbia University and would later serve on President Dwight Eisenhower's Council of Economic Advisors. His first book was an examination of monetary theory: *Contemporary Monetary Theory: Studies of Some Recent Theories of Money, Prices, and Production* (New York: AMS Press, 1970; reprint, Columbia University Press, 1938).

55. Thomas F. Divine, S.J., "The Nature of Economic Science and Its Relation to Social Philosophy," *American Catholic Sociological Review* 1, no. 3 (1940): 133, 136–37. Divine did not ignore the contribution of historical economics. He perceived that, for applied economics, knowledge of market conditions and the institutional framework of exchange and production was vital. He disagreed when the historical critics went so far as to deny the validity of the theoretical principles (135).

56. Divine, "Nature of Economic Science," 136–37; Divine, "On Yoking the Economic Forces to the Social Car," *RSE* 1 (December 1942): 6–11.

57. For a Catholic response to Knight, see John L. Shea, S.J., "Discussion," *RSE* 1 (December 1942): 19–22. On Knight's place in the development of economics in the United States, see Dorothy Ross, *The Origins of American Social Science* (New York: Cambridge University Press, 1991), 420–27; Purcell, *Crisis*, 41–43; Joseph Dorfman, *The Economic Mind in American Civilization*, 5 vols. (New York: Viking Press, 1959 [1949]), vol. 5, 467–79.

58. Frank H. Knight and Thornton W. Merriam, *The Economic Order and Religion* (New York: Harper and Brothers, 1945), 24, 27, 33–34.

59. Ibid., 41.

60. Ibid., 26, chap. 6.

61. John A. Ryan, "Two Objectives for Catholic Economists," *RSE* 1 (December 1942): 1–2.

62. Bernard W. Dempsey, S.J., "Economics Implicit in the Social Encyclicals," *RSE* 1 (December 1942): 12–13. Dempsey did note that, by its own terms, *Quadragesimo* did not consider the purely technical dimensions of economics to be within its proper scope (13); cf. *Quadragesimo Anno*, n. 41.

63. John F. Cronin, S.S., *Economic Analysis and Problems* (New York: American Book Company, 1945), 65–66.

64. Ibid., 3, 68, 527.

65. Ibid., 537.

66. Cronin, "Implementing the Social Encyclicals in American Economic Life," *RSE* 5 (June 1947): 7–8.

67. Ibid., 15–16.

68. Thomas Divine, "On the Place of 'Profit' in a Capitalistic Economy," *RSE* 2 (January 1944): 57–67; Brother Robert L. Sherman, F.S.C., "The Industry Council Plan as an Instrument of Reconstruction," *RSE* 2 (January 1944): 87–99; Franz H. Mueller, "The Principle of Solidarity in the Teachings of Father Henry Pesch, S.J.," *RSE* 4 (January 1946): 31–39. A number of articles concerned with ethics appeared in the *RSE*, vol. 7 (1949).

6

Catholics and Capitalism in the Fifties

The 1950s, like the 1960s, maintain iconic status for many Americans. For observers on the left, the fifties represent the worst aspects of American life while the sixties represent the best. For many on the right, the judgment is reversed. The 1950s have been called "extraordinarily senseless and unnatural," "a moral disaster, an amusing waste of life," "more an era of fear than fun"; in sum, it was "one of the worst decades in the history of man." The Eisenhower era was "tired, dull, cautious, and anxious," one survey has concluded. "Domesticity, religiosity, respectability, security through compliance with the system" were the "essence of the fifties." Whittaker Chambers's accusation against Alger Hiss, Communist takeovers in Czechoslovakia and China, and the detonation of an atomic weapon by the Soviet Union tinged the last two years of the forties with uncertainty and set the stage for a fearful decade of Cold War.[1]

Yet, the fifties were simultaneously an era of supreme American confidence. Militarily, the United States was one of two superpowers to emerge from World War II. Economically, the United States indisputably dominated the rest of world. By some markers, America was at its cultural and intellectual apogee. The death of Stalin, the election of Eisenhower, and the end of the Korean conflict early in the decade provided grounds for optimism.[2]

In many cases, of course, observers with divergent interpretations have been reacting to the same phenomena. What is for one critic a suburban wasteland of stiflingly conformist social pressures is for another a sign of opportunity and prosperity—working-class families moving into the middle class and achieving economic and family stability. What is for one observer the rise of a vapid American civil religion is for another a widespread religious awakening.

Among Catholics, confidence was readily detectable. "By the 1950s," Jay Dolan has written, "Catholicism in the United States had clearly come of age. More accepted by the Protestant majority, Catholics entered the 1950s confident about their place in American society. Being Catholic was indeed compatible with being American."[3] The increasing certainty Catholics felt about their place in American society was in part simply an indication of the assimilation of an immigrant church that was now three decades removed from the last significant wave of immigration. In addition, the combination of patriotism during World War II and unstinting anticommunism thereafter ensured Catholics' acceptance as full-blooded Americans by most of their fellow citizens.

Catholics joined with other Christians in welcoming the continuation of the religious revival noted in the previous chapter. The increasing attention paid to religion penetrated academia as well, with the result that theologians such as Reinhold Niebuhr, Paul Tillich, Jacques Maritain, Martin Buber, and Karl Barth enjoyed "a prominence with the intellectual elite that no religious thinkers had possessed since the days of Jonathan Edwards." In a seeming reversal of its 1948 *McCollum* ruling, the Supreme Court allowed release time for religious instruction in *Zorach v. Clausen* (1952), with Justice William O. Douglas writing for the majority: "We are a religious people whose institutions presuppose a Supreme Being."[4]

Disquieting voices persisted, however, both inside and outside the Catholic community. Liberal activist Paul Blanshard, in *American Freedom and Catholic Power* (1949) and *Communism, Democracy, and Catholic Power* (1950) continued to assault Catholics' place in American life, and his tracts remained enormously popular, including among intellectuals. Catholic University historian John Tracy Ellis called into question Catholics' intellectual prowess, indicated by their lack of standing among the academic elite. Conversely, some wondered whether Catholics' increasingly smooth assimilation into American life itself bespoke a danger—of eliding what was distinctively Catholic in the attempt to gain status. Archbishop Patrick O'Boyle of Washington was among those who thought that the religious awakening was simply a case of people turning to religion "as they would a benign sedative to soothe their minds and settle their nerves."[5]

Confronted with the challenges of maintaining religious integrity in the midst of assimilation and material success, Catholics continued to debate the relationship between their Church's social teaching and their nation's economic life. Increasingly, Catholics identified with political conservatism, and Catholic intellectuals became leaders in that cause. Simultaneously, many Catholic economists questioned the assumptions of orthodox economics that lay at the root of much conservative political and economic analysis.

Christianity and Capitalism

The differences among Catholic commentators on social and economic life continued to be pronounced in the 1950s. Some Catholics viewed Congress of Industrial Organizations (CIO) president Philip Murray's Industrial Council plan as a promising initiative in the drive for the kind of corporatist arrangement called for by Pius XI. The deliberations of a National Catholic Welfare Conference (NCWC) group formed to discuss the plan provide a glimpse of the concerns that characterized intra-Catholic debates.[6]

Goetz Briefs, professor of economics at Georgetown, took exception to a memo by Father Raymond McGowan, who had succeeded John Ryan as director of the Social Action Department. Briefs's comments bring to light the fact that, in part, differences of application with respect to papal encyclicals were due to differences in understanding the method by which that application would occur. In other words, the text of the documents of Catholic social teaching, for some social thinkers, could be applied in fairly simple and straightforward fashion to various national and local contexts. For Briefs and others, however, such application involved a much more complicated process of understanding the situations in which social principles might be used.

"The memo seems to mistake the moral law," Briefs wrote to the Industry Council Committee (ICC) members, "for a code of norms easily applied to even the most complex and complicated situations economic and social life can produce." Invoking the hallowed scholastic philosophical tradition, Briefs reminded his interlocutors of "the enormous difficulties the schoolmen encountered in their day, although the moral law then had the optimum of conditions of application." Referring to the "long controversies" of the late medieval scholastics on the issues of "justice of prices, usury, etc.," Briefs observed that Aquinas's disciples had themselves resolved the problem by "recourse . . . to the *pretium fori*, that is, to the market as a regulating factor."[7]

Briefs observed that the economy in the present was even more complex than it had been for the schoolmen and that, therefore, "we should not present the moral law as something perfectly codified and ready-made for application."[8] While it would be inaccurate to characterize Briefs as an advocate of laissez-faire economics, it is clear that, on certain questions, such as that of the justice of prices, Briefs thought that the information provided by the market was the most accurate one could hope to obtain. It was wrong, therefore, to attempt to improve upon what the market offered by some other method of price determination; no other method could possibly take into account the myriad of interrelating factors contributing to the setting of a price.[9]

The attempt to apply social teaching in this way was not the only aspect of McGowan's memo to which Briefs objected. Briefs also called into question McGowan's emphasis on the potential for direction of the economy by organized bodies: "In its belief in organization on a variety of levels the memo fails to assign a proper role and function to that degree of freedom, self-determination, self-interest, self-responsibility and competition, without which no economy can fulfill the very goals of the memo: high output tied to a degree of technological progress, family and saving wages, economically rational distribution, etc."[10] Briefs can be seen brushing up against the conservative American view of John Dos Passos, for whom "organization is death." Once again, the status of American Catholic social thought is exemplified: consensus on the goals to be attained (just distribution), disagreement as to the means of their attainment.

For Briefs, the market played an indispensable role in attaining these goals. "The Christian moral order," he wrote, "presupposes an *Ordo* within which the market can fulfill its function without producing socially destructive consequences." Briefs's understanding of what Catholic social teaching called for with respect to the market was different from that of many of his coreligionists. While McGowan and others were fundamentally suspicious of the market and believed it needed to be adjusted by the intervention of government and other institutions, Briefs saw the market as fundamentally sound, yet needing to be circumscribed and supplemented by other institutions, including the family, the church, and the government. Tinkering with the market was arrogant, demonstrating indifference toward the irreplaceable role of the market. "If we obliterate the function of the market entirely, we are confronted with the same problems on another level—on a more explosive one I dare say." In this somewhat oblique reference, Briefs seems to be warning against transferring the function of the market to the sphere of politics. Briefs was at pains to emphasize his dissatisfaction, nonetheless, with the status quo: "These observations are not meant to minimize the need for social reconstruction along the lines suggested by the papacy. They are however meant to convey an inkling of the terrific job we have to face."[11]

Briefs was not the only member of the ICC to criticize aspects of McGowan's paper. Jesuit Benjamin Masse also found misplaced emphasis. Masse questioned McGowan's insistence that there be a widely distributed ownership of productive property. "It seems to me," he opined, "that in a modern industrial society the majority of the people never will own any productive property, unless indirectly through their insurance policies. I would hate to think that they are thus deprived of something essential to economic freedom." Like John Courtney Murray, for whom the experience of the Church in America called into question the conventional articulation of church-state theory, Masse was led by the experience of workers in the United States to rethink the conventional insistence on a wide distribution of productive property. "In contemporary society," he observed, "many people enjoy economic freedom who own no productive property, never expect to, and don't want to." It was important, he admitted, that, "enough people own productive property to give a private-property character to the society. I think that would satisfy Pius XII." It was assumed, moreover, that workers would share indirectly in the "riches of nature," through a living wage.[12]

Masse's stance vis-à-vis industrialization is noteworthy. In this instance, there is no call to return to medieval economic structures, no exhortation to reorder modern economy fundamentally. Instead, Masse accepts the modern situation as a given and strives to achieve the goals of Catholic social teaching within those parameters.

Goetz Briefs was more explicit in his refusal to participate in advocacy of a return to a guild-like economic system. In another communication to the ICC, Briefs objected to a report distributed to the members. "I am afraid we might be accused of medievalism and neo-feudalism." He pointed to the industrial groups recommended by the reports, groups that apparently would have the backing of legal compulsion: "All this sounds like feudalism adapted to modern conditions." Undoubtedly, "feudalism adopted to modern conditions" was exactly what some Catholic thinkers had in mind; Briefs read the encyclicals as calling for nothing of the sort. "However it may be," he warned, "one cannot avoid the shortcomings of the guilds in the Middle Ages by having the modern equivalent operate in a frame of public policy."[13]

Briefs also thought that the importance of competition was given inadequate attention: "Cooperation and competition belong together: in the framework of cooperation there should be room for a degree of competition. Let us not ignore that competition itself is a form of cooperation; it has its function in the rule of the game precisely for purposes of cooperation."[14] Here was a controversial claim for an American Catholic social theorist, whose colleagues had more often derided the competitive, individualist American system. Briefs's view did not represent a facile acceptance of individualism, however, as is obvious when coupling his remarks here with his earlier comments in response to McGowan's memo. Competition, in tandem with the market, had a role in the economy not because it was good for its own sake, but because it served the end of the common good. In short, in a rightly ordered society, good citizens would cooperate by competing.

Briefs also criticized the report for insufficiently addressing the role of "technological and economic ingenuity, of business organization, of managerial function." "Natural resources and labor are not all," he continued. "Unless technology and management organize them rationally, they are just potentialities, not actualities of wealth."[15]

Finally, Briefs summarized his objections by imputing to the report an idealistic tenor that did not square with the tradition of Catholic thought on social questions:

> I cannot share the optimism which permeates the report. To the social order is ascribed smooth social cooperation, maximum output, and just distribution. . . . I think we should not indulge in such Utopian expectations. . . . We Catholics should be realists. . . . Under modern conditions the rational use of scarce means is very complex and complicated. More than one judgment is possible and can be vindicated.[16]

Briefs's assertion notwithstanding, some Catholic thinkers insisted that certain judgments on economic issues were beyond the pale of acceptability. In

1950, Edward Keller published *Christianity and Capitalism*, an expansion of his views expressed in the *Ave Maria* series. Joseph Fitzpatrick, S.J., attacked Keller's statement of compatibility between capitalism and Christianity. Fitzpatrick was astounded that Keller seemed "to be unaware of the rather general agreement of Catholic scholars on particular economic and political questions on which he expresses a contrary opinion." Fitzpatrick wrote wryly: "To anyone who wishes to remain quite satisfied with American Big Business as it is, or rather as it would be without Big Government and Big Labor, the book will offer great support and consolation."[17]

Viewing big labor and big government as antidotes to the evils of big business, Fitzpatrick had no sympathy for Keller's assessment of the positive role of business. Keller admitted that reform was necessary to effect the realization of a "Christian social order" but he insisted that such reforms "would not require radical changes in the institutions of American Capitalism." There was the danger, moreover, that reform too quickly or radically undertaken might end in fascism or communism, "which would be worse than allowing our present system to continue unchanged."[18] Keller continued in the tradition of both American Catholic social thought and American conservatism by tempering the enthusiasm of reform with caution against radicalism.

A possible indication of convergence of Catholic and American conservatism appears in Keller's views finding a hearing among the sometimes-critics of capitalism at the Catholic Central Verein. In a series of articles in the *Social Justice Review* (changed from *Central Blatt and Social Justice* in 1940), Keller upheld the validity of profit-making in the American economy. The prominent role of Catholics such as William Buckley in the blossoming conservative movement has led one historian to surmise, "The new conservatism was, in part, an intellectual cutting edge of the postwar 'coming of age' of America's Catholic minority."[19]

If Catholics could be seen, in general, to be moving increasingly toward sympathy with conservative viewpoints on economic questions, American conservatism remained a problematic candidate for a potential synthesis with Catholic teaching. One problem is that conservatism itself was not a unified school of thought. In historian John Diggins's estimation, "In no discipline were the differences greater than in economics, which encompassed the corporatist capitalism of Peter Drucker, the classical laissez-faire school of Friedman, and the anarcho-libertarianism of Murray Rothbard."[20]

Even among Catholics identified with conservative politics, views toward capitalism varied widely. If Edward Keller and William Buckley were enthusiastic about the character of the American economic system, Frederick Wilhelmsen and Garry Wills were equally skeptical of its compatibility with Catholic social teaching. Some approaches to economic questions gained little traction, even among conservative Catholics, such as the strict libertarianism and individualism represented by Murray Rothbard and Ayn Rand.[21]

While some Catholics were solidifying their place in the conservative movement, others were becoming more closely identified with the political and economic viewpoints of the left. One indication of this bifurcation occurred in the editorial decisions of the Jesuit journal *America*. Friedrich Baerwald attacked Keller's economics in a 1954 piece, and in 1955, *America* ceased accepting for publication the work of Russell Kirk and Erik von Kuehnelt-Leddihn, who had previously contributed. The pair had begun writing for *National Review*.[22]

John Cronin

Even within the Social Action Department of the NCWC, a shift toward greater appreciation of the market system was noticeable. The shift was reflected in John Cronin's tenure as assistant director of the SAD through the late fifties. Having already established his reputation as a thorough and serious student of economics in his earlier work, he focused his efforts on applying Catholic social teaching to the American situation.

Cronin began by revealing his adherence to traditional Catholic approaches to the economy. The main problem of economic life was its disorganization, he claimed, its lack of "organic" unity. The consequent concentration of wealth and power led to calls for increasing state power, which only compounded existing problems. What was needed, instead, was the "diffusion of economic power" so as to promote "real personal independence." The tendency to increasing concentration of wealth and power was, at root, a "moral and spiritual" problem. Cronin did not single out any segment of society for blame: business, government, labor, and farmers all suffered from the same tendency to self-aggrandizement at the expense of the common good. Social justice required acting in concert, as organized groups rather than individuals.[23]

Economic life, in Cronin's outline, was divided into three "phases." The technical phase of production and distribution, he explained, "leans heavily upon the physical sciences and is in turn governed by physical law." The organization of resources is an economic problem, "regulated by the laws of economics." The third phase encompassed the direction of organization and the use of physical instruments, which "can often be a moral problem, subject to the dictates of ethics and religion." When all three were "properly coordinated and subordinated," he concluded, "we have a smoothly running economic system."[24]

Cronin believed that there were economic laws, such as supply and demand, that, though knowledge of their working may be limited, "may not be flouted." This being the case, "ethical demands must be framed within the limits of economic as well as physical possibility." In addition to economic laws, however, economic life is governed by "patterns of organization" (socialism, various forms of capitalism), which may influence the range of available possibilities for economic action.[25]

With respect to the Church's social teaching, Cronin was clear: "The Church teaches moral law, not economics." This fact did not excuse individual Catholics from the obligation to apply ethical principles to concrete situations. "At the same time," he continued,

> In making such concrete applications, they must know their place. They can no longer speak unequivocally for the Church. There is always a margin of error, due to the limitations of their own prudential judgment. On this level there is disagreement between Catholics applying identical principles. Disputes at this stage cannot normally be resolved by an appeal to authority, but must be settled on the merits of the concrete issues.[26]

Cronin distinguished what was and was not binding within the social encyclicals based on the wording of the teaching. If the expression of a particular point were intended to be authoritative, it would be stated in a way so as to make this clear. A recommendation, on the other hand, would be more provisionally stated.[27]

Cronin continued to exhibit his earlier trademark by attempting to stake out a middle ground between apologists for capitalism and radical reformers. He rejected the position that the current system, though imperfect, was better than any conceivable alternative, considering such a view as showing "a deep pessimism in regard to the improvement of human institutions, or else a shallow optimism regarding our achievements thus far."[28]

Ambivalent about the status quo, Cronin nonetheless cautioned against facile recourse to supposed halcyon eras of economic utopia located in the past. Industrial organization with its attendant phenomena of specialization and division of labor could not be rejected out of hand, since they were necessary for sustaining the exponentially increasing population of the modern world. Nor should agrarian economies be romanticized, he instructed: Farming itself was not devoid of tedium. "The scribes who copied out medieval manuscripts," he added, "would probably have welcomed a typewriter, even if it meant a stint at the assembly line to produce one."[29]

Cronin criticized the contemporary American economy, but his target was *individualism* rather than *capitalism*. Individualism he explained, which had been regnant in large industrial nations (especially the United States), was marked by widespread belief that there is no role for the state in economic life, that wealth is an end in itself rather than a means to other ends, and that the individual has no social responsibilities. Competition, he added, following Pius XI, cannot be the "ruling principle of economic life" or the "sole regulating principle in the business field." A major problem with competition, in Cronin's estimation, was its intrinsic insecurity—its inability to provide a hedge against depression.[30]

Cronin's analysis was dependent on certain economic assumptions. The nature of the causes of and remedies for business cycle troughs had been a matter of debate in economics for decades.[31] In addition, Cronin's perception that Pius XI's condemnation of "economic dictatorship" applied to the United States was dependent on a historical interpretation of the nineteenth century that was reflected most famously in Matthew Josephson's *The Robber Barons*, but which remains open to question and qualification.[32]

Cronin's engagement of contemporary historical and economic literature was indicated further in the course of his description of the organic economic system that he proposed as an improvement. Disagreeing with those who viewed the papal program as far-fetched in the American context, Cronin argued that well-known mainstream American economists had proposed similar ideas. John Maurice Clark, for instance, in *Alternative to Serfdom* (1947), elaborated economic reform that depended on nongovernmental social institutions.[33]

The economic reform gleaned from social encyclicals looked more feasible to Cronin because he was less radical than others in his appropriation of that reform. His appreciation of industrialization has already been mentioned. He also recognized the value of competition and allowed latitude regarding its being circumscribed: "The determining of the proper limits of competition is a prudential matter, to be handled under the principles of social justice." The social institutions ("industry councils") that were to be the engine of reform, moreover, were not to possess political power, he declared.[34]

Other Catholic thinkers, most notably Frederick Kenkel, had made similar claims with respect to the intermediate institutions that would organize a cooperative economy. Cronin seemed more aware, however, of the difficulty of creating and maintaining such groups in the context of the American situation. The relationship between government and the industry councils, Cronin admitted, was a "delicate" one. Government must foster the councils and provide "general regulatory power for the sake of the common good," but must not simultaneously dominate or absorb the councils. The overall result, he joined with Kenkel and other corporatists in claiming, would be decentralization and the diminution of state power, as the councils would take on some of the economic functions currently lodged in government.[35]

Again, Cronin's interpretation of the industry council plan demonstrated his critical but essential acceptance of the American system. The plan did not imply drastic changes in the economy, he judged: "In most cases it would involve merely broadening the functions and perspectives of existing groups." The immediate task, he explained further, "is to minimize selfishness and stimulate concern for the common good in present-day trade unions, employers' associations, professional groups, and farmers' organizations." He distanced himself explicitly from commentators such as John Ryan and Francis Haas, arguing that industrial councils should not exert extensive economic controls; wages and prices would be justly set by the market within the cooperative environment created by the councils.[36]

Cronin's departure from Ryan's views was further evident in his discussion of wages. He shared Ryan's view that a living wage was the right of a worker, but he qualified the obligation on the part of the employer to honor it fully. In some cases, including the employer's inability to pay or insufficient productivity of workers, the employer would not be morally compelled to offer a living wage. Cronin thus more tightly bound the paying of a living wage with productivity. He made clear that the feasibility of the living wage depended not primarily on government mandate but on increasing productivity.[37]

The shift in emphasis from distribution to productivity marked Cronin's departure from Ryan's work. Cronin did not strictly disavow Ryan's dependence on Hobson's underconsumption theory, but he observed, "Economists today are approaching a synthesis between the classical and the underconsumption theories." Government pump priming was widely accepted, he wrote, but business crises could not be blamed entirely on maldistribution of income.[38]

Moderately critical of Ryan, Cronin was more pointed in his assessment of various other American Catholic interpreters of the social teaching, including Paul Hanly Furfey and, more emphatically, the Catholic Worker. Both overspiritualized the faith, Cronin thought, not allowing sufficiently for a worldly vocation. "We must sanctify and transform this world, not flee from it," he declared. "We need apostles as well as martyrs."[39]

Cronin also presented a careful account of the often-polemical term, *capitalism*. According to "general American usage," he observed, capitalism connoted private ownership, free enterprise, the profit motive, and the use of invested funds by a significant portion of business enterprise. Attachment of the term to these morally acceptable aspects of the American system rendered European condemnations of capitalism unintelligible to Americans. With the American definition in hand, Cronin argued, it was false to make statements such as "The Church condemns capitalism and communism alike."[40]

The consonance of Cronin's basic acceptance of the American system with Catholic social teaching received confirmation from Oswald von Nell-Breuning, a key adviser in the drafting of Pius XI's 1931 encyclical *Quadragesimo Anno*. Nell-Breuning wrote to Cronin that the social order envisioned by Pius "does not only conform to the free governmental system of the United States, but also to the free concept of economy which is accepted by large groups of employers and employees in the United States."[41]

Still, Cronin cannot be categorized as an ally of Edward Keller. He was sympathetic with Keller's effort to correct distortions of Catholic teaching by the political left, but he found fault with some of Keller's analysis as well. Keller's treatment, in Cronin's opinion, left the impression that the encyclicals endorsed the status quo and portrayed wealth distribution as being fairer than it actually was. Additionally, Cronin objected to Keller's defense of the 1920s, asserting, "certainly the dominant mentality was individualistic."[42]

Right-to-Work Debate

Keller's own focus shifted in the later 1950s from income distribution to unionism. Labor unions had enjoyed substantial support from American Catholics since their inception in modern form in the 1870s. Cardinal James Gibbons interceded on behalf of the Knights of Labor to prevent Vatican condemnation of the group as a secret society. Early scattered opposition primarily among Poles and Germans notwithstanding, by 1900, Catholic support of unionism was virtually unanimous. During the progressive era, Catholics made up a majority of union membership. By the 1930s, some bishops had established training programs for their priests, who were then assigned to full-time work in the labor movement. They added to the ranks of the "labor priests," who included such prominent figures as John Boland, Charles Rice, and George Higgins. In 1937, the Catholic presence in the labor movement was institutionalized in the Association of Catholic Trade Unionists.[43]

In some quarters, the identification of unionism with Catholic social teaching persisted, even to the present. Consensus on that position, however, began to erode substantially in the 1950s. Part of the impetus for the reconsideration that occurred was the meteoric growth of union membership in the decade following the validation of the Wagner Act by the Supreme Court (1937). Among Catholics and non-Catholics alike, there were those who viewed the increasing clout of organized labor with alarm.[44]

The immediate cause of a voluminous debate among Catholics was the state-level proposal—and, in many places, passing—of so-called "right-to-work" laws. Federal law, encoded in the Railway Labor Act (1926), the Wagner Act (1935), and the Taft-Hartley Act (1947) and interpreted by the courts, outlawed the closed union shop but permitted other forms of union security arrangements, such as the agency shop (requiring a worker to pay dues after he is hired). With passage of Taft-Hartley, however, the states were explicitly granted the privilege of legislatively forbidding almost any union security arrangement.[45] Proponents of such prohibitions, such as Keller, touted the laws as preserving the freedom of workers not to join unions as a condition of employment (i.e., "right-to-work").

Keller believed that voluntary unionism was necessary to protect Catholic workers from the spiritual dangers attendant with joining the main American unions. Besides the strong presence of communists and organized crime within the unions, he warned, there was also the political activism conducted by the unions, which often conflicted with the political preferences of individual members. Catholic members, he argued, should not be forced to support financially an organization's activities that are at odds with the members' political or moral judgments.[46]

Keller allied with the political right on this issue. Barry Goldwater, U.S. senator from Arizona and future Republican presidential candidate, wrote to the priest-economist in 1958 to thank him for his work on the issue. He appreciated Keller's "putting in words my position on voluntary unionism" and admitted plagiarizing from Keller's book for the purposes of a Senate speech on the topic.[47] Keller, for his part, privately supported Goldwater's bid for the presidency in 1964.[48]

In a letter to James Wick, editor of the conservative periodical *Human Events*, moreover, Keller indicated that he self-identified with the conservative movement in American politics. At the same time, the Notre Dame professor was circumspect about making public his political views. Asked by the conservative group Americans for Constitutional Action to join their organization, Keller wrote Notre Dame president and fellow Holy Cross priest Theodore Hesburgh about the matter. Hesburgh was of the opinion that such membership was acceptable, but Keller decided not to join after all, citing the canon law imperative that priests "eschew politics."[49]

A man of decided political positions, Keller was cautious about the public impression created by a cleric identifying with particular candidates or political movements. With respect to his political participation, then, he occupied ground somewhere between John Ryan and Virgil Michel. At one end of a spectrum was Michel, who seldom commented on any particular political item but articulated broad principles that were theologically expressed. At the other end was Charles Coughlin, who was direct and reckless in his political engagement, attacking politicians by name and practically creating a political party of his own. Closer to Coughlin than Michel (though closer to Michel in terms of his alignment with the political left), John Ryan did not engage in politics as directly as the radio priest, but he did defend Roosevelt publicly and participated in his administration. Keller, then, occupying a broad middle ground with Ryan, articulated ideas with direct political relevance, but remained closer to Michel than Coughlin because he refused to align himself publicly with any politician or political group.

In a piece written for fellow priests in the *Homiletic and Pastoral Review*, Keller continued his advocacy of voluntary unionism. The central claim buttressing Keller's case was his insistence that the nature of the union had changed over the course of the previous half-century. "The opposition to voluntary unionism by so many Catholic social scientists," he postulated, "can be attributed to an uncritical attitude toward modern unionism which results in a failure to comprehend the significant changes that have occurred in the past generation in the union movement."[50] Far from being weak institutions needing government protection and encouragement, Keller observed, unions had become powerful and capable of running roughshod over not only employers but workers as well, particularly those who wished not to join the union.

Although Keller was decidedly in favor of right-to-work laws, his main targets were not those who merely did not share his enthusiasm and remained neutral, but instead, those who declared that Catholic social teaching called for opposition to such legislation. On that score, Keller cited the backing of American Catholic theologians, such as Gerard Rooney, C.P., and Francis J. Connell, C.S.S.R., dean of Catholic University's school of theology. Keller's quotation of Connell articulated the pivotal distinction: The principle of Catholic social teaching at issue was the right of workers to form organizations to further their welfare. Whether right-to-work laws supported or vitiated this principle was open to debate. Well-meaning Catholics might agree on the principle, then, yet disagree as to the desirability of right-to-work legislation. Both positions of support for and opposition to such laws, Connell (and Keller) insisted, were compatible with Catholic social teaching.[51]

Keller also marshaled evidence in support of the contention that right-to-work legislation had as its aim the protection of individual workers, not the emasculation of labor unions. The average increase in union membership among states that had outlawed compulsory unionism, Keller observed, was greater than that among states without such laws.[52] Unions did not need the union shop mechanism, in Keller's estimation, either to survive or to remain a vital force in American industry.

A Jesuit priest and University of Detroit professor, John Coogan, took the pro-legislation argument to the pages of the *American Ecclesiastical Review.* Like Keller, Coogan was particularly distressed at the claims by labor priests that the authentic Catholic position must be one in favor of the union shop. Coogan, too, cited Connell's judgment that Catholics were free to disagree on this matter. Coogan's article emphasized the theological dimension of the union problem, harkening to the early-twentieth-century popes' stress on Catholic organizations and only-grudging concession to secular unions. For Coogan, non-Catholic unions, for which "secularism is almost their breath of life," represented an increasing danger to Catholics' faith. This secularism manifested itself in the generally low contemporary moral state of union leadership, methods, and goals, and seeming indifference to the common good.[53]

Other Catholic scholars corroborated the claim that the character of unions had changed dramatically since the time of their formation. In *Unionism Reappraised: From Unionism to Union Establishment*, Goetz Briefs argued that the character of American unions had changed qualitatively since the early twentieth century when they had to fight for their existence and for acceptance. Briefs believed that unions in 1960 enjoyed immense power but had failed to consider the responsibilities that were entailed by the possession of that power. Like Keller, Briefs thought that union wage scales were generally excessively high, compared to product demand and the national balance of payment. This artificial inflation of wages, he complained, while serving the interests of union members, had a detrimental effect on the national economy.[54]

With national power, however, the unions must consider the national economic impact of their actions, Briefs insisted. Unions were at a crossroads, he observed. Their options were to "fashion a new economic order in their own image," or to "adjust their programs and policies to those leeways for union action which an efficient free enterprise economy periodically widens and contracts." If unions chose the former course, he warned, free enterprise would be destroyed and "unions would have won their battle, but the workingmen and workingwomen might discover that they had lost the war."[55]

Briefs was neither an ardent foe of unions nor an apologist for laissez-faire capitalism. He denounced the nineteenth-century brand of liberalism that argued that society can function without regulation or institutional structure and that "natural" economic laws supersede social rules. It was the rise of this kind of liberal mindset among business leaders, according to Briefs, that in turn led to the initial need for unions. The development of an antagonistic relationship between unions and business, he explained, could not be blamed on the unions, but instead was the result of a reaction by the unions to the decline of ethical behavior among businessmen—a real decline occasioned by their acceptance of a liberal ideology that placed self-interest and competition at the pinnacle of the business values hierarchy.[56]

Unions, then, had as their original impetus a valid desire to fill the "vacuum" created by the "absence of established social standards and institutions" that could curtail the abuses of capitalists and harmonize the interests of labor and capital. Liberals were wrong, Briefs contended, in thinking that economic competition automatically delivered justice to everyone.[57]

The vacuum that unions perceived, then, was real, Briefs determined. "Whether or not they were intrinsically suited to fill the vacuum," he continued, "is another question." With this hint of doubt cast, Briefs offered his interpretation of the decreasing value of the social role played by American unions. The era of "classical unionism" in the United States ended with the New Deal, he argued, and by the 1940s there had occurred a shift to union establishment. "It is no longer true," wrote Briefs, "that the union presupposes the worker, the worker the job, and the job the private employer.... The balance has been shifted in favor of union power over worker and employer alike."[58]

With union establishment, Briefs continued, there developed a "divorce of concerted action and group liability." This separation "shrouds the consequences of concerted action in a veil of anonymity," a development that foreshadows the next predictable step: "the cry for government intervention."[59] To avoid these undesirable outcomes, Briefs argued, there must be some connection made between union actions (e.g., on wages) and the economy-wide impact of those actions (e.g., on price levels).

Briefs's central concern, then, was that organized labor in the United States, created to serve an important need, had failed to develop institutionally in a way that would preserve its value to society. "Formerly designed to protect members," he wrote, "the large union of today is equally if not primarily concerned with its institutional survival and expansion." "The two concerns," he added, "may go together and, again, they may not."[60]

Despite scattered counterexamples such as Keller, Coogan, and Briefs, most Catholic commentators on the issue remained firmly pro-union.[61] The degree to which there was consensus led some to overstate the case.[62] Others made careful arguments in opposition to right-to-work laws.

J. R. Dempsey's defense of compulsory unionism is a good example of such an argument and demonstrates the ways in which different interpretations of the contemporary situation of organized labor influenced positions on the right-to-work debate. Dempsey, pace Keller's claim that right-to-work laws were not intended to endanger unions, argued that opponents viewed the union shop, unionism, and collective bargaining as standing or falling together. This view, Dempsey, observed, had been borne out in practice, as right-to-work laws had been extended by court decisions to prohibit not only coercive union member-ship but also other union activities, such as picketing.[63]

Tendentiously pointing out that right-to-work laws had been supported mainly by business interests (without noting who had been their main oppo-nents), Dempsey nonetheless allowed that some advocates had favored the laws on the basis of principle rather than self-interest. At the same time, he argued that such laws had pinned some employers in a dilemma: They could honor the laws and face business-damaging union picketing, or they could ignore the laws and face government fines.[64]

Ultimately, Dempsey's assessment of the contemporary state of unionism and the impact of right-to-work laws led him to a judgment contrary to that of Keller and Briefs. Laws against compulsory unionism would destroy unionism altogether, he predicted, thereby abrogating the right of free association upheld by Catholic social teaching.[65] Dempsey's presentation was, then, an instance of the kind of that debate Keller considered valid: Dempsey shared devotion to the principle of association but thought that right-to-work laws undermined rather than promoted that principle.

The CEA in the Fifties

The Catholic Economics Association (CEA) continued to host a variety of view-points through the 1950s. Thomas Divine defended the assumptions of orthodox theory, while Bernard Dempsey and others offered heterodox treatments of eco-nomic issues based explicitly on papal encyclicals. The connection between ethics and economics remained an important topic. In 1955, an entire issue of the *Review* was devoted to the question of the role of moral judgments in economic analysis.[66]

Gradually, however, the more orthodox contingent gained ascendancy within the organization. By the end of the decade, people within the association noticed the shift and the observation led to an interrogation of the association's purpose for existence. Cornelius Eller's incisive 1958 article encapsulated and prefigured the set of concerns that would trouble—and sometimes transform—all Catholic scholarly organizations over the course of the following decade.[67]

Some of the CEA's convention programs, Eller observed, "appear to differ very little, if at all, from those of the American Economics Association." Moral analysis, Eller worried, was not central enough to the CEA's programs. Importantly, however, Eller's call was not one of separatism. The point of the CEA from the beginning, he argued, was to complement the AEA. If its focus and methods simply mirrored the AEA, then it became not complementary but competitive—or, more likely, simply redundant.[68]

Eller proposed, then, that the CEA be broadened to include "*everyone* who is interested in the relations between economics and morals." The CEA, in Eller's vision, would not be composed of economists who happened to be Catholics, but of economists who wanted to investigate a particular dimension of economics. It was a vision that in some ways saw its realization by the end of the following decade, when the ranks of orthodox economists had thinned. The society changed its name to the Association of Social Economics and the main point of commonality shifted from Catholicism to criticism of mainstream economics.[69]

Catholics Against Communism

The role of 1950s anticommunism in making Catholicism more respectable to mainstream America has been well recognized.[70] Significant for present purposes is the relationship between Catholic participation in anticommunist thought and Catholic views on economics. The first point to be made in this connection is that, for most Catholics, opposition to communism proceeded from theological—not economic—tenets.

The second is that, even as economics was not central to Catholic opposition, Catholic cooperation with American anticommunism helped to move at least some Catholics toward a more benign view of the capitalist economy. As antifascism had contributed to the discrediting of economic corporatism (perceived to be connected to fascism), so anticommunism abetted the discrediting of leftist economic views more generally (perceived to be connected to communism). A young William F. Buckley Jr., articulated succinctly the linking of religion and economics: "I myself believe that the duel between Christianity and atheism is the most important in the world. I further believe that the struggle between individualism and collectivism is the same struggle reproduced on another level."[71]

American intellectuals in general were compelled to line up on one side or the other of Buckley's antinomy. This trend (noted in the previous chapter) more often than not led to scholars' viewing America, and American capitalism more specifically, more favorably than they had in the past. A 1952 symposium in one of the left's premier publications, *Partisan Review*, indicated the trajectory of American thought. In the last decade, the introductory editorial observed, a shift had occurred among the American elite: "Many writers and intellectuals now feel closer to their country and its culture." There was a recognition, it continued, "that the kind of democracy which exists in America has an intrinsic and positive value: It is not merely a capitalist myth but a reality which must be defended against Russian totalitarianism."[72] For an increasing number of liberal intellectuals, including former antagonists such as Sidney Hook, Soviet Communism easily overtook Catholicism in the 1950s as the major threat to American democracy.[73]

Catholic friendliness toward Will Herberg evinced the changing situation. An ardent anticommunist, Herberg also provided optimistic Catholics an example of a prominent American intellectual who recognized that the strife with communism was fundamentally religious in nature. In 1954, Herberg gave a speech to the National Conference on the Spiritual Foundations of American Democracy. The event, opined the Jesuit editor of *Thought*, was "one of the most noteworthy of a series of recent indications that the nation is increasingly concerned, at this critical time in history, to examine its own meaning and religious roots." Herberg's speech, he continued, was "one of the highest moments of the meeting."[74]

With Catholics, Herberg argued, "At its deepest level, the conflict between Soviet Communism and the free world is a religious conflict.... Quite literally, it is a struggle for the soul of modern man." Herberg also shared the Catholic (and neoorthodox Protestant) belief in original sin and its consequences. He warned against the proclivity to pursue utopias, "to idolize ourselves and our works, to attribute quite uncritically final significance to our institutions."[75]

Instead of the utopian scheme of communism, which refused to recognize the consequences of the fallen nature of man, Herberg urged a reinvigoration of biblical faith. Such faith "calls upon man never to rest so long as there is evil in the world, but warns him against deluding himself into believing that it is by his hand or in his time that the work can be completed." It was this biblical faith, moreover, that "in however diluted and secularized a form, has served as the underlying dynamic of the vast movement for social reform that is perhaps the chief glory of western civilization." Secular folk who were in favor of goals such as social justice and equality, in Herberg's estimation, were pursuing ends that had their underpinnings in the Judeo-Christian tradition. Their activities might be laudable, but their failure to recognize the connections to religion rendered them dangerously susceptible to utopianism, which led to totalitarianism. Herberg, the ex-Communist turned devout Jew, should know—it had happened to him.[76]

Ironically, as Herberg was pointed to as an example of the recovery of America's religious roots, Herberg himself was less sanguine about the religious revival being detected around him. In another Catholic vehicle, a book edited by Notre Dame history professor Thomas McAvoy, Herberg warned against seeing gratuitous displays of religiosity as indicative of genuine embrace of religion. Catholicism and Judaism had joined Protestantism in the ranks of respectable and fully accepted American religious traditions. The result, however, had in some ways been the diminishment of the potency of these faiths.[77]

Herberg pointed to the popularity of Fulton Sheen as evidence of the capitulation of Catholicism to the American civil religion. Herberg may have misread Sheen on this point. Sheen did not in fact, mute his Catholicism in the interest of appealing to non-Catholics. He was, moreover, adamantly anticommunist on religious, not political or economic, grounds.[78]

The issue of Herberg's interpretation of Sheen aside, Herberg's question remained pointed: How could Catholicism be a fully American religion without succumbing to becoming merely one strand of an American civil religion?

Although economic issues were not at the heart of Herberg's critique of communism, increasing numbers of Catholics were turning away from New Deal liberalism and toward the kind of conservative economic views that Herberg and his colleagues held. It is difficult, of course, to locate precisely the causes of this turn, but it seems plausible that one factor was the shifting allegiances of anticommunism. The previous chapter already noted the stream of formerly communist intellectuals who found their way into the conservative movement. Some of these, such as Herberg, rediscovered the power of religious faith in the process and became allies of Catholics against the secularization of American culture.

There was no similar phenomenon on the Left. Although many leftist thinkers reasserted the value of democracy and made more evident their anticommunist credentials, their intellectual development did not involve public celebrations of religion and assertions of its indispensability as the foundation of democracy, freedom, and the American way of life. Brought into communication with American conservatism by anticommunism and antisecularism, Catholics would begin to find conservative economic arguments more convincing, too.

Jacques Maritain is not usually considered a member of the American conservative movement, but his reflections on capitalism can be seen as part of the broader trend of diminishing skepticism toward the American economic system. Maritain, resident in the United States since leaving France in 1940, was respected in both Catholic and non-Catholic circles. With his European origins, Thomistic credentials, and secular appeal, Maritain's opinions carried enormous weight among American Catholics, who considered his a voice at once authentically Catholic and intellectually sophisticated.[79]

In a wide-ranging commentary published in 1958, Maritain addressed Americans as their (not uncritical) defender against the stereotypes of the European elite. In the United States, he had discovered, there obtained a situation historically unique: The "gigantically developed" industrial civilization was "by a strange paradox" paired with "the most humane and the least materialist among modern peoples which had reached the industrial stage." The tension between the people and the system within which they lived, Maritain concluded, "is transforming from within the inner dynamism and historical trends of the industrial regime. It is causing this regime to pass beyond capitalism."[80]

Maritain did not downplay the harmful aspects of American life, including racism, the tendency toward a facile optimism, and the commodification of ideas. He argued, however, that two phenomena were in the process of transforming the structure of the American economy into a system that promoted rather than undermined the common good. The first factor, the growth of organized labor into a power that "confronts big corporations as an equal," had made possible a decent standard of living for American workers.[81]

The second development was the evolution of industry and management. The rise of arrangements such as profit-sharing, the "proddings" of government regulations, the systematic planning provided by company economists, and the spread of humane management practices had contributed to the "old merciless struggles between management and labor" giving way to "a new relationship in which the antagonisms are still basically serious, but in the last analysis are reduced to a kind of cooperative tension. . . ." In light of these developments, Maritain suggested, while "Capitalism" remained indefensible, the system Americans defended could no longer meaningfully be denoted by that name.[82]

The Sixties

The election of 1960 was a ratification of Herberg's *Protestant, Catholic, Jew* thesis. It represented the exorcism of the demons of 1928 and solidified Catholicism's place in American society. At the same time, the vehemence with which Kennedy was compelled to denounce religion's role in his public life reflected the domestication of Catholicism that Herberg feared would be necessary to effect that solidification. In this sense, it is not coincidence that the nation's first Catholic president would also come to be called the "first completely secular American President."[83] Catholic response to the Kennedy campaign also reflected continued diversity in Catholic political and economic views. Conservative Catholics did not rally around the Democratic candidate on the basis of religion; they opposed him on political and economic grounds.[84]

Some perceived the increasing vituperation between Catholic liberals and conservatives as damaging to the potential for a unified Catholic program of social reform. *Ave Maria* editor Donald Thorman, for instance, called for a truce between the two camps for the purpose of supporting a common program based on areas of agreement.[85]

The release of *Mater et Magistra* in 1961, however, did not contribute to a more unified front on economic question issues. Among non-Catholic conservatives, Will Herberg was miffed at what he saw as Pope John XXIII's capitulation to secular values in the pope's emphases on world peace and the drawbacks of capitalism. Conservatives such as Herberg and William F. Buckley Jr., joined liberals in misreading the pope's writings as indicative of a Vatican shift to the left, when viewing encyclicals through the lens of a left-right political spectrum was an intrinsically flawed eneterprise.[86]

The waves created by *Mater et Magistra*, however, turned out to be but ripples compared to what lay on the horizon. In 1962, the bishops of the world convened in Rome for the beginning of the defining event of twentieth-century Catholicism, the Second Vatican Council. New formulations of Church teaching on ecumenism and religious freedom, new emphasis on engagement of the world, and new liturgical norms confronted a 1960s American culture that was itself in the throes of change. As a result, American Catholicism before and after the decade of the sixties, in many ways, looked very different. The obvious changes overshadowed the essential continuity, but it is true that the range of disputed issues widened considerably. No longer was it only the application of papal teaching that was in question; instead, dissent from moral principles themselves became widespread. Discord regarding economic questions persisted.

Notes

1. Douglas T. Miller and Marion Nowak, *The Fifties: The Way We Really Were* (Garden City, N.Y.: Doubleday, 1977), 13. Quotes are from Miller and Nowak, 6–7; and from Paul Goodman, Michael Harrington, and Norman Mailer, quoted in Miller and Nowak, 6.

2. Miller and Nowak, *The Fifties*, 14–15. Paul A. Carter, *Another Part of the Fifties* (New York: Columbia University Press, 1983), is one more positive assessment of the 1950s. Chapter 6 contains evidence of cultural and intellectual vitality. For a good description of the period that captures the combination of fear and confidence, see Robert S. Ellwood, *1950: Crossroads of American Religious Life* (Louisville, Ky.: Westminster John Knox, 2000), chap. 1.

3. Jay P. Dolan, *The American Catholic Experience: A History from Colonial Times to the Present* (Garden City, N.Y.: Doubleday, 1985), 417.

4. Miller and Nowak, *The Fifties*, 88–89. On the growth of Protestant churches at the beginning of the decade, see Ellwood, *Crossroads*, chap. 5.

5. John Tracy Ellis, "American Catholics and the Intellectual Life," *Thought* 30 (Autumn 1955): 351–88. On the reaction to Ellis's essay, see Philip Gleason, *Contending with Modernity: Catholic Higher Education in the Twentieth Century* (New York: Oxford University Press, 1995), 287–88. O'Boyle is quoted in Miller and Nowak, *The Fifties*, 102.

6. On Catholic response to the Industry Council plan, see Aaron I. Abell, *American Catholicism and Social Action: A Search for Social Justice, 1865–1950* (Garden City, N.Y.: Hanover, 1960), 267–72.

7. G. A. Briefs, "Some Remarks to Father McGowan's Memorandum of October, 1950," CKEL 1/02. On the economic thought of the Late Scholastics, see Joseph A. Schumpeter, *History of Economic Analysis* (New York: Oxford University Press, 1954), 94–107; Bernard W. Dempsey, *Interest and Usury* (London: D. Dobson, 1948); Marjorie Grice-Hutchinson, *The School of Salamanca: Readings in Spanish Monetary History, 1544–1605* (Oxford: Clarendon Press, 1952), and *Early Economic Thought in Spain, 1177–1740* (London: Allen and Unwin, 1975); Alejandro A. Chafuen, *Faith and Liberty: The Economic Thought of the Late Scholastics* (Lanham, Md.: Lexington Books, 2003). For an example of Late Scholastic scholarship, see Juan de Mariana, S.J., "A Treatise on the Alteration of Money," trans. Patrick T. Brannan, S.J., *Journal of Markets & Morality* 5 (Fall 2002): 523–93.

8. G. A. Briefs, "Some Remarks to Father McGowan's Memorandum of October, 1950."

9. This view coincided with that of free-market economists such as Friedrich Hayek, which gained popularity in American conservative circles in the late 1940s; see George H. Nash, *The Conservative Intellectual Movement in America, Since 1945* (Wilmington, Del.: Intercollegiate Studies Institute, 1996), chap. 1. F. A. Hayek, *The Fatal Conceit:*

The Errors of Socialism, vol. 1 of *The Collected Works of F. A. Hayek*, ed. W. W. Bartley III (Chicago: University of Chicago Press, 1988), esp. chaps. 5–6.

10. G. A. Briefs, "Some Remarks to Father McGowan's Memorandum of October, 1950."

11. G. A. Briefs, "Some Remarks to Father McGowan's Memorandum of October, 1950."

12. Father Masse, untitled, undated typescript (evidently response to McGowan Memo, October 1950), CKEL 1/02.

13. G. A. Briefs, "Memorandum Concerning the Report of August 4," unpublished typescript, p. 3, CKEL 1/05.

14. Ibid., 2.

15. Ibid., 2.

16. Ibid., 3–4.

17. Fitzpatrick, "The Encyclicals and the United States: What of the Human Person?" *Thought* 29 (Autumn 1954): 392–96.

18. Keller, *Christianity and Capitalism* (Chicago: Heritage Foundation, 1953), 90, 92.

19. Keller's articles in *Social Justice Review* include: "Are Profits Too High?" *Social Justice Review* 43 (July–August 1950): 113–17; "The Morality of Profits," *Social Justice Review* 43 (September 1950): 147–49; "The Morality of Profits [continued]," *Social Justice Review* 43 (October 1950): 187–89; Nash, *Conservative Movement*, 71, 81. On Catholics and political conservatism in the 1950s, see also Patrick Allitt, *Catholic Intellectuals and Conservative Politics in America, 1950–1985* (Ithaca, N.Y.: Cornell University Press, 1993), chap. 2.

20. John P. Diggins, *Up from Communism: Conservative Odysseys in American Intellectual History* (New York: Harper and Row, 1975), 401.

21. Allitt, *Catholic Intellectuals*, 70–82. On Catholic conservatives' denunciations of Rothbard and Rand, see 73, 92–93.

22. Friedrich Baerwald, "Who Gets Our National Income?" *America*, April 17, 1948, 21–24; Allitt, *Catholic Intellectuals*, 89–90.

23. John F. Cronin, S.S., *Catholic Social Principles: The Social Teaching of the Catholic Church Applied to American Economic Life* (Milwaukee: Bruce Publishing Company, 1955), 25–27, 112ff. The book was updated, condensed, and republished as *Social Principles and Economic Life* (Milwaukee: Bruce Publishing Company, 1959).

24. Ibid., 51.

25. Ibid., 52–53.

26. Ibid., 54.

27. Ibid., 55–61. As an example of such a recommendation, Cronin cited paragraph number 65 in *Quadragesimo Anno*.

28. Ibid., 62.

29. Ibid., 85.

30. Ibid., 146–53.

31. Joseph Dorfman, *The Economic Mind in American Civilization*, 5 vols. (New York: Viking Press, 1959 [1949]), vol. 5, 727–37.

32. Cronin cites Josephson on 154. For challenges to the robber baron thesis, see Burton W. Folsom, Jr. *The Myth of the Robber Barons: A New Look at the Rise of Big Business in America*, 3d ed. (Herndon, Va.: Young America's Foundation, 1996); and Peter J. Hill and Seth Norton, "Nineteenth-Century Robber Barons and Their Impact on

Economic Welfare," unpublished paper, APEE Conference, Las Vegas Nevada, April 2003. Hill and Norton provide a summary of economic-historical studies that call into question the conventional robber baron depiction.

33. Cronin, *Catholic Social Principles*, 220.

34. Ibid., 153, 224.

35. Ibid., 224–25.

36. Ibid., 232, 237–53, 722.

37. Ibid., 351–79.

38. Ibid., 621–23.

39. Ibid., 684–92.

40. Ibid., 264–65.

41. Nell-Breuning to Cronin, October 22, 1950 (trans.), CKEL 1/03.

42. Cronin, *Catholic Social Principles*, 699–710.

43. Neil Betten, *Catholic Activism and the Industrial Worker* (Gainesville: University Presses of Florida, 1976), 9, 74, chaps. 5, 8. Gibbon's intercession in Rome has led at least one scholar to argue that the American Catholic experience of unionism influenced papal opinion toward a more favorable view of labor organization. Marvin L. Krier Mich, *Catholic Social Teaching and Movements* (Mystic, Conn.: Twenty-Third Publications, 1998), 17–18. For a summary of papal teaching and American episcopal views concerning unions, see Edward B. McLean, *Roman Catholicism and the Right to Work* (Lanham, Md.: University Press of America, 1985), chaps. 1–2. McLean's otherwise useful summaries lack a discussion of Catholic ecclesiology that would make an important distinction between the respective authoritative characters of papal and episcopal documents.

44. On the growth of unions, see Christopher L. Tomlins, *The State and the Unions: Labor Relations, Law, and the Organized Labor Movement in America, 1880–1960* (Cambridge: Cambridge University Press, 1985), 252. For a non-Catholic view of alarm, see Donald R. Richberg, *Labor Union Monopoly: A Clear and Present Danger* (Chicago: Henry Regnery, 1957).

45. Howard Dickman, *Industrial Democracy in America: Ideological Origins of National Labor Relations Policy* (La Salle, Ill.: Open Court, 1987), 9, 285; Tomlins, *State and Unions*, chap. 8.

46. Keller, "A Defense of Voluntary Unionism," unpublished manuscript, dated August 9, 1957, CKEL 1/24. See also Keller, *The Case for Right to Work Laws: A Defense of Volun-tary Unionism* (Washington: Heritage Foundation, 1956).

47. Barry Goldwater to Keller, February 5, 1958, KEL 1/18 "Barry Goldwater (1958–1970)."

48. See various correspondence between Keller and Goldwater in CKEL 1/18 "Barry Goldwater (1958–1970)." Goldwater wrote later that Keller, "has had a great deal to do with the shaping of my life and my philosophy." August 19, 1968, KEL 1/18 "Barry Goldwater (1958–1970)."

49. Keller to James L. Wick, December 11, 1963, KEL 1/13 "Father Keller's Personal Correspondence, 1961–1965." On the ACA invitation, see Keller's correspondence with Ben Morrell and Theodore Hesburgh, CKEL 1/13 "Father Keller's Personal Correspondence, 1961–1965."

50. Keller, "Right-to-Work Laws: Just and Beneficial," *Homiletic and Pastoral Review* 58 (October 1957): 34. Jerome L. Toner, O.S.B., offered an opposing view in the same issue of the *Review*, 59–71.

51. Keller, "Right-to-Work Laws," 38. Keller cites personal correspondence from Connell: Connell to Very Rev. Msgr. Philip M. Hannan, May 31, 1955.

52. Keller, "Right-to-Work Laws," 39. Subsequent studies have essentially corroborated Keller's claim, although some evidence suggests that right-to-work laws exert a small negative influence on initial organizing among non-union workers. William J. Moore and Robert J. Newman, "The Effects of Right-to-Work Laws: A Review of the Literature," *Industrial and Labor Relations Review* 38 (July 1985): 571–86; David T. Ellwood and Glenn Fine, "The Impact of Right-to-Work Laws on Union Organization," *Journal of Political Economy* 95 (April 1987): 250–73.

53. John E. Coogan, S.J., "Can Nothing Be Said for State 'Right to Work' Laws?" *American Ecclesiastical Review* 133 (December 1955): 370–76. For a list of Coogan's writings on the subject, see Edward B. McLean, *Roman Catholicism and the Right to Work* (Lanham, Md.: University Press of America, 1985), 161–62, nn. 6–13.

54. G. A. Briefs, *Unionism Reappraised: From Classical Unionism to Union Establishment* (Washington, D.C.: American Enterprise Association, 1960), 1–6.

55. Ibid., 7.

56. Ibid., 8–11, 17–19.

57. Ibid., 20.

58. Ibid., 20, 44.

59. Ibid., 47.

60. Ibid., 63.

61. McLean, *Roman Catholicism*, chap. 3. See also Abell, *American Catholicism*, 280–2, for a summary of the right-to-work debate in Catholic circles. The *Review of Social Economy* devoted an issue to the subject: *Review of Social Economy* 18 (March 1960).

62. Francis Downing, for instance, in a mid-century account of Catholics and unionism, practically equates organized labor with Catholic social teaching; "Catholic Contributions to the American Labor Movement," in *Church and Society: Catholic Social and Political Thought and Movements 1789–1950*, ed. Joseph N. Moody (New York: Arts, 1953), 845–904.

63. J. R. Dempsey, S.J., *The Operation of the Right-to-Work Laws* (Milwaukee, Wis.: Marquette University Press, 1961), 16, 52ff.

64. Ibid., 19–21, 27, 106.

65. Ibid., 127.

66. Divine, "On the Assumption of 'Rational Conduct' in Economic Science," *RSE* 8 (September 1950): 85–88; J. R. Dempsey, "The Worker as Person," *RSE* 12 (March 1954): 16–24; Geza B. Grosschmid, "Pesch's Concept of the Living Wage in *Quadragesimo Anno*," *RSE* 12 (September 1954): 147–55; *RSE* 13 (March 1955).

67. William R. Waters, "Evolution of Social Economics in America." In *Social Economics: Retrospect and Prospect*, ed. Mark Lutz (Boston: Kluwer Academic, 1990), 93–94; Cornelius A. Eller, S.J., "Is the CEA Achieving Its Purpose?" *RSE* 16 (September 1958): 69–73. Waters notes that Goetz Briefs, disillusioned with the shift away from solidarism, left the CEA shortly after he served as president in 1956 (91–92). On the crisis among Catholic scholarly organizations, see Gleason, *Contending with Modernity*, 319–20.

68. Eller, "Purpose," 70–71.

69. Eller, "Purpose," 71; Waters, "Social Economics," 91–92, 98–99.

70. Donald F. Crosby, S.J., *God, Church, and Flag: Senator Joseph P. McCarthy and the Catholic Church, 1950–1957* (Chapel Hill: University of North Carolina Press, 1978), 243–46; Paul A. Carter, *Another Part of the Fifties* (New York: Columbia University Press, 1983), 126–31.

71. William F. Buckley Jr., *God and Man at Yale* (Chicago: Henry Regnery, 1951), lx–lxi. Many Catholics rejected Buckley's analysis. See, for instance, Christopher Full-man, O.S.B., "God and Man and Mr. Buckley," *CW* 175 (May 1952): 104–8.

72. "Editorial Statement," *Partisan Review* 19 (May–June 1952): 282, 284. The symposium continues in the July–August 1952 and September–October 1952 issues.

73. John T. McGreevy, "Thinking on One's Own: Catholicism in the American Intellectual Imagination, 1928–1960," *Journal of American History* 84 (June 1997), 127–30.

74. "Editor's Note," preceding Will Herberg, "The Biblical Basis of American Democracy," *Thought* 30 (March 1955), 37.

75. Herberg, "Biblical Basis," 37–38.

76. Ibid. 43.

77. Herberg, "Religion and Culture in Present-Day America," in *Roman Catholicism and the American Way of Life*, ed. Thomas T. McAvoy, C.S.C. (Notre Dame, Ind.: University of Notre Dame Press, 1960), 4–19. The argument was a reprisal of that presented in *Protestant-Catholic-Jew: An Essay in American Religious Sociology* (Garden City, N.Y.: Doubleday, 1955).

78. Mark Massa, *Catholics and American Culture: Fulton Sheen, Dorothy Day, and the Notre Dame Football Team* (New York: Crossroad, 1999), 85, 96; Thomas C. Reeves, *America's Bishop: The Life and Times of Fulton J. Sheen* (San Francisco: Encounter Books, 2001). Many commentators have shared Herberg's view of Sheen as the Catholic equivalent of Norman Vincent Peale with respect to the creation of an American civil religion. See, for instance, Carter, *Another Part*, 131–34.

79. For various aspects of Maritain's life and thought, see *Understanding Maritain: Philosopher and Friend*, eds. Deal W. Hudson and Matthew J. Mancini (Macon, Ga.: Mercer University Press, 1987).

80. Jacques Maritain, *Reflections on America* (New York: Charles Scribner's Sons, 1958), 21–23.

81. Ibid., 31, 45–46, chap. 6, 101–3.

82. Ibid., 105–9.

83. Quoted in Massa, *Catholics and American Culture*, 5. On Kennedy's privatization of religion, see Massa, *Catholics and American Culture*, chap. 6.

84. Allitt, *Catholic Intellectuals*, 84–89.

85. Ibid., 91.

86. Diggins, *Up from Communism*, 363, 407. On the discord following *Mater et Magistra*, see Allitt, *Catholic Intellectuals*, 93–97.

CONCLUSION

Catholics genuinely devoted to the teachings of their Church have differed widely and strenuously over both how and whether those teachings apply to a particular political question. It is expected that this will continue to be the case. Points of doctrine, which Catholics are obliged to believe, must, therefore, always be sufficiently distinguished from fluid issues of economic and political judgment that are subject to the vicissitudes of changing data, circumstances, and political momentum. As these pages have indicated, this distinction has sometimes, but not always, been maintained adequately.[1]

This study has sought to elucidate the reasoning and, thereby, the lines of influence that led American Catholics to apply the social teachings of their Church in the ways that they did. In so doing, it has tried to avoid pigeonholing individual thinkers by lumping them in categories (such as "liberal") that do more to obscure than to clarify the positions taken and the reasons for doing so. Connections and allegiances among Catholic social thinkers shifted over time, along with the political and economic contexts in which their thought occurred.

The difficulty of establishing groupings is indicated, for instance, in the case of John Ryan and Frederick Kenkel. While Ryan considered Kenkel an ally, Kenkel was less enthusiastic about Ryan's work and grew more critical over the course of the 1930s. To split Catholic social thinkers in the period under question into two groups, such as "liberals" and "conservatives," involves insurmountable difficulties. It is at the least highly simplistic, for example, to combine under one heading such figures as John Ryan, Virgil Michel, Jacques Maritain, and Emmanuel Mounier.[2]

The engagement of the economic sphere by Catholics of the period examined in this study, like any such engagement, displayed both strengths and limitations. The "premodern" sensibility that characterized much of the work of Frederick Kenkel and Virgil Michel—and certain aspects of John Ryan's writing—was an important and insightful voice of reform in the early decades of the twentieth century. This approach to economic and social issues, with its appealing vision of an organic society based on shared theological values and characterized more by concord than competition, continues to attract adherents in the twenty-first century.

Historian Christopher Shannon, for instance, has argued for the need to detach from the contemporary "culture of irony," to renew a sense of tradition, and to "engage premodern thought in an attempt to live within some kind of non-ironic social and intellectual world."[3] Taking a cue from philosopher Alasdair MacIntyre, Shannon views countercultural Catholic social thinkers as exemplars of the premodern way of thinking about the individual's relationship to knowledge. This way of thinking sees knowledge as inescapably communal and founded on acceptance of authority and location within a tradition. The recovery of social and intellectual community, Shannon writes, "requires acceptance of the premodern insistence that God, not man, is the measure of all things, and that man connects himself to God through ritual, prayer, and contemplation, not work." The problems of modernity, he concludes, can only be addressed by premodern religious traditions such as Judaism, Roman Catholicism, Orthodoxy, and Islam.[4]

Loosely speaking, a number of disparate strands of communitarian thought can be included under this approach to economic and social questions, including the scholars associated with the journal *Communio*, distributists in the tradition of Hilaire Belloc and G. K. Chesterton, and participants in the "radical orthodoxy" movement.[5]

While these traditions of social thinking have much to offer a modern world that often suffers from solipsistic individualism and materialism, they also flirt with the danger of remaining aloof from the world that they hope to reform. John Ryan was roundly criticized in his day for endangering the credibility of Catholic social teaching by aligning it too closely with a particular political program, and this study has largely shared that critique. At the same time, Ryan's willingness to befriend and engage non-Catholic persons and movements gave him access to and credibility in secular circles that was rarely accorded his coreligionists.

Catholic businessmen, too, were uniquely positioned to bring Catholic social teaching to bear on their particular situations. Individuals accomplished this with greater or lesser degrees of success, but their experience and thoughtful reflection on the relationship of their faith to their profession represented an important voice in debates over the application of Catholic teaching to the American economy. Unfortunately, their reflections failed to be incorporated adequately in the work of most academic social theorists, and many Catholic social thinkers fostered a spirit of conflict between Catholic teaching and businessmen.

This study has noted the sociological reasons for this conflict, including predominant Catholic sympathy for organized labor. It has also noted that some of the blame lies with Catholic managers and employers, many of whom failed sufficiently to educate themselves in the teaching of their Church and assumed that such teaching, being theological rather than practical, had nothing to say to the practice of their professional lives. Nonetheless, the failure of theologians and business leaders to create an adequate dialogue is a significant weakness characteristic of the period in question. The lives of managers and executives were consumed within the market strife as much as those of wage laborers, and deserved as much attention and deference.

In general, the reflections of American Catholic churchmen, academics, and lay people over the seven decades that this study covers can be seen as falling into the pattern of antimodern modernism described by Jackson Lears.[6] Antimodern modernism, for Catholics, though, can be viewed as a phenomenon eminently normal—even endemic to their faith. It can be seen, in other words, simply as a form of the perennial Christian grappling with being "in the world but not of it." In this sense, it is expected that Catholics will at once seek to appreciate what is good about modernity and criticize what is at odds with the moral and theological doctrines that constitute the deposit of faith. Social and economic commentary has been one part of this dual activity of appreciation and criticism.

The distance between the appraisals of the American economy offered by Virgil Michel and Edward Keller indicates the latitude that Catholics enjoyed in their efforts to filter Catholic social teaching into the American context through their own observations and economic analysis. Although clerics such as Michel and Keller played a dominant role in such efforts during the period in question, the Second Vatican Council and its aftermath would bring about a shift in emphasis toward the role of the laity in bringing the faith to bear on the world. Such a shift could only encourage the understanding that, on matters of economics and politics not directly involving clear moral teaching, Catholics could take a wide variety of positions.

While there has been much justified dismay at the breakdown of American Catholic unity on core theological and moral issues in the post-Vatican II era, such dismay should not extend to the disparity of Catholic voices on economic issues. Within the professions of academic economics and business management, considerable differences of opinion exist concerning the efficacy of particular government policies and the nature and extent of reform needed in the economy in general and in business practice more particularly. It is to be expected that the opinions of Catholics on these issues will differ similarly. The oft-cited apothegm coined in an era of religious strife can serve as well as a guide for Catholics on economic questions: "In essentials, unity; in non-essentials, liberty; in all things, charity."[7]

Notes

1. See Michael Warner, *Changing Witness: Catholic Bishops and Public Policy, 1917–1994* (Washington, D.C./Grand Rapids, Mich.: Ethics and Public Policy Center/ William B. Eerdmans, 1995), 169, for the argument that statements from the United States bishops' conference, especially in the 1980s, failed to maintain this distinction.

2. Most historians, nonetheless, have found it difficult to escape these categories. For a recent example, see Jay Corrin, *Catholic Intellectuals*, in which the four figures cited belong to the "liberal" camp. The preponderance of Corrin's magnificent book, detailing as it does the complex relationships and political positions among prominent American and European social thinkers, belies those moments when his treatment falls into the conventional categories.

3. Christopher Shannon, *Conspicuous Criticism: Tradition, the Individual, and Culture in American Social Thought, from Veblen to Mills* (Baltimore: Johns Hopkins University Press, 1996), 177.

4. Shannon, *Conspicuous Criticism*, 179–80, 185, 188.

5. Besides the numerous articles on social issues published in *Communio*, some social commentary can be found in David Schindler, *Heart of the World, Center of the Church: Communio Ecclesiology, Liberalism, and Liberation* (Grand Rapids, Mich.: William B. Eerdmans, 1996). A recent, positive appraisal of the "Chesterbelloc" distributist program is Corrin, *Catholic Intellectuals*. Social and economic criticism along distributist lines continues to be published in organs such as the *New Oxford Review*. For a statement of radical orthodoxy's social implications, see D. Stephen Long, *Divine Economy: Theology and the Market* (London: Routledge, 2000).

6. See also Staf Hellemans, "From 'Catholicism Against Modernity' to the Problematic 'Modernity of Catholicism,'" *Ethical Perspectives* 8 (Summer 2001): "Antimodernist modernization is indeed the label that, in my view, best captures the double and ambiguous 'performance' of Catholicism in the modern world: objectively rooted in, and yet subjectively stubbornly resisting modernity" (122). Hellemans, like many others, however, fails to recognize that the Church's being at once modern and antimodern is not a quirk to be eliminated, but is of its nature.

7. The saying, sometimes attributed to Augustine, was first stated by seventeenth-century Lutheran theologian Peter Meiderlin. See Hans Rollman, "In Essentials Unity: The Prehistory of a Restoration Movement Slogan," *Restoration Quarterly* 39 (1997): 129–39.

BIBLIOGRAPHY

General Catholic Social and Economic Thought

Abell, Aaron I. "Introduction." In *American Catholic Thought on Social Questions*, edited by Abell. Indianapolis: Bobbs-Merrill, 1968.

Abell, Aaron I. *American Catholicism and Social Action: A Search for Social Justice, 1865–1950*. Garden City, N.Y.: Hanover, 1960.

Benestad, J. Brian. "Henry George and the Catholic View of Morality and the Common Good I." *American Journal of Economics and Sociology* 44 (July 1985): 365–78.

Caldez, Jean-Yves, S.J., and Jacques Perrin, S.J., *The Church and Social Justice: The Social Teaching of the Popes from Leo XIII to Pius XII*. Chicago: Henry Regnery, 1961.

Chafuen, Alejandro A. *Faith and Liberty: The Economic Thought of the Late Scholastics*. Lanham, Md.: Lexington Books, 2003.

Corrin, Jay P. *Catholic Intellectuals and the Challenge of Democracy*. Notre Dame, Ind.: University of Notre Dame Press, 2002.

Curran, Charles E. *American Catholic Social Ethics: Twentieth-Century Approaches*. Notre Dame, Ind.: University of Notre Dame Press, 1982.

Curran, Robert Emmett, S.J., "The McGlynn Affair and the Shaping of the New Conservatism in American Catholicism, 1886–1894." *Catholic Historical Review* 66 (April 1980): 184–204.

Dempsey, Bernard W. *Interest and Usury*. London: D. Dobson, 1948.

Downing, Francis. "Catholic Contributions to the American Labor Movement." In *Church and Society: Catholic Social and Political Thought and Movements 1789–1950*, edited by Joseph N. Moody, 845–904. New York: Arts, 1953.

Gallagher, Sister Vera, R. G. S., *Hearing the Cry of the Poor: The Story of the St. Vincent de Paul Society*. Liguori, Missouri: Liguori Publications, 1983.

Grabill, Stephen J., Kevin E. Schmiesing, and Gloria L. Zúñiga. *Doing Justice to Justice: Competing Frameworks of Interpretation in Christian Social Ethics*. Grand Rapids, Mich.: Acton Institute, 2002.

Grice-Hutchinson, Marjorie. *The School of Salamanca: Readings in Spanish Monetary History, 1544–1605*. Oxford: Clarendon Press, 1952.

———. *Early Economic Thought in Spain, 1177–1740*. London: Allen and Unwin, 1975.

Kelley, John J., S.M. *Freedom in the Church: A Documented History of the Principle of Subsidiary Function*. Dayton, Ohio: Peter Li, 2000.

McLean, Edward B. *Roman Catholicism and the Right to Work*. Lanham, Md.: University Press of America, 1985.

Mich, Marvin L. Krier. *Catholic Social Teaching and Movements*. Mystic, Conn.: Twenty-Third Publications, 1998.

Misner, Paul. *Social Catholicism in Europe: From the Onset of Industrialization to the First World War*. London: Darton, Longman and Todd, 1991.

Mueller, Franz H. *The Church and the Social Question*. Washington, D.C.: American Enterprise Institute, 1984 (1963).

Nolan, Hugh J., ed. *Pastoral Letters of the United States Catholic Bishops*. Vol. 1, 1792–1940. Washington, D.C.: United States Catholic Conference, 1984.

Novak, Michael. *The Catholic Ethic and the Spirit of Capitalism*. New York: Free Press, 1993.

Nuesse, C. Joseph. "Henry George and *Rerum Novarum*." *American Journal of Economics and Sociology* 44 (April 1985): 241–54.

Pecklers, Keith F., S.J. *The Unread Vision: The Liturgical Movement in the United States of America, 1926–1945*. Collegeville, Minn.: Liturgical Press, 1998.

Quinn, John F. "Father Mathew's Disciples: American Catholic Support for Temperance, 1840–1920," *Church History* (December 1996): 631.

Roohan, James Edward. *American Catholics and the Social Question, 1865–1900*. New York: Arno, 1976 (reprint of Ph.D. diss., Yale University, 1952).

Sacerdotal Communities of Saint-Severin of Paris and Saint-Joseph of Nice. *The Liturgical Movement*. Translated by Lancelot Sheppard. New York: Hawthorn, 1964 (1960).

Schumpeter, Joseph A. *History of Economic Analysis*. New York: Oxford University Press, 1954.

Shields, Leo W. "The History and Meaning of the Term Social Justice." Ph.D. diss., University of Notre Dame, 1941.

Wallace, Lillian Parker. *Leo XIII and the Rise of Socialism*. Durham, N.C.: Duke University Press, 1966.

Warner, Michael. *Changing Witness: Catholic Bishops and Public Policy, 1917–1994*. Washington, D.C./Grand Rapids, Mich.: Ethics and Public Policy Center/William B. Eerdmans, 1995.

General History of American Catholics

Carey, Patrick W. "Political Atheism: *Dred Scott*, Roger Brooke Taney, and Orestes A. Brownson," *Catholic Historical Review* 87 (April 2002): 207–29.

Dolan, Jay P. *The American Catholic Experience: A History from Colonial Times to the Present*. Garden City, N.Y.: Doubleday, 1985.

Fisher, James T. *Communion of Immigrants: A History of Catholics in America*. New York: Oxford University Press, 2002 (2000).

Fogarty, Gerald P., S.J. *The Vatican and the Americanist Crisis: Denis J. O'Connell, American Agent in Rome, 1885–1903.* Rome: Università Gregoriana, 1974.

Gleason, Philip. *Contending with Modernity: Catholic Higher Education in the Twentieth Century.* New York: Oxford University Press, 1995.

———. "The New Americanism in Catholic Historiography." *USCH* 11 (Summer 1993): 1–18.

Greeley, Andrew M. *The Catholic Experience.* New York: Image, 1969 (1967).

Halsey, William M. *The Survival of American Innocence: Catholicism in an Era of Disillusionment, 1920–1940.* Notre Dame, Ind.: University of Notre Dame Press, 1980.

Hennesey, James, S.J. *American Catholics: A History of the Roman Catholic Community in the United States.* New York: Oxford University, 1981.

Huff, Peter A. *Allen Tate and the Catholic Revival: Trace of the Fugitive Gods.* New York: Paulist Press, 1996.

McAvoy, Thomas T., C.S.C. *The Great Crisis in American Catholic History, 1895–1900.* Chicago: Henry Regnery, 1957.

———. *A History of the Catholic Church in the United States.* Notre Dame, Ind.: University of Notre Dame Press, 1969.

McGreevy, John T. "Thinking on One's Own: Catholicism in the American Intellectual Imagination, 1928–1960." *Journal of American History* 84 (June 1997): 97–131.

Morris, Charles R. *American Catholic: The Saints and Sinners Who Built America's Most Powerful Church.* New York: Times, 1997.

O'Brien, David. *Public Catholicism.* 2d ed. Maryknoll, N.Y.: Orbis, 1996 (1988).

Reher, Margaret Mary. *Catholic Intellectual Life in America: A Historical Study of Persons and Movements.* New York: Macmillan, 1989.

Slayton, Robert A. *Empire Statesman: The Rise and Redemption of Al Smith.* New York: Free Press, 2001.

American Catholics in the Age of Reform

Abell, Aaron I. "The Reception of Leo XIII's Labor Encyclical in America, 1891–1919." *Review of Politics* 7 (October 1945): 464–95

Appleby, R. Scott. *"Church and Age Unite!": The Modernist Impulse in American Catholicism.* Notre Dame, Ind.: University of Notre Dame Press, 1992.

Baxter, Michael, C.S.C. "Reintroducing Virgil Michel: Towards a Counter-Tradition of Catholic Social Ethics in the United States." *Communio* 24 (Fall 1997): 515.

Betten, Neil. *Catholic Activism and the Industrial Worker.* Gainesville: University Presses of Florida, 1976.

Broderick, Francis L. *Right Reverend New Dealer: John A. Ryan.* New York: Macmillan, 1963.

Carey, Patrick W. "After *Testem Benevolentiae* and *Pascendi*," *Catholic Southwest* 7 (1996): 13–33.

Coy, Patrick G., ed. *A Revolution of the Heart: Essays on the Catholic Worker.* Philadelphia: Temple University Press, 1988.

Cross, Robert D. *The Emergence of Liberal Catholicism in America.* Cambridge, Mass.: Harvard University Press, 1967.

Ellis, Marc H. *Peter Maurin: Prophet in the Twentieth Century*. New York: Paulist, 1981.

Ellis, William E. *Patrick Henry Callahan (1866–1940): Progressive Catholic Layman in the American South*. Lewiston, N.Y.: Edwin Mellen, 1989.

Finn, Seamus Paul. "Virgil Michel's Contribution to Linking the Liturgical and Social Apostolate in the American Catholic Church: A Fifty Year Perspective." Th.D. diss., Boston University, 1991.

Franklin, R. W., and Robert L. Spaeth. *Virgil Michel: American Catholic*. Collegeville, Minn.: Liturgical Press, 1988.

Gearty, Patrick W. *The Economic Thought of Monsignor John A. Ryan*. Washington, D.C.: Catholic University Press, 1953.

Gleason, Philip. *The Conservative Reformers: German-American Catholics and the Social Order*. Notre Dame: University of Notre Dame Press, 1968.

Gribble, Richard, C.S.C. *Guardian of America: The Life of James Martin Gillis, C.S.P.* New York: Paulist Press, 1998.

Himes, Kenneth R. "Eucharist and Justice: Assessing the Legacy of Virgil Michel." *Worship* 62 (May 1988): 201–36.

Marx, Rev. Paul, O.S.B. *The Life and Work of Virgil Michel*. Washington, D.C.: Catholic University of America Press, 1957.

McKeown, Elizabeth. *War and Welfare: American Catholics and World War I*. New York: Garland, 1988).

McShane, Joseph M., S.J., *"Sufficiently Radical": Catholicism, Progressivism, and the Bishops' Program of 1919*. Washington, D.C.: Catholic University, 1986.

Miller, William. A. *Harsh and Dreadful Love: Dorothy Day and the Catholic Worker Movement*. New York: Liveright, 1973.

Miscamble, Wilson, D., C.S.C. "The Limits of American Catholic Antifascism: The Case of John A. Ryan." *Church History* 59 (December 1990): 523–38.

Moloney, Deirdre M. *American Catholic Lay Groups and Transatlantic Reform in the Progressive Era*. Chapel Hill: University of North Carolina Press, 2002.

Piehl, Mel. *Breaking Bread: The Catholic Worker and the Origin of Catholic Radicalism in America*. Philadelphia: Temple University Press, 1982.

Roberts, Nancy L. *Dorothy Day and the Catholic Worker*. Albany: State University of New York Press, 1984.

Werner, Stephen A. *Prophet of the Christian Social Manifesto: Joseph Husslein, S.J.* Milwaukee: Marquette University Press, 2001.

Woods, Thomas E., Jr. "Assimilation and Resistance: Catholic Intellectuals and the Progressive Era." *Catholic Social Science Review* 5 (2000): 297–312.

American Catholics and the New Deal

Billington, Monroe, and Cal Clark. "Catholic Clergymen, Franklin D. Roosevelt, and the New Deal." *Catholic Historical Review* 79 (January 1993): 65–82.

Blantz, Thomas E., C.S.C. *A Priest in Public Service: Francis J. Haas and the New Deal*. Notre Dame, Ind.: University of Notre Dame Press, 1982.

Broderick, Francis L. *Right Reverend New Dealer: John A. Ryan*. New York: Macmillan, 1963.

DeSaulniers, Lawrence B. *The Response in American Catholic Periodicals to the Crises of the Great Depression, 1930–1935*. Lanham, Md.: University Press of America, 1984.

Flynn, George Q. *American Catholics and the Roosevelt Presidency, 1932–1936*. Lexington: University of Kentucky, 1968.

Gleason, Philip. *The Conservative Reformers: German-American Catholics and the Social Order*. Notre Dame: University of Notre Dame Press, 1968.

Greene, Thomas R. "The Catholic Conference on Industrial Problems in Normalcy and Depression," *Catholic Historical Review* 77 (July 1991): 442 and passim.

Gribble, Richard, C.S.C. *Guardian of America: The Life of James Martin Gillis, C.S.P.* New York: Paulist Press, 1998.

Heineman, Kenneth J. *A Catholic New Deal: Religion and Reform in Depression Pittsburgh*. University Park: Pennsylvania State University Press, 1999.

Lally, Francis J. *The Catholic Church in a Changing America*. Boston: Little, Brown, 1962.

O'Brien, David J. *American Catholics and Social Reform: The New Deal Years*. New York: Oxford University Press, 1968.

Schmiesing, Kevin E. "Catholic Critics of the New Deal: 'Alternative' Traditions in Catholic Social Thought." *Catholic Social Science Review* 7 (2002): 145–59.

Shapiro, Edward S. "Catholic Agrarian Thought and the New Deal." *CHR* 65 (October 1979): 583–99.

American Catholic Economic Thought, 1940–1962

Allitt, Patrick. *Catholic Intellectuals and Conservative Politics in America, 1950–1985*. Ithaca, N.Y.: Cornell University Press, 1993.

Corrin, Jay P. "H. A. Reinhold: Liturgical Pioneer and Anti-Fascist," *Catholic Historical Review* 82 (July 1996): 436–58.

Cort, John C. *Dreadful Conversions: The Making of a Catholic Socialist*. New York: Fordham University Press, 2003.

Fisher, James Terence. *The Catholic Counterculture in America, 1933–1962*. Chapel Hill: University of North Carolina Press, 1989.

Hudson, Deal W. and Matthew J. Mancini, eds. *Understanding Maritain: Philosopher and Friend*. Macon, Ga.: Mercer University Press, 1987.

Massa, Mark. *Catholics and American Culture: Fulton Sheen, Dorothy Day, and the Notre Dame Football Team*. New York: Crossroad, 1999.

McLean, Edward B. *Roman Catholicism and the Right to Work*. Lanham, Md.: University Press of America, 1985.

Reeves, Thomas C. *America's Bishop: The Life and Times of Fulton J. Sheen*. San Francisco: Encounter Books, 2001.

Waters, William R. "Evolution of Social Economics in America." In *Social Economics: Retrospect and Prospect*, edited by Mark Lutz. Boston: Kluwer Academic, 1990.

General American Economic History and Thought

Anderson, Benjamin M. *Economics and the Public Welfare: A Financial and Economic History of the United States, 1914–1946*. Indianapolis: LibertyPress, 1979 (1949).

Boller, Paul F. *American Thought in Transition: The Impact of Evolutionary Naturalism, 1865–1900*. Washington, D.C.: University Press of America, 1981 (1969).

Brinkley, Alan. *The End of Reform: New Deal Liberalism in Recession and War*. New York: Vintage, 1995.

Cotkin, George. *Reluctant Modernism: American Thought and Culture, 1880–1900*. New York: Twayne, 1992.

Dickman, Howard. *Industrial Democracy in America: Ideological Origins of National Labor Relations Policy*. La Salle, Ill.: Open Court, 1987.

Dorfman, Joseph. *The Economic Mind in American Civilization*, 5 vols. New York: Viking Press, 1959 (1949).

Dorman, Robert L. *Revolt of the Provinces: The Regionalist Movement in America, 1920–1945*. Chapel Hill: University of North Carolina Press, 1993.

Ellwood, David T., and Glenn Fine. "The Impact of Right-to-Work Laws on Union Organization." *Journal of Political Economy* 95 (April 1987): 250–73.

Engelbourg, Saul. *Power and Morality: American Business Ethics, 1840–1914*. Westport, Conn.: Greenwood Press, 1980.

Folsom, Burton W., Jr. *Urban Capitalists: Entrepreneurs and City Growth in Pennsylvania's Lackawanna and Lehigh Regions, 1800–1920*. Baltimore: Johns Hopkins University Press, 1981.

———. *The Myth of the Robber Barons: A New Look at the Rise of Big Business in America*, 3d ed. Herndon, Va.: Young America's Foundation, 1996.

Greenfeld, Liah. *The Spirit of Capitalism: Nationalism and Economic Growth*. Cambridge, Mass.: Harvard University Press, 2001.

Horowitz, Daniel. *The Morality of Spending: Attitudes toward the Consumer Society in America, 1875–1940*. Baltimore: Johns Hopkins University Press, 1985.

Howe, Daniel Walker. "Charles Sellers, the Market Revolution, and the Shaping of Identity in Whig-Jacksonian America." In *God and Mammon: Protestants, Money, and the Market, 1790–1860*, edited by Mark A. Noll, 54–74. New York: Oxford University Press, 2002.

Kates, Steven, ed. *Two Hundred Years of Say's Law: Essays on Economic Theory's Most Controversial Principle*. Cheltenham, U.K.: Edward Elgar, 2003.

Katz, Michael B. *In the Shadow of the Poorhouse: A Social History of Welfare in America*. New York: Basic Books, 1986.

Lasch, Christopher. *The New Radicalism in America, 1889–1963: The Intellectual As Social Type*. New York: W. W. Norton, 1965.

Lasch, Christopher. *The True and Only Heaven: Progress and Its Critics*. New York: W.W. Norton, 1991.

Moore, William J. and Robert J. Newman. "The Effects of Right-to-Work Laws: A Review of the Literature." *Industrial and Labor Relations Review* 38 (July 1985): 571–86.

Morgan, Mary S., and Malcolm Rutherford, eds. *From Interwar Pluralism to Postwar Neoclassicism*. Durham, N.C.: Duke University Press, 1998.

Olasky, Marvin. *The Tragedy of American Compassion*. Washington, D.C.: Regnery Gateway, 1992.

Purcell, Edward A., Jr. *The Crisis of Democratic Theory: Scientific Naturalism and the Problem of Value*. Lexington: University Press of Kentucky, 1973.

Ross, Dorothy. *The Origins of American Social Science*. New York: Cambridge University Press, 1991.

Seckler, David. *Thorstein Veblen and the Institutionalists: A Study in the Social Philosophy of Economics*. Boulder: Colorado Associated University Press, 1975.

Sellers, Charles. *The Market Revolution: Jacksonian America, 1815–1846*. New York: Oxford University Press, 1991.

Shannon, Christopher. *Conspicuous Criticism: Tradition, the Individual, and Culture in American Social Thought, from Veblen to Mills*. Baltimore: Johns Hopkins University Press, 1996.

Veysey, Laurence R. *The Emergence of the American University*. Chicago: University of Chicago Press, 1965.

White, Morton. *Social Thought in America: The Revolt Against Formalism*. Boston: Beacon Press, 1957 (1949).

General American Religious History

Carpenter, Joel. "The Fundamentalist Leaven and the Rise of an Evangelical United Front." In *The Evangelical Tradition in America*, edited by Leonard Sweet, 257–88. Macon, Ga.: Mercer University Press, 1984.

Carter, Paul A. *The Decline and Revival of the Social Gospel: Social and Political Liberalism in American Protestant Churches, 1920–1940*. Ithaca, N.Y.: Cornell University Press, 1954.

Carwardine, Richard. "Charles Sellers's 'Antinomians' and 'Arminians': Methodists and the Market Revolution." In *God and Mammon: Protestants, Money, and the Market, 1790–1860*, edited by Mark A. Noll, 75–98. New York: Oxford University Press, 2002.

Cogliano, Francis D. *No King, No Popery: Anti-Catholicism in Revolutionary New England*. Westport, Conn.: Greenwood, 1995.

Ellwood, Robert S. *1950: Crossroads of American Religious Life*. Louisville, Ky.: Westminster/John Knox, 2000.

Garrett, James Leo, Jr. *Reinhold Niebuhr on Roman Catholicism*. Louisville, Ky.: Seminary Baptist Book Store.

Gaustad, Edwin Scott. *A Religious History of America*. New rev. ed. San Francisco: Harper and Row, 1990.

Handy, Robert T. *Undermined Establishment: Church-State Relations in America, 1880–1920*. Princeton, N.J.: Princeton University Press, 1991.

Hardman, Keith J. *Issues in American Christianity: Primary Sources with Introductions*. Grand Rapids, Mich.: Baker Books, 1993.

Hart, D. G. *Defending the Faith: J. Gresham Machen and the Crisis of Conservative Protestantism in Modern America*. Baltimore: Johns Hopkins University Press, 1994.

Higham, John. *Strangers in the Land: Patterns of American Nativism, 1860–1925*. New Brunswick, N.J.: Rutgers University Press, 1955.

Hutchison, William R. *The Modernist Impulse in American Protestantism*. Cambridge, Mass.: Harvard University Press, 1976.

Kuklick, Bruce. *Churchmen and Philosophers: From Jonathan Edwards to John Dewey*. New Haven: Yale University Press, 1985.

Leonard, Ira M. and Robert D. Parmet. *American Nativism, 1830–1860*. New York: Van
    Nostrand Reinhold Co., 1971.
Marsden, George M. *The Soul of the American University: From Protestant Establishment
    to Established Nonbelief*. New York: Oxford University Press, 1994.
Moberg, David. *The Great Reversal: Evangelism Versus Social Concern*. New York: J.B.
    Lippincott Company, 1972.
May, Henry F. *Protestant Churches and Industrial America*. New York: Harper
    Torchbooks, 1967 (1949).
McCarraher, Eugene. *Christian Critics: Religion and the Impasse in Modern American
    Social Thought*. Ithaca, N.Y.: Cornell University Press, 2000.
Miller, Robert Moats. *American Protestantism and Social Issues, 1919–1939*. Chapel
    Hill: University of North Carolina Press, 1958.
Moore, R. Laurence. *Religious Outsiders and the Making of Americans*. New York:
    Oxford University Press, 1986.
Noll, Mark A. *A History of Christianity in the United States and Canada*. Grand Rapids,
    Mich.: William B. Eerdmans, 1992.
Smith, Timothy L. *Revivalism and Social Reform: American Protestantism on the Eve of
    the Civil War*. Baltimore: Johns Hopkins University Press, 1980 (1957).
Tobin, Kathleen A. *The American Religious Debate Over Birth Control, 1907–1937*.
    Jefferson, N.C.: McFarland and Company, 2001.
Wills, Garry. *Under God: Religion and American Politics*. New York: Simon and
    Schuster, 1990.

The Social Gospel, Populism, and Progressivism

Beckley, Harlan. *Passion for Justice: Retrieving the Legacies of Walter Rauschenbusch,
    John A. Ryan, and Reinhold Niebuhr*. Louisville, Ky.: Westminster/John Knox, 1992.
Chambers, John Whiteclay, II. *The Tyranny of Change: America in the Progressive Era,
    1900–1917*. New York: St. Martin's Press, 1980.
Crunden, Robert M. *Ministers of Reform: The Progressives' Achievement in American
    Civilization, 1889–1920*. New York: Basic Books, 1982.
Curtis, Susan. *A Consuming Faith: The Social Gospel and Modern American Culture*.
    Baltimore: Johns Hopkins University Press, 1991.
Dawley, Alan. *Struggles for Justice: Social Responsibility and the Liberal State*.
    Cambridge, Mass.: Belknap, 1991.
Dumenil, Lynn. "'The Insatiable Maw of Bureaucracy': Antistatism and Education
    Reform in the 1920s." *Journal of American History* 77 (September 1990): 499–524.
Elshtain, Jean Bethke, *Jane Addams and the Dream of American Democracy*. New York:
    Basic Books, 2002.
Fink, Leon. *Progressive Intellectuals and the Dilemmas of Democratic Commitment*.
    Cambridge, Mass.: Harvard University Press, 1997.
Fones-Wolf, Ken. *Trade Union Gospel: Christianity and Labor in Industrial Philadelphia,
    1865–1915*. Philadelphia: Temple University Press, 1989.
Foster, Gaines M. "Conservative Social Christianity, the Law, and Personal Morality:
    Wilbur F. Crafts in Washington." *Church History* 71 (December 2002): 799–819.
Goodwyn, Lawrence. *The Populist Moment: A Short History of the Agrarian Revolt in
    America*. New York: Oxford University Press, 1978.

Gordon, Linda. *Woman's Body, Woman's Right: A Social History of Birth Control in America*. New York: Grossman Publishers, 1976.

Gorrell, Donald K. *The Age of Social Responsibility: The Social Gospel in the Progressive Era, 1900–1920*. Macon, Ga.: Mercer University Press, 1988.

Handy, Robert T. "Introduction." In *The Social Gospel in America, 1870–1920: Gladden, Ely, Rauschenbusch*, edited by Handy. New York: Oxford University Press, 1966.

Hicks, John D. *The Populist Revolt: A History of the Farmers' Alliance and the People's Party*. Minneapolis: University of Minnesota Press, 1931.

Hofstadter, Richard. *The Age of Reform: From Bryan to F. D. R.* New York: Alfred A. Knopf, 1989 (1955).

Hopkins, Charles H. *The Rise of the Social Gospel in American Protestantism, 1865–1915*. New Haven, Conn.: Yale University Press, 1940.

Johnson, Paul E. *A Shopkeeper's Millennium: Society and Revivals in Rochester, New York, 1815–1937*. New York: Hill and Wang, 1997 (1978).

King, "'History as Revelation' in the Theology of the Social Gospel." In *Protestantism and Social Christianity*, edited by Martin E. Marty, 145–65. Munich: K. G. Saur, 1992.

King, William McGuire. "An Enthusiasm for Humanity: The Social Emphasis in Religion and Its Accommodation in Protestant Theology," In *Religion and Twentieth-Century American Intellectual Life*, edited Michael J. Lacey, 49–77. New York: Cambridge University Press, 1989.

Kloppenberg, James T. *Uncertain Victory: Social Democracy and Progressivism in European and American Thought, 1870–1920*. New York: Oxford University Press, 1986.

Kolko, Gabriel. *The Triumph of Conservatism: A Reinterpretation of American History, 1900–1916*. New York: Free Press, 1963.

Lane, James B. *Jacob A. Riis and the American City*. Port Washington, N.Y.: Kennikat Press, 1974.

Lears, T. J. Jackson. *No Place of Grace: Antimodernism and the Transformation of American Culture, 1880–1920*. New York: Pantheon, 1981.

Link Arthur S., and Richard L. McCormick. *Progressivism*. Arlington Heights, Ill.: Harlan Davidson, 1983.

Marsden, George. "The Gospel of Wealth, the Social Gospel, and the Salvation of Souls in Nineteenth-Century America." In *Protestantism and Social Christianity*, edited by Martin E. Marty. Munich: K. G. Saur, 1992. First published in *Fides et Historia* 5 (Fall 1972 and Spring 1973): 10–21.

May, Henry F. *The End of American Innocence: A Study of the First Years of Our Own Time, 1912–1917*. New York: Alfred A. Knopf, 1969 (1959).

Nash, Roderick. *The Nervous Generation: American Thought, 1917–1930*. Chicago: Rand McNally, 1970.

Nugent, Walter T. K. *The Tolerant Populists: Kansas Populism and Nativism*. Chicago: University of Chicago Press, 1963.

Palmer, Bruce. *"Man Over Money": The Southern Populist Critique of American Capitalism*. Chapel Hill: University of North Carolina Press, 1980.

Pollack, Norman. *The Humane Economy: Populism, Capitalism, and Democracy*. New Brunswick, N.J.: Rutgers University Press, 1990.

Rader, Benjamin G. *The Academic Mind and Reform: The Influence of Richard T. Ely in American Life*. Lexington: University of Kentucky Press, 1966.

Rodgers, Daniel T. *Atlantic Crossings: Social Politics in a Progressive Age*. Cambridge, Mass.: Harvard University Press, 1998.

Rubin, Joan Shelley. "Henry F. May's The End of American Innocence." *Reviews in American History* 18 (March 1990): 142–49.

Sanders, Elizabeth. *Roots of Reform: Farmers, Workers, and the American State, 1877–1917*. Chicago: University of Chicago Press, 1999.

Sizer, Sandra. "Politics and Apolitical Religion: The Great Urban Revivals of the Late Nineteenth Century." In *Protestantism and Social Christianity*, edited by Martin E. Marty, 15–32. Munich: K. G. Sour, 1992. First published as "Politics and Apolitical Religion: The Great Revivals of the Late Nineteenth Century," *Church History* 48 (March 1979): 81–98.

Sklar, Martin. *The Corporate Reconstruction of American Capitalism, 1890–1916*. Cambridge, Mass.: Harvard University Press.

Smith, Gary Scott. "The Men and Religion Forward Movement of 1911–1912: New Perspectives on Evangelical Social Concern and the Relationship between Christianity and Progressivism." In *Protestantism and Social Christianity*, edited by Martin E Marty, 166–193. Munich: K. G. Saur, 1992.

Smith, Gary Scott. *The Search for Social Salvation: Social Christianity and America, 1880–1925*. Lanham, Md.: Lexington Books, 2000.

White, Ronald C., and C. Howard Hopkins. *The Social Gospel: Religion and Reform in Changing America*. Philadelphia: Temple University, 1976.

Wiebe, Robert H. *The Search for Order, 1877–1929*. New York, Hill and Wang, 1967.

Woodward, C. Vann. *Tom Watson: Agrarian Rebel*. New York: Oxford University Press, 1963.

The New Deal

Anderson, Benjamin M. *Economics and the Public Welfare: A Financial and Economic History of the United States, 1914–1946*. Indianapolis: LibertyPress, 1979 (1949).

Best, Gary Dean. *Pride, Prejudice, and Politics: Roosevelt Versus Recovery, 1933–1938*. New York: Praeger, 1991.

Brinkley, Alan. *The End of Reform: New Deal Liberalism in Recession and War*. New York: Vintage, 1995.

Cohen, Lizabeth. *Making a New Deal: Industrial Workers in Chicago, 1919–1939*. New York: Cambridge University Press, 1990.

Cooney, Terry A. *Balancing Acts: American Thought and Culture in the 1930s*. New York: Twayne, 1995.

Dawley, Alan. *Struggles for Justice: Social Responsibility and the Liberal State*. Cambridge, Mass.: Belknap, 1991.

Fraser, Steve, and Gary Gerstle, eds. *The Rise and Fall of the New Deal Order, 1930–1980*. Princeton, N.J.: Princeton University Press, 1989.

Leuchtenberg, William Edward. *Franklin D. Roosevelt and the New Deal, 1932–1940*. New York: Harper & Row, 1963.

McKenna, Marian C. *Franklin Roosevelt and the Great Constitutional War: The Court-Packing Crisis of 1937.* New York: Fordham University Press, 2002.

Rothbard, Murray N. *America's Great Depression.* Los Angeles: Nash, 1972 (1963).

Stone, Albert E., Jr. "Seward Collins and the American Review: Experiment in Pro-Fascism, 1933–1937." *American Quarterly* 12 (Spring 1960): 3–19.

Temin, Peter. *Did Monetary Policy Cause the Great Depression?* New York: W. W. Norton, 1976.

Vedder, Richard, and Lowell Gallaway. *Out of Work: Unemployment and Government in Twentieth-Century America.* New York: Holmes and Meier, 1993.

Conservatism, Anticommunism, and General American History, 1940–1962

Carter, Paul A. *Another Part of the Fifties.* New York: Columbia University Press, 1983.

Crosby, Donald F., S.J., *God, Church, and Flag: Senator Joseph P. McCarthy and the Catholic Church, 1950–1957.* Chapel Hill: University of North Carolina Press, 1978.

Crunden, Robert M., ed. *The Superfluous Men: Conservative Critics of American Culture, 1900–1945.* Austin: University of Texas Press, 1977.

Diggins, John P. *Up From Communism: Conservative Odysseys in American Intellectual History.* New York: Harper and Row, 1975.

Hoeveler, J. David, Jr. *The New Humanism: A Critique of Modern America, 1900–1940.* Charlottesville: University Press of Virginia, 1977.

Matusow, Allen J. *The Unraveling of America: A History of Liberalism in the 1960s.* New York: Harper & Row, 1984.

Miller, Douglas T., and Marion Nowak. *The Fifties: The Way We Really Were.* Garden City, N.Y.: Doubleday, 1977.

Nash, George H. *The Conservative Intellectual Movement in America, Since 1945.* Wilmington, Del.: Intercollegiate Studies Institute, 1996.

Stewart, John L. *The Burden of Time: The Fugitives and Agrarians.* Princeton, N.J.: Princeton University Press, 1965.

Tomlins, Christopher L. *The State and the Unions: Labor Relations, Law, and the Organized Labor Movement in America, 1880–1960.* Cambridge: Cambridge University Press, 1985.

INDEX

intervention. *See* government intervention
Ireland, John (Archbishop), 4, 29, 46n7

Jefferson, Thomas, 69
Jewish immigrants, 46n3. *See also*
 immigrants
John, XXIII, *Mater et Magistra*, 151
Johnson-Reed Act of 1924, 62
just distribution, 135
justice, economic, 87–92, 146
justice of prices, 135
just wage, 17, 37–39, 94, 141

Keane, Monsignor John J., 17, 46n7
Keller, Fr. Edward, 115–19, 138, 142–45,
 146–47, 154n48; *Christianity and
 Capitalism*, 138
Kenkel, Frederick: economic thought,
 39–40, 43–44, 46, 51n54, 67–70,
 71–72, 79n51, 141; New Deal
 critique, 92–94; social reform, 67–71
Kennedy, John F., 151
Kerby, William, 27–29, 85
King, William McGuire, "An Enthusiasm
 for Humanity: The Social Emphasis
 in Religion and Its Accommodation
 in Protestant Theology," 49n36;
 "History as Revelation," 50n43
Klein, Félix, 4
Kloppenberg, James, 24–25, 48n34,
 53n88; *Uncertain Victory*, 51n51
Knight, Frank, *Risk, Uncertainty, and
 Profit*, 125
knowledge, economic, 34–35, 125, 126,
 127
Ku Klux Klan, 61

labor movement: Catholic thought,
 14n35, 14n36, 18, 43, 69, 87, 138,
 154n43; child labor amendment
 (CLA), 70–72, 93–95, 109n53;
 laborers, 27, 98, 102; social reform,
 9, 11n12, 16, 19. *See also* unions
labor priests, 143, 145
LaFarge, John, 91

laissez-faire, 17, 114, 135. *See also*
 government intervention; wealth
Lasch, Christopher, 24, 47n22
Lears, Jackson, 40, 41
legislation. *See* child labor amendment
 (CLA); New Deal; right-to-work
Leo XIII, 12n18, 117; *Quod Apostolici
 Muneris*, 14n36; *Rerum Novarum*, 2,
 14n39, 15, 16–18, 29, 35, 37, 38;
 Testem Benevolentiae, 4, 12n13
liberal: economics, 5, 114–15, 145–46;
 theology, 6, 7, 22–24, 64–65, 151
liberty, 31, 71–72, 159
Lincoln, Abraham, 79n51. *See also*
 subsidiarity, principle of
Lissner, Will, 121, 122
liturgical reform, 88, 89, 90, 107n25
living wage, 37–39, 42, 43, 45, 136,
 141–42. *See also* Agricultural
 Adjustment Act (AAA)

Machen, J. Gresham, 64–65; *Christianity
 and Liberalism*, 78n25
Maguire, J. W. R., 42, 72
mainstream, defined, 55n103. *See also*
 liberal; orthodox economics
management, humane, 150–51
Man Over Money, Palmer, Bruce,
 47nn22–25
marginalism, 32–33. *See also* liberal
Maritain, Jacques, 150–51
market system, 20, 98, 136, 139–42. *See
 also* capitalism
Marsden, George, 7
Marshall, Alfred, *Principia*, 34
Martin, Clarence E., 94–95
Marxism, 33, 54n88, 120–21
Massa, Mark, 91–92
Masse, Benjamin, 136–37
Mater et Magistra, John XXIII, 151
materialism, 28, 50n45, 89, 96, 120. *See
 also* Catholic Worker movement;
 Keller, Fr. Edward; living wage
Maternity and Infancy Act, 81n62
Maurin, Peter, 90–91

ABOUT THE AUTHOR

KEVIN E. SCHMIESING (Ph.D., University of Pennsylvania) is a research fellow in history at the Acton Institute in Grand Rapids, Michigan. Author of *American Catholic Intellectuals and the Dilemma of Dual Identities, 1895–1955* (2002), he has written on a variety of subjects within the fields of Catholic social thought and American religious and intellectual history. His articles have appeared in the *Journal of Church and State, Logos*, the *Journal of Markets and Morality*, the *Josephinum Journal of Theology*, and the *Catholic Social Science Review*.